A ROAD TRIP INTO

AMERICA'S HIDDEN HEART

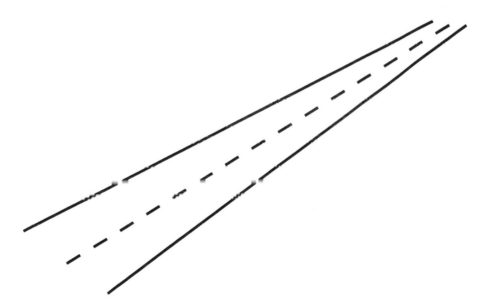

Traveling the Back Roads, Backwoods and Back Yards

Published by AKA-Publishing

ISBN 978-1-936688-39-5

A ROAD TRIP INTO AMERICA'S HIDDEN HEART

Traveling the Back Roads, Backwoods and Back Yards

John Drake Robinson

Acknowledgments

Love and thanks to the pair who awakened my mutant travel gene: Dad and sister Susan. A wave to six million Missourians I drove past, and to their ancestors who didn't see me coming.

I found 32,314 stories on the road. Three storytellers showed me how to tell them: Bob Smith, Bob Carnett and Vance Heflin. Editors Mary V. Helsabeck, Rita Dallmeyer and Sarah Alban helped me sift and select and stay focused.

Thanks to local historians and researchers who keep the flame, and guides like Kaye Malins, Janeen Aggen, Angela Da Silva, Alan Peters and Maryellen McVicker.

I consulted detailed histories like Switzler's 1889 *Illustrated History of Missouri*, and Walter Williams' 1913 *History of Northeast Missouri*.

Thanks to the Missouri Division of Historic Preservation, storykeeper for properties on the National Historic Register, and to the State Historical Society of Missouri's *Robert L. Ramsay Missouri Place Names File*. I tapped the well of three great geologists: Jerry Vineyard, Wally Howe, and Tom Beveridge's *Geologic Curiosities and Wonders of Missouri*.

Cheers to the underappreciated workforce at Missouri's Departments of Transportation, Conservation, Natural Resources, Divisions of Parks, Tourism, and the Board on Geographic Names.

Thanks to the 285 newspapers of the Missouri Press Association. Thanks to *Inside Columbia Magazine*, *Missouri Life Magazine*, and *Show Me Missouri Magazine* for allowing me to recount bits and pieces of my past articles from their pages.

Most important, my loving gratitude to Cheryl and our children and grandchildren for excusing my absences.

And Mom.

Erifnus thanks University Garage, her Car Spa. They think she'll make it to 500,000 miles. I do too.

Table of Contents

Truant

"Got a ham bone?" I asked the undertaker. I pulled a two-pound bag of great northern beans out of my overcoat pocket and plopped it on his desk. He looked puzzled.

"Last request," I said, and told him about my sister.

She made the wish a few years back, during the funeral of an aunt. She told me, "When I die, I don't want my visitation to smell like flowers. Put on a pot of ham and beans."

I knew Susan was serious. But she was 47 years old when she told me. Healthy. Or so I thought. I put her request out of my mind. Six months later she died of a heart attack. So I brought beans to the undertaker. "Crock pot's in the car," I said. "I'll go get it."

The funeral director found a ham hock. We fired up the crock pot ten hours before visitation.

It was a fragrant funeral. And a hearty meal. My recipe, "Nearer My God to Bean Soup," never made it into any church cookbooks. I understand.

Susan was a teacher. She told me she could always identify the children who had traveled, who had seen other parts of the world beyond their beaten path. "Well-traveled kids seem to adjust better to life," she said. "They understand how things fit together." But she worried. "Kids are spending more time with video games, less time with real life."

She was right. Kids can tell you more about Grand Theft Auto than the Grand Canyon. When they ride in the family SUV they're watching movie screens. Most of 'em can't find Paris or Chicago on a map.

Bit by bit, I was drifting into a similar trap. My TV remote offered instant escape into a thousand channels. The Internet showed me the world so vividly, so easily that I scarcely noticed that more and more, I wasn't touching or smelling or tasting it.

Like a lot of people, I took a job that strapped me to a cell phone. The phone grew into a Blackberry. If television is an opiate, Blackberry is heroin. I quickly became dependent on it. Every buzz stopped me until I peeked at the message.

I was adapting to the society of electrons, well-connected to friendly faces on my tiny screen, but oblivious to anything outside its circuit. I had become a prisoner, an addict attached to my wireless like a marionette, moving through hallways and streets and airports with my eyes fixed a foot in front of me where my tiny master made my thumbs dance.

But one message kept coming from outside my service area. "Well-traveled kids seem to adjust better to life," Susan's voice played in my mind. "They understand how things fit together."

It made me stop and take inventory. My passport has two dozen stamps. I've been to every state. To reassure myself, I got out my state map to trace the roads I'd traveled. I was shocked. Aside from wearing deep grooves in a few skeletal routes, I'd bypassed 90 percent of the capillaries, those little roads where real America lives. I knew more about Iraq than I knew about the neighbors living just beyond my treadmill.

So I set out to touch them all. I drove every mile of every road on my state map. Driving was the easy part. Writing down notes at 60 mph was an adventure. After I finished, and began to decipher 40 notebooks full of disjointed scribbles, I realized a big problem: This wasn't a trip from point A to point B. It was more like mowing a 68,000 square mile lawn. I struggled to organize my notebooks, and I fumbled for a way to tell this tale.

Then a sign came to me, a vision from a trusted source. My father spoke to me from the grave.

"Gravy," I think he said. The voice was muffled, coming from the grave and all. But I knew what he meant. Find good food, because that's where the good stories are. He was right.

Dad was a gravy freak. Pretty much everybody who knew about his addiction was surprised he lived to be 93. But gravy kept him going. And he scoured the globe for the world's best gravy. Across five continents, in thousands of restaurants, he searched for his next fix. At every meal, he asked the server to load his plate with extra gravy.

Gathered around him at the dinner table, our family showed a full range of reactions to Dad's gravy Jones: amusement, irritation, disgust. Truth is, gravy served him well. It was gravy that trained his arteries to form new branches around the blockage to his heart. It was gravy that made him happy, even while it made his children fearful for his health. We told the doctor; the doctor remained unfazed. He looked at us like we were narcs. "Your dad is 93. Let him eat what he wants."

Dad did. After the beans and onions of his Depression-era youth, he launched into a lifetime obsession with gravy. And in between bites, he told great stories about dead people.

Like Injun Joe.

Around Dad's home town of Hannibal, Joe Douglas is the town's second-favorite son.

Sam Clemens, of course, is the town's first favorite son. You know him as Mark Twain. He isn't buried among the 15,000 headstones at Mt. Olivet Cemetery. But his mom and dad are, and most of the rest of his Hannibal family. So is Injun Joe, or, more precisely, the man Hannibalians think served as Twain's model for Injun Joe.

Joe Douglas was a decent man, and his life was pretty good except for his reputation as the model for a raging bloody cutthroat killer. Even in his later years, bathing in the spotlight of Tom Sawyer and Huckleberry Finn, Twain never fingered Joe Douglas as the model for Injun Joe. He remained mum on the subject, carrying his thoughts to his grave a thousand miles away from Hannibal.

Joe Douglas outlived Twain by a dozen years. A century after Twain's death, his autobiography finally sees the light of day, and Twain says that Injun Joe was patterned on somebody else.

But the folks of Hannibal hold tight to their own beliefs about Mark Twain. There were 19,000 people in Hannibal at the time Twain sat on his porch in Hartford, Connecticut and wrote about Injun Joe, and almost all of them were convinced that Joe Douglas served as Twain's model. Through no fault of his own, Joe Douglas had the physical characteristics to play Injun Joe. If he was in a police lineup with a dozen other fellows, where folks could finger a villain, they'd point to poor Joe Douglas. He was a towering figure of Osage Indian and African descent, with deep facial scars from smallpox, and a red wig hiding a bald head.

Dad knew Joe Douglas. They met when Dad was seven years old. Joe was 102. "He used to come into the service station where I washed windshields as a kid," Dad said. "Even as an old man, every Saturday Injun Joe would ride into Hannibal from his home outside Spalding, in the back seat of a car driven by a neighbor family. They would buy some gasoline, and sell some produce, and Injun Joe would laugh and joke with us kids. But nobody ever called him Injun Joe, or even brought up the subject. We were respectful of him, or maybe just afraid."

I set out to find Injun Joe. Along the way, many more stories, buried by time, kept surfacing—like the story about the boys who were buried alive.

Smacking into Missouri's east coast, I made a beeline down Highway 79 to the base of Lover's Leap, a sheer cliff that towers over the Mississippi River. Across America, 30 dozen Lover's Leaps stand ready to oblige the nation's forlorn, and each tells the same story: love denied, somebody jumps. Lovers and leapers have combined to name seven such sites in Missouri alone. But behind the face of this cliff, within the mountain that forms a massive southern bookend to Hannibal, another mystery remains unsolved.

I remember when it happened. Back in 1967, three boys younger than my 15 years set out for adventure around the rugged bluffs and caves that surround Hannibal. They never came home. Right beside the Mississippi River, workers were blasting a new roadcut to straighten the twists and turns of Highway 79, and searchers believe the boys are still entombed in a man made cave-in somewhere beneath Roadcut 79.

Sounds like a Twain story. Except there's no happy ending.

As a boy, Sam Clemens prepared for his adult career by hiding. Mark Twain Cave is where he did some of his best hiding, as anybody who was a school kid knows. Of course, when Twain was a schoolboy it wasn't called Mark Twain Cave, because he wasn't called Mark Twain. It was called McDowell's Cave, named for the doctor who owned it. In his novels, Twain called it McDougal's Cave, which later was renamed Mark Twain Cave for the obvious reasons of honor and tourism. But back in the 1840s, when the butterfly named Twain was still a caterpillar named Clemens, a real live Dr. McDowell bought the cave, walled the front entrance and used the cool cavern confines to perform research on corpses. Rumors persisted among neighbors that one of the doctor's cadavers was his own infant daughter, kept in a glass jar in the cave. It doesn't matter whether any of those tales are true. The stories are true in the minds of true believers. And then, as now, true believers hear ghastly cadaver stories, do their duty to spread them, and anybody who hears these dark tales never forgets them.

Mark Twain draws liberally from that cave and its gruesome reputation as a trade center, a chop shop for body snatchers. In *The Adventures of Tom Sawyer*, two cretins, Injun Joe and Muff Potter, steal dead bodies from the local cemetery to feed the research needs of Dr.

Robinson. But when Injun Joe kills the doctor in a moonlit graveyard, scientific advancement screeches to a halt.

In Twain's tale, Injun Joe dies too. Twain makes the cave dark and Devilish, and he portrays his villain's death at a manhole-sized back entrance to the cave, where searchers find Joe's dead eyes shining out of the darkness, the bony fingers of his corpse clutching the iron bars that blocked his escape. But that was Twain's version of events, greatly exaggerated.

As Twain transformed his experiences along these bluffs into a collection of the world's greatest adventures, his silence about Joe Douglas created one more tragedy. The proof lies in Mt. Olivet Cemetery. I turned onto Route T and drove two minutes to the scene.

Like most old cemeteries, Mt. Olivet hides plenty of forgotten history beneath a stonecutter's art gallery. It sprouts plenty of character. The most noticeable sprout is a 10-foot tall tombstone chiseled in the image of a tree trunk. Less flamboyant is the simple military marker for the admiral of the Great White Fleet. Nearby lie the bones of a guy who couldn't afford a lawyer. His Supreme Court case paved the way for suspects without money to get counsel. But I hadn't intended to get caught up in graveyard biographies. I was seeking the tragedy that Twain had allowed to happen: the branding of the real Joe Douglas as the fictional Injun Joe.

To his dying day, Joe denied that he was the Injun Joe in Twain's tale. But the descendants of Mark Twain's Hannibal can't let go. They erected a headstone on his grave a few years ago, and I found it in Mt. Olivet: "Joe Douglass [sic], known to many in Hannibal as Injun Joe, died September 29th, 1923 at age 102. He was found, an infant, in an abandoned Indian camp by a man named Douglass who raised him. He denied that he was the Injun Joe in Mark Twain's writings, as he had always lived an honorable life...."

Joe Douglas met a tragic end of his own. He died of apparent ptomaine poisoning after eating pickled pigs' feet. Old legends die hard.

I left Joe Douglas to rest in peace, and drove downtown to find Abe & Higgies, a scary old Hannibal tavern down by the railroad tracks. At least the tavern was scary the first time I went there as a wide-eyed child. Mom and Dad took me there to teach me a lesson. Even before we entered the tavern, the building's exhaust fan pumped out hot air currents saturated with the aroma of stale beer and cigarette smoke and grilled onions and grease from the open grill. The tavern's dark wood paneling absorbed the dim light offered by a hanging lamp that somehow had trapped a tiny team of Clydesdales pulling a tiny beer wagon. The little plastic Clydesdales trudged round and round inside that greasy lamp, trapped in horse Hell, pulling a beer wagon to nowhere. But nightmares in horse Hell vanished when the server set a breaded pork tenderloin in front of me. I can't recall if there was a plate underneath it, the sandwich was so big.

"It could smother a snappin' turtle," said a voice from a distant table. I looked toward the voice, and saw a solitary silhouette backlit by a window that grudgingly admitted daylight through fifty years of smoky greasy film. "That sandwich is so big, ol' pap owes property tax on it," the silhouette chuckled. Even today I believe that silhouette was a descendant of Huck Finn. On that day I learned this lesson: The best food can be found in the dim-lit taverns and roadhouses with cracks in the foundation and grease on the walls and blue plates on top of cheap Formica tabletops.

Sometime in the years I wasn't paying much attention to Hannibal, the scary old tavern bit the dust. I'm not sure why Abe & Higgies didn't survive. Maybe they went belly up serving tenderloins the size of your head.

I took solace up the hill where a giant water tower-sized root beer mug hovers over the Mark Twain Dinette. They serve giant tenderloins, too, and root beer floats, and Maid-Rite burgers and plenty of photos of the dinette's namesake, the bard of the Mississippi, whose boyhood home and girlfriend's house and a bevy of museums are half a block downhill.

I'd seen the Mark Twain museums countless times, since I'd done a fair amount of growing up in Hannibal myself, bouncing between two sets of grandparents and boulevards full of aunts and uncles and cousins. Back then Mark Twain's Hannibal worshiped its hometown hero, the writer with the white hair and the white suit and the white ash at the end of his cigar. But locals seemed to embrace only the good side of his characters. So it was hard to find anything but sanitary vestiges of Twain throughout the city dubbed "America's Home Town." Tom This. Becky That. Everything in Twain's downtown seemed a bit tidy, whitewashed in a way that just might annoy Samuel Clemens.

For years the town seemed to shuck Huckleberry Finn and Jim, the way it shunned them in the novel. Oh, there's a statue of Tom 'n' Huck at the base of Cardiff Hill, Hannibal's north bookend with the lighthouse on top. For a century, Huck got little local recognition other than that statue, and the marquee at Huck Finn Shopping Center. But recently, the town took a meaningful step to embrace the true Huck. They built the Huck Finn House on a nearly vertical avenue called Hill Street, aptly named even for Hannibal's undulous standards.

Twain agrees with Hannibalians that his childhood friend Tom Blankenship is the model for Huckleberry Finn. I suspect Tom Blankenship's soul is soaring—wherever it ended up—to see a $300,000 structure represent the shack where Huck plotted when his Pap passed out. No matter what Tom Blankenship thinks, a high-rent shack signals a step forward for the citizens of Hannibal to embrace their culture, warts and all, in a fashion befitting their favorite son. It's a tougher leap for the town to come to grips with acknowledging Huck's costar Jim, the runaway slave. For folks whose eyeballs are between their ears, it's common knowledge that racism can surface in a small town But it's particularly difficult to deal with the vestiges of racism in this famous river town, named after an African genius.

One by one, all my Hannibal family died and each time one died, we'd gather after the burial for a meal at the Mark Twain Dinette. Now, they're all in one cemetery or another, so I consumed my giant tenderloin alone, uninterrupted, in no hurry to visit much of anything else in Hannibal on this trip

I slept that night in a place that was built for reclining but not sleeping. Lula Belle's is a bed & breakfast down by the river and the railroad tracks, those two commercial conduits that supplied a steady stream of business for Lula Belle's original purpose. Dad was just a young kid when his neighborhood gang, the RinkyDinks, would ride their bicycles to the riverfront, and hide in the weeds across the street from Lula Belle's.

Back then, the place wasn't called Lula Belle's. And callers didn't stick around for breakfast. The kids would gasp and squeal as they recognized pillars of the community slipping in, sneaking out.

Lying in that old bordello with the ghosts of the oldest profession, I fell asleep repeating the mantra, "Nothing's better than a good night's sleep." Next morning I aroused to the scent of brewing coffee, and the next great adventure.

* * *

Before he died, John Clemens, Mark Twain's father, was an early partner in building the old Hannibal and St. Joseph Railroad, which, as one might suspect, leads from Hannibal to St. Joseph. Nobody rides those rails anymore, since a modern highway can deliver a driver from Hannibal to St. Jo between meals.

That was my goal when I left Hannibal, to be seated for dinner at the old Hoof & Horn, a historic steakhouse on the hide of St. Jo's stockyards.

But on my way, I took a detour. And another. With no plan, I began a string of shortcuts that lasted beyond a dozen years, a journey that left my tire tracks along every mile of every road on my highway map.

My traveling companion was with me, the only partner that accompanied me on every mile of every Missouri road. It wasn't Cheryl, who married me 35 years ago. She tolerates my travels, but has no desire to ride shotgun. Can't blame her. Not everybody has the good sense to spend whole days crisscrossing county roads for the simple reason that they exist, checking off an alphabet soup of road signs, intent on discovering nothing in particular.

Our two daughters, having real lives of their own, agree with their mother about my foolish compulsion. Truth is, only one partner could put up with my aimless wandering: I met her in a car lot a dozen years ago. She was sleek and new and lipstick red, and even though I didn't realize it at the time, she would carry me faithfully from beginning to end of this journey.

The car's name is Erifnus Caitnop. She shares in every discovery herein, so the "we" in this odyssey refers to my ride and me. Erifnus and I covered more miles than the combined travels of Marco Polo and Magellan, Columbus and Zebulon Pike, Lewis and Clark and Dr. Livingstone. The only difference between us and those other explorers is that their amazing feats of bravery, skill and sacrifice changed the world. We just drove around. A lot.

Aside from the few intrepid reporters who rode along with me from time to time, I rarely could interest anybody to take these long treks into the middle of nowhere.

Can't blame them.

The Avenue of the Greats

During the Great Depression, Dad was a hitchhiker by necessity. He was a poor college student in Kirksville, Missouri, with no car, not even money for a bus ticket. So he used his thumb.

In those days, Truman State University was called Kirksville State Teachers College. It was a suitcase school, and every weekend Dad would hitchhike back to his home on the outskirts of Hannibal, to a town called Oakwood where the only thing harder than Depression life was the well water. One Friday afternoon after his class, he packed his cardboard suitcase and walked to the highway to thumb a ride home.

On Highway 63 near Kirksville's south city limits, he dropped his bag with the purple college pennant plastered on its side, and he stuck out his thumb. His goal was to reach the Macon junction and head east to Hannibal. A multitude of cars bypassed him as he stood with his thumb out. In the distance, he noticed a sleek black limousine approaching. He figured it was useless to stick out his thumb, but he did anyway out of habit. The limousine slowed. He couldn't see anything through the car's window shades. The car rolled past him and pulled to the shoulder. He was still hesitant to run after the car. The chauffeur got out. Dad picked up his bag and ran to catch up.

"Where ya headed?" the chauffeur asked.

"Hannibal."

"Are you a Kirksville student?"

"I am."

"Well, we'd like to give you a lift, at least as far as Macon. We'll have to let you out there, since you're going east and we're headed west."

The driver put Dad's bag in the trunk and opened the passenger door. Seated inside was a distinguished white-haired man who could have passed for Mark Twain's ghost. But Dad knew it wasn't Mark Twain's ghost, since the car wasn't headed to Hannibal.

The chauffeur made the introduction: "This is J.C. Penney." Even back in the '30s, Penney was in his sixties. "We're happy to have a Kirksville student to ride with us," he welcomed Dad.

"Well, I appreciate the ride, especially with you...." Dad stammered.

Penney explained why he stopped: "It's Friday, you look like a student, you have the emblems on your bag. I enjoy conversations with college students because I get ideas about merchandising. I don't get enough opportunities to talk to people directly about what they want."

They talked for the hour it took to reach Macon. Dad told Penney about the things he'd like to buy in a department store, a long list from a kid mired at the bottom of the Great Depression. Dad hopped out, thanked Penney and the chauffeur, and thumbed east to Hannibal. Penney headed west, home to Hamilton. They both were following a road that would become the Avenue of the Greats.

* * *

West of Hannibal just off that highway, Dad's grandfather lies in a peaceful cemetery next to a church that struggles against time. Like the pastoral setting where he's buried, Daniel O'Dwyer was a man of peace—mostly. Oh, there's strong evidence that he liked whiskey more than gravy. He'd stand in the churchyard after services and get drunk with his cronies while their families waited in wagons, shivering cold. And yes, sometimes when he got drunk he would fight, but never in the churchyard and never in front of the family.

Years before, he had been a Catholic priest in his native County Cork, Ireland, until the church excommunicated him for falling in love with a girl who became my great-grandmother. They came to this country and dropped the overtly Irish "O'" from their name. He became a teacher, and she became a mother to their nine children, and when he died—murdered by horse thieves who tied him to railroad tracks—she scraped together money to pay the church a ransom to bury the pieces of his body in consecrated ground.

Dad always told me to "live recklessly for good." I guess it's a family trait.

So I drove west to get to Daniel Dwyer's grave.

Over the decades, the unique personalities of legendary routes have earned them colorful nicknames: Burma Road. Tobacco Road. The Mother Road.

This road to St. Jo deserves a nickname, too. So I call it the Avenue of the Greats. Nobody else does. Regardless, this road is the birthplace of your modern concepts of literature, religion, fighting, driving, shopping, sinking, eating and armed robbery. Seriously.

Locals still refer to it as Route 36, because that's what it is. Nobody says, "I'm going down the Avenue of the Greats to get some gas." A few years ago lawmakers gave the road a formal name: the V.F.W. Memorial Highway. But nobody calls it that. More recently, a group of tourism promoters tried to nickname it The Way of American Genius. Nobody calls it that, either. Nicknames take time to stick. Some never do.

Like a headband, the Avenue of the Greats stretches across Missouri's brow and attaches to America's great jugular veins, the Missouri River on the western edge of the state and the Mighty Mississippi on the eastern edge. From that narrow nerve passage between Missouri's temporal lobes evolved some of the globe's most influential individuals.

How influential? Two decades ago a London newspaper polled its readers with one simple question: "Who is your favorite American?" Respondents picked Mark Twain, Jesse James and Mickey Mouse. All three were born along this road.

Those are world-famous names. But this highway is the estuary for other greats who made their marks on the world. Even before Erifnus and I left downtown Hannibal, we passed the house where the Unsinkable Molly Brown grew up, on a hillside so steep it taught her how to remain buoyant during a lifetime of ups and downs. Down the road and around the bend, I was about to stumble onto the story of a man who should be a candidate for sainthood.

A few miles off the Avenue of the Greats, Route DD turns its pavement over to a gravel road. Just past a fork in the road, Brush Creek Cemetery sits in peaceful seclusion. There, I'd revisit the grave of Daniel Dwyer, the Irish Catholic priest who became my great grandfather, and I'd bask in his special brand of evangelical fervor, with its heavy emphasis on liquor and procreation.

Meantime, in that same country churchyard, I discovered a story with a meaning as deep as Huckleberry Finn. Unlike Huck's tale, though, this story is true. It's just not as well known. Beside that cemetery on a bluff above the Salt River, where Samuel Clemens roamed as a boy and ran as a rebel, there sits a very unique window to Missouri's past.

St. Peter's Church casts its short shadow beside the cemetery, awaiting parishioners from Monroe City and Perry, Spalding and

Rensselaer, as it has ever since the church was built back at the beginning of the Civil War. Nowadays, the faithful come to the country church less often. There are no regularly scheduled masses. But on the church wall a small plaque would help lead to a revival in its proud ministry.

The plaque hails this home parish of Father Augustine Tolton, a man who would break the color barrier in the American priesthood. Augustine was trained and ordained in Rome, because America would afford him no such opportunity. He was born a slave.

Despite that barrier, nearly 60 years before Jackie Robinson broke baseball's color line and 70 years before Rosa Parks inspired the Montgomery Bus Boycott, the young priest who would become known as Good Father Gus said his first mass in the United States, thus becoming America's first African-American Roman Catholic priest. His long journey began here, in this little chapel.

I surveyed the scene. Here, in the middle of nowhere, a tiny church was losing its struggle against weather and time, abandonment and neglect. Despite the best efforts of local supporters and a spot on the National Historic Register, the building was in danger of collapsing before its 150th birthday. Because the good Catholic families who live nearby had migrated to other parishes, the diocese discontinued regular mass at St. Peter's. The building's roof sagged. A peek through the church's windows revealed crumbled ceiling plaster covering dust-caked pews. The tiny living quarters for a priest, attached to the back of the church like a lean-to, was a wooden box not much bigger than a horse stall. It was past mere decay. But even as the lean-to collapsed and the roof sagged and the incense was replaced by the smell of water damage, the church's rock walls remained as strong as the last time young Augustine John Tolton saw them.

At his birth, the church's baptismal record gave no name: "A colored child born April 1, 1854, son of Peter Tolton and Martha Chisley, property of Stephen Elliott; Mrs. Stephen Elliott, sponsor; May 29, 1854." Peter and Martha, Augustine's parents, were enslaved separately to neighboring families, so when Peter and Martha wed in St. Peter's, the families agreed that any children would be owned by Martha's owners, the Elliotts. Martha was Mrs. Elliott's personal slave. As a child, Augustine was raised in the influence of the Brush Creek parish of St. Peter's.

But in 1861 as parishioners were building the rock-walled church that struggles to survive today, Augustine's father left to join the Union army. Soon after, Augustine left with his mother and two siblings. Stories differ about whether they were freed by the Elliotts or ran away. Regardless, the family rowed one night across the Mississippi River into Illinois and freedom.

Illinois offered freedom from slavery. But racism infected rural Illinois the same as it infected Missouri. When he wasn't working in a tobacco factory in Quincy, Illinois, young Augustine attended a private parochial school at the urging of a local priest. The community howled in protest at this mixing of races. Parents threatened to take their children out of the school and quit the Catholic Church. They even threatened violence. Augustine was forced to leave the school, and years passed before another priest enrolled him in a different parochial school. Once again, parishioners threatened violence. But the priest insisted that Augustine stay in school. He ultimately graduated from Quincy College, taught by Franciscan friars.

Along the way, he knew he wanted to become a priest. But that ambition hit a solid wall of prejudice. He was rejected by every American seminary to which he applied, even schools that trained white priests to serve the black community. Supporters believed so strongly in his calling that they applied for him to study at Pontifical Urbaniana University in Rome. Eventually he was accepted, with the understanding he likely would be sent to Africa or New Guinea as a missionary.

Instead, in a move that disappointed Augustine, the Vatican sent him back to Quincy, amid the same racism and hate he had endured as a child. Yet the young priest quickly became well-known as Father Gus, with a reputation for giving inspirational sermons at St. Joseph Negro Church, where his powerful messages attracted an audience of blacks and whites alike.

Again, Father Gus heard protests about mixing races. He felt the heat from white citizens who targeted his ministry and even a few black preachers who bristled at his success. Some of the strongest protests actually came from the local Catholic Church hierarchy, who told him to stop taking money from white parishioners for his black church. Further, they ordered him to minister "only to Negroes."

Not long after, Father Gus angered the gentrified community by agreeing to perform a wedding ceremony between a society girl and, according to the girl's mother, an "unacceptable" person. Eventually Father Gus, his local superiors and the Vatican all agreed it was time for him to move on.

So he moved to Chicago, where the archbishop gave him "full pastoral jurisdiction" over the more than 27,000 blacks who lived in the city during the late 1880s. Augustine's calm demeanor, punctuated by a passionate speaking voice, again attracted blacks and whites to his sermons.

On a hot summer day in 1897, he was returning from a retreat south of Chicago when he succumbed to the 105-degree heat and collapsed on a Chicago street. Hospital records say he died of heat exhaustion and uremia. Many of his contemporaries believe he worked himself to death. He was 43 years old.

As he requested, he is buried in a Quincy cemetery for priests. Yet prejudice followed him to his grave. He was buried deep in the ground to allow another priest's coffin to be interred above his. Yet now the Catholic Church is considering him for sainthood.

Today the little church where Augustine Tolton was baptized appears to have survived its painful period of neglect, thanks to a spirited rescue effort powered by one lady. I remember how that rescue came together.

A dozen years ago, speaking to a cultural heritage conference in St. Louis, I asked attendees if they knew about Augustine Tolton or where he lived. None did.

But after the event, one lady asked me for directions to the little church. Her name was Gwendolyn Crimm, and at the time she worked as the ethnic coordinator for the Catholic Archdiocese of St. Louis.

A year later, my family was on a Memorial Day tour of graveyards when we rolled up the long path through a canopy of tall cedars, into the St. Peter's Church grounds. There was Gwen Crimm with a dozen young scouts from St. Louis chopping brush, mowing grass and painting the trim on the church. For Gwen, this was just the first step.

The next year, the church had a new roof, and the interior was restored. The bishop said a mass at the tiny church. On that Sunday morning, the scores of visitors were greeted by something else: Several dozen simple wooden crosses stood atop the unmarked graves on the perimeter of the cemetery. Those are the graves of the slaves who lived and worked in the farms and fields around the parish. Locals say one mass grave contains as many as 30 bodies—victims of a deadly cholera epidemic.

Father Augustine Tolton's bones lie in nearby Quincy. But his influence extends well beyond that, reaching out from his roots in tiny St. Peter's Church, where Monroe and Ralls counties meet along a line of unmarked graves.

The Dinner Table

Taking the Highway 15 exit ramp off the Avenue of the Greats, I can get to anywhere in tiny Shelbina in five minutes, as long as a freight train isn't crawling through the middle of town.

It wasn't, and that was a good thing because the chime on my radio signaled it was straight-up noon, and as the newscaster began his first story, I knew lunch was already on the table.

From different directions, Robert Shoemyer and I arrived at the table at the same time. We exchanged greetings as we sat down to the glorious task of absorbing a 15-course meal. Robert is a family friend—and my hero. He farms for a living. And like most folks who toil the whole time the sun is watching, he stays young behind his weather-beaten face that looks all the more leathery as he sits hatless across the table from me, his balding pate a pasty white above a tan line as stark as the rustline in a porcelain tub. That tan line is testament to five dozen seasons on the seat of a tractor, sowing soybeans and feeding cattle. Robert has the energy and the enthusiasm of a kid despite his 75 years. He owes his stamina to early rising and hard work and clean living, but mostly to his companion for 50-some odd years.

Dorothy Shoemyer's kitchen table looks like a Grandma Moses painting. Everything is on it. Everything. Her face would be on the label of the grocery-store package that says "grandma's home cooking," if there was such a package. Robert and I dug into a home-grown, sit-down, all-you-can-eat, family-style, "don't stop now because there's only a spoonful of cottage cheese left and finish up those peaches 'cause I can't keep up with 'em fallin' off the trees and here, have some more fried chicken 'cause there's not enough room to put all this stuff back in the fridge" dinner from Dorothy Shoemyer's kitchen table, featuring beef and gravy and new potatoes with green beans from the garden and sliced home-grown tomatoes and cucumbers from her garden, too, and corn and relish and pickled beets and bread and butter.

Robert watched me coax the last drops of chocolate syrup out of a Hershey's squirt bottle onto a dish of vanilla ice cream. I worked the squeeze bottle like a bellows, violently expelling a few drops of syrup in a flatulent whoosh, then waited as the air wheezed back into the plastic bottle.

"Give it here," Robert said. He grabbed the squeeze bottle and decapitated it, held it in one hand and a gallon milk jug in the other. He poured milk into the syrup bottle.

"Chocolate milk," he explained," and I don't even have to dirty a glass." Dorothy Shoemyer chuckled as she flitted like a hummingbird from stove to table to sink.

"More ice cream?" she asked.

"No, thanks," I demurred, as I watched Robert shake his squirt bottle to make his chocolate milk. I was stuffed. It's rare that a weary road traveler gets a home-cooked meal, especially for lunch.

Robert's work ethic is impressive, and he's married to Saint Cook. But that's not why he's my hero. Robert finds a use for everything. Or a short cut. And I knew that as soon as he finished his chocolate milk, the squeeze bottle would find the recycling bin. This lunch was a refreshing oasis in my sojourn through this big, throwaway world.

Back on the Avenue of the Greats, I was still three hours away, as the crow flies, from St. Joseph. Damn the crows. My hands and my wheels worked together to steer me through the landscape like a trackless Tilt-A-Whirl. The trip was a dream for a guy who battles attention deficit disorder. And in the beginning, when nothing lay before me but untraveled roads, I didn't obsess about completing the long journey. Truth is, I really didn't have a plan or a system to reach this fuzzy, forming goal of driving everywhere. But I kept track, marking my map, taking notes, dodging turtles and squirrels, stray calves and texters. I chipped away at my map, line by squiggly line.

Along every mile, I counted every yellow dash in the road's center line, one after the other. I counted them all, a whole state's worth. My mental abacus wore thin counting yellow dashes, as I retraced routes a hundred times to get to fresh pavement, and I counted the dashes then too. Their number is staggering but unimportant. It's only one more burden in my quiver of compulsions. The yellow dashes speak only one language, but the places and the people along the roadside, even the dead ones—especially the dead ones—they have better stories, and those stories connect the dots in this journey.

I packed along the eyes of Everyman and my car provided the persistent "putt putt" of *Pac Man*. The spirits of Chief Tatschaga and Black Dog guided me past the menacing signs of doom, always reminding that the end is near. The highways themselves reminded me of that, because each highway has an end. Highways have souls. They showed me.

My map's cover spells Missouri. But the adventure could just as easily be Texas or Manitoba or Lilliput. The map called out the names; I traced the stories. Every fold in the Ozarks, every bend in the rivers, every drive down the main drag in 700 towns reminded me that even as my map sets the stage, it can't produce the play. Maps squish miles into millimeters. They conceal identities even as they reveal names. They're lazy and they won't work on their own, preferring to doze, folded tight as a sleeping dog, gravitating to dark out-of-the-way spots like glove compartments and magazine racks.

Maps are threatened by a lot of things—by GPS devices that talk to us in a soothing female voice, by TV shows that tell us where to go even as they hinder us from getting started, by packaged tours that lead us by the nose, and by airlines that require us to be on time so we can wait, and stand in lines and take direction from people who wish they were on vacation. But mostly maps suffer from those twin bookends that fence the borders of our lives: familiarity and neglect. We drive toward familiar. We neglect almost everything else.

I drove up Highway 15 and took the back roads to Looney Creek. It's a peaceful spot, like most country cemeteries. Gentle hillsides, breeze flowing through the trees. It's where my mother's great-grandfather is buried. But his demise was anything but peaceful. He was murdered in Macon during the Civil War, executed by Union soldiers who had arrested him and nine other local men suspected of being Southern sympathizers.

That was the Macon Massacre, September 26, 1862.

After the massacre, eleven-year-old Edgar Davis Drake helped family members bury his dad at Looney Creek Cemetery. And then Edgar returned to work the family farm on Tiger Fork with his mother and brother and sister. The war raged on around Shelby County, but it was over for the fatherless Drake family. Edgar would tell my mother the story until he died in 1942 and joined his father at Looney Creek.

Beyond this peaceful spot, on this autumn afternoon, the Great Impressionist had turned expansive soybean fields into giant green-and-gold palettes. Some fields, planted earliest in the spring, already had turned brown, the beans ready for harvest. The drive through the patchwork of soybean fields was reminiscent of a Monet canvas or a Van Gogh landscape. Green, speckled with bright yellows and bordered by buckskin browns. These vibrant fields were framed by hardwood forests, themselves changing into their autumn dress of maroon and orange and gold. On some of the fields, farmers were beginning to harvest the grain, and flocks of red-tailed hawks followed the combines as they chopped up the cornstalks and exposed the once secret trails of a thousand mice.

Back on the road, only minutes west of here, I knew my car would stop at Main Street USA. The real one.

The World's Imagineer

It was cocktail hour when they cornered me. We were churning up the Tennessee River toward Chattanooga on an old paddle-wheel steamboat. Four hundred travel agents had turned the steamer into a floating tourism convention. A couple from Carolina put me on the defensive. They couldn't resist the temptation to ask, "Why would anybody go to Missouri?"

My answer was a question. "Do you book family vacations to Orlando?"

"Hundreds," they said.

"And Disneyland, too?"

"Of course," they answered, and eyed me like I was an idiot.

"Well, after they've seen Main Street at the Disney parks, send 'em to Marceline to see the real thing," I said. They looked puzzled at my blasphemy against the Great Disney. After all, on the world stage, Marceline's main street remains a secret.

That's understandable. A tiny Midwest town founded with little fanfare by the Santa Fe Railroad surely can't have a main street that competes with the bright lights of Broadway, the music on Bourbon Street, the stars along Hollywood Boulevard.

Nevertheless, perhaps the most replicated street in the world runs through the middle of Marceline.

Flash back to 1955: Walt Disney had long since moved away from Marceline and made his mouse tracks in the world. But a half century hadn't dulled Disney's memories of the happiest time of his life. That's why Marceline's main street inspired Walt's blueprint for Main Street at Disneyland. For sure, the Magic Kingdom's Main Street was a communal effort among Walt and his art directors, who jazzed it up with bells and whistles and walking photo-ops in the forms of life-size cartoon characters. But every element of Disney's Marceline is represented at the theme parks. The train station. The locomotive. The gazebo. The picture show. Walt described the essence of his Main Street vision: "Main Street is everyone's hometown—the heart line of America. To tell the truth, more things of importance happened to me in Marceline than have happened since, or are likely to in the future."

Even with Hollywood success, Disney remained loyal to his roots. "I'm glad I'm a small-town boy," he said, "and I'm glad Marceline was my town." So Main Street in Disneyland maintains that Marceline feel, albeit with more window dressing. Ditto for Disney World and for the other magic kingdoms from Paris to Tokyo. Walt Disney wanted them that way.

Marceline's main drag wasn't always known as "Main Street." For most of its history, street signs carried its given name, Kansas Avenue. And the Missouri state highway map calls it Route JJ. But to anybody who sees it now, it's Main Street USA, right down to the black wrought-iron street signs sprouting mouse ears.

It's nearly impossible to travel more than one block in Marceline without opening a page in the storybook of young Walt's life. The icons pop up everywhere, testament to Walt Disney's influence on the town, and the town's influence on Walt. The Walt Disney Post Office. The Walt Disney Elementary School. The picture show where Disney's "The Great Locomotive Chase" premiered.

Kaye Malins' eyes sparkle when she tells stories about the young imagineer. Her dad and Walt were pals. She showed me around town, pointing out the spots where young Walt first discovered the world. When he wasn't hanging out downtown in a vacant lot beside a giant wall painted with a Coca-Cola logo, he might be found in his back yard engaged in what he later called "belly botany." Lying on his stomach in a field, he'd conduct an up-close study of ants and aphids, crickets and critters. Indeed, the descendants of Jiminy Cricket still live here.

On every trip back home, Walt would depart the train and walk through Marceline's Santa Fe depot, a building that fell into disrepair after his death. But Kaye Malins and crew brought it back to life as the Walt Disney Hometown Museum, with hundreds of artifacts like the Midget Autopia kiddie-car ride. Kaye says it's the only ride Walt allowed to leave a Disney property and operate elsewhere.

Kaye is a walking encyclopedia on Walt's Marceline years. She literally dreams Disney, living in his boyhood home on the outskirts of town. That's a Disney tale in itself. Her father, Rush Johnson, became a business associate of Walt Disney. The partners agreed to re-purchase the old Disney farmhouse and eventually establish a living-history farm. Although both partners are gone, Kaye has taken steps to enhance living history at Walt's boyhood home. She showed me the house, including the bedroom Walt and brother Roy shared, unchanged from their childhood.

Behind the house, young Walt's Dreaming Tree still stands un-bowed in the fields behind the Disney home. One of the oldest cot-tonwood trees standing in Missouri, it was mature even when Walt was a boy. The tree has survived two lightning strikes, which only added power to the inspiration that flows from its branches.

Not fifty paces from the Dreaming Tree sits the barn. In typical Disney style, the townspeople raised a new barn in 2001 to replicate the structure where eight-year-old Walt got his showbiz start. It's a faithful replica, with a swayback roof—like the one that faithful Mouseketeers remember on TV—a shrine on the spot where his imagination began.

The original barn was the venue for Walt's first showbiz produc-tion, a circus. He charged neighborhood kids a dime apiece to see barnyard animals dressed in toddlers clothes. Most of his fellow eight-year-olds left the show less than satisfied. Locals testify that Walt's mother made him return the proceeds to his disgruntled patrons. Therein he learned his first valuable showbiz lesson: When promot-ing a show, under-promise and over-deliver. In retrospect, the attend-ees probably consider the admission price a bargain for the memories those thin dimes bought the lucky crowd.

From all over the world, pilgrims visit the new barn, scribbling thousands of notes, verses, and signatures in every language on the rough-hewn wood walls and beams.

Somewhere, a belly botanist is beaming.

Blackjack, Zack and the Bread Rack

We drove west toward a horizon smeared with smoke. Even from a distance I could tell it wasn't the steamy cloud produced when volunteer firefighters pour water on a burning barn, or the black-orange roiling of a gasoline fire from a wreck. We got closer and veered off the Avenue of the Greats to investigate. What we encountered was surreal. Crossing the boundary into this domain, we were surrounded by scorched earth on all sides. Smoke rose from the smoldering ground, commanding the senses to yield to confusion. Slowly, Erifnus and I felt our way forward, immersed in the conflagration that might've been Verdun.

But it wasn't. The road led us through the forests and fields that were the playground of a child named John Pershing. Young John would grow up with the ambition to be a school teacher. But an education at West Point changed his course, and he rose through the ranks to become General of the Armies. With a nickname he picked up during his command of the army's vaunted Buffalo Soldiers, General Blackjack Pershing led doughboys to save the world, in his role as Commander-in-Chief of the American Expeditionary Force during World War I. His remains lie beneath a simple marker in Arlington National Cemetery.

But on this day, his ghost moved in the cover of smoke that rose from his childhood playground, now called Pershing State Park. Park rangers had set a series of controlled grass fires that burned through leaves and brush. The fires would energize the soil, but as we moved deeper into the smoke, it was an eerie, unintended remake of a battle during the War to End All Wars.

Obviously, that first visit to Pershing State Park was not what I expected. But that's the beauty of exploring new territory. And it's a reminder that indeed, you never step into the same burning battlefield twice.

I'm just grateful to the state park personnel, who unwittingly welcomed me in a way I'll never forget.

Across the highway from that state park is Pershing's home. As a boy, born at the outbreak of the Civil War, he didn't have to worry about crossing busy highways to get to his playground, like kids do today. And Highway 36 didn't roll past his house until 1922, long after he had left to vanquish the Axis powers, at least for a while. But when he came back from Europe, leaders asked him to turn his logistical skills to highway planning. His 1921 Pershing Map for a national highway grid is the grandfather of the Interstate Highway System, finally funded during President Eisenhower's administration.

Today, the Avenue of the Greats doesn't go through Laclede, Missouri, anymore. And Pershing's hometown looks much like it did when he lived here: Sleepy. Comfortable.

On the edge of this little town, big concrete pillars once propped the overpass where Highway 36 crossed Highway 139. Now the pillars prop only sky. A middle-aged man with crooked teeth rode a go-kart through the town's empty streets. Bordering the city park were a dozen American flags.

A block away, a statue of the man who saved Europe stands near his boyhood home. I paused in front of that house and thanked his mother for raising a son who envisioned our modern highway system. Then Erifnus motored down the road to Chillicothe, where I discovered a story that led to national outrage.

Back in 1928 a jeweler from St. Joseph named Otto Rehwedder invented the first automatic bread slicer, which he sold to the Chillicothe Baking Company. The invention was heralded by kitchen help everywhere, and even though some folks claim the first automatic bread slicer was used in Battle Creek, Michigan, that wasn't the ruckus. When a St. Louis inventor named Gustav Papendick improved the process by inventing a cardboard tray that kept the sliced loaf together before it got wrapped, the future looked bright for sliced bread.

But then Hitler invaded Poland and Japan bombed Pearl Harbor, and America went to war. As a wartime conservation effort, America's food administrator banned sliced bread, claiming that the heavy wrapping was a wasteful step, and needless in our consumption of bread. The ban lasted 49 days, crumbling under the outrage of cooks and moms and sandwich eaters everywhere, and the ghosts of Prohibition, too, who reminded leaders about the last time the government tried to control yeast.

So sliced bread flourished, and so did Chillicothe, which adopted the slogan "Home of Sliced Bread" and painted its 13th downtown mural to celebrate the feat. I indulged in a yeasty treat while my eyes feasted upon the baker's-dozen tasty murals downtown. Among other scenes of wheat fields and flour mills and streetscapes, a Burlington Northern locomotive belches smoke and steam. The murals are proof that Chillicotheans promote their town better than most do, offering mural mugs and mural magnets. As good as Chillicothe is at promotion, the recognized father of modern mercantile hails from just down the road.

Tiny Hamilton, Missouri, actually produced two legendary Americans. Hamilton marks the intersection of the Avenue of the Greats and the Zack Wheat Highway. Most folks probably know more about Cream o' Wheat than Zack Wheat. Casey Stengel called Zack "one of the kindliest men God ever created." Kindliness doesn't guarantee fame, and it's likely that more folks can identify Casey's General Store than Casey Stengel. Well, Casey and Zack are baseball icons, in a league with Babe Ruth and Ty Cobb. Zack played baseball in Polo, Missouri, and the Polo Grounds, too. Nowadays, more folks know about Polo shirts than the Polo Grounds, but that's what happens to immortals over time. Anyway, now Highway 13 from Polo to Hamilton is Zack Wheat Highway.

Hamilton is also J.C. Penney's birthplace. While there doesn't appear to be a J.C. Penney Highway near here, or anywhere in Missouri, there is a J.C. Penney Memorial Highway in Florida.

In Hamilton, it's easy to find the 500th store built by J.C. Penney, right on the main highway, one block from the local Casey's General Store. It's a museum now, since his hometown isn't big enough to support a J.C. Penney store. It shares space with the town library, which probably increases traffic for both places. Hey, it's a small town. I was the only visitor on the morning I walked through the displays of Penney's life, his photos and memorabilia. I learned how one of 12 children in the Penney household revolutionized the mercantile business. Mostly self-taught, his employee-training regimen is legendary. Even as a kid, while he raised feeder pigs, he sold lemonade and watermelons and livery stalls to playmates with stick horses. But I respect him most for his conservation ethic: He insisted that employees turn off the light when they exited the bathroom.

The museum is very much the way it might've looked in 1950, when merchandise stacked the shelves. In fact, much of the room looks like it hasn't been changed since 1950. That's not an indictment of the good people of Hamilton, who operate on a budget that's, well, pennies. They make do with what they have. A life-size wax figure of Penney is held stationary by a wire around its neck that gives the unfortunate impression of a garrotte. The Penney Museum could benefit from the creative touch of a cadre of J.C. Penney corporate display designers and marketers. The company could install some interactive displays, online stuff that would attract youngsters, challenge them, maybe even create brand awareness and loyal customers. Old James Cash Penney would approve, I suspect. But neither of us are holding our breath.

Erifnus and I motored north, systematically driving blacktops and marking them off the map, when we drove into a line of thunderstorms. Ahead, a bridge was closed for repairs. Backtracking to pick a detour, I smacked into a torrential downpour. Driving too fast for conditions, I forced Erifnus through a curve her tires couldn't hold. We did a 360-degree spinout in the middle of the road, but we stayed on the pavement. It wasn't my car's fault. This spin was totally self-inflicted. We regrouped, took a deep breath, and motored into the storm.

In the confusion and the downpour, I spent an hour compensating for two wrong turns, and by the time we rejoined the intended route, daylight yielded to dusk, and then to darkness. I could only catch strobe-like glimpses of our surroundings through constant flashes of lightning.

It was a rough day driving the back roads of Missouri.

Driving through one downpour after another, losing count of the lightning flashes, we pressed toward our destination, and with every passing neon diner sign, I knew my chances dwindled for a sit-down dinner.

Just before midnight we reached St. Jo, originally called Black Snake Landing, and rolled into the perfect setting for a horror movie. The city looks as old as Dracula's coffin, as ornate as a Victorian mansion.

Thunder punched us as Erifnus pointed up a steep hill, the kind of incline that's unavoidable in river towns. Ahead, backlit by theatrical lightning flashes, sat my destination, the mansion atop Museum Hill.

Beth Courter loves her old mansion. And it shows in every corner, every comfort of the Museum Hill B&B. She and husband John pour heart and soul into this house. He's a retired navy chef with a nickname right out of Hollywood: Cookie Courter. Late as it was, Beth showed me the house, and fed me leftovers. Quiche and fruit salad. No gravy.

"Tomorrow, you'll see scores of wonderful old homes in these surrounding neighborhoods," she promised.

She wasn't exaggerating. The whole town is a museum, a bridge to a Golden Age when St. Jo capitalized on the insatiable hunger of westward expansion. But after that golden age, the town's robust economy slowed. Commerce rolled out of town like wagon trains, and townspeople found it impossible to save all the old stately mansions. Oh, some lucky houses revel in their restoration. Others await the capital punishment that comes from years of neglect. In these old neighborhoods, the houses stand together like teeth, some strong, some gone. And the tweeners beg for salvation.

Mawmaw's Boy

Almost every St. Joseph museum tells some part of the town's most sensational story, the killing of Mawmaw's boy.

Mawmaw raised some ornery children. Hellraisers. But she knew it wasn't their fault. Other folks made 'em mean. Other folks caused young Jesse to take up swearing. Some folks even think he invented the term "Dingus," a nickname brother Frank started calling him. Nobody else did, to his face anyway.

Mawmaw was a nickname, too, of course, and by that name or any other name, Zerelda James was the family's matriarch. To the children she was Mawmaw. To adults she was a force to be reckoned with. She must've been a role model of toughness for the boys. She must've earned some respect from the girls, too, or at least their parents, because Zerelda's son Jesse married his first cousin Zerelda, who was named for his mother. When the feds swept through and put a noose around Mawmaw's husband's neck and strung him up, she cut him down, saved his life. The Union later threw her in prison, accusing her of being a spy. And years after that, because of transgressions committed by two of her grown boys, the Pinkertons firebombed her house, blowing off her hand and killing her youngest son.

In downtown St. Joseph I parked right in front of the little house where Dingus died. The house used to be on the edge of town, but promoters moved it next to the Patee House museum downtown. I

walked around back and entered through the back door. Jesse probably felt more comfortable going in that back door, too, even though
around St. Jo he used an alias. Back when he and Zerelda lived there,
most neighbors called him Mr. Howard.

The back door opened into the kitchen, where I stuck my fee in
a jar and walked into the killer's living room. It was ugly, Victorian,
dated. The ugliest decoration was on the wall, a frame around a bullet hole. I knew the significance of the bullet hole, the one made after
the bullet exited Jesse's head. The existing wallpaper shouted like bad
drapes, but within the frame the old wallpaper looked like Vincent
Price picked it out. It was hideous, in a way that could highlight a
130-year-old bullet hole.

Jesse's bed still sits in his bedroom, along with other personal
items. The walls are covered with family photos. But among all that
history, that tiny square of the living room's original wallpaper with the
bullet hole may be the single most scary background since the movie,
"The Pit and the Pendulum."

On my way out of town, I passed one more museum. It also does
business as the Heaton-Bowman-Smith & Sidenfaden Funeral Home.
Back in 1882, the Sidenfaden Funeral Home was on 4th Street, near
the spot of Jesse's murder. When the victim's family notified the undertaker to pick up the body, Sidenfaden brought a wicker corpse basket to carry Jesse's remains. That basket is on display at the modern
funeral home, along with a ledger showing an entry for the Jesse James
funeral, and a few other relics from the past, like an icebox casket for
long-distance transport.

Jesse's body didn't need an icebox casket, since he was buried nearby. Some folks think Jesse's body was stolen by grave robbers. Others
believe that Jesse faked his death. All this modern brouhaha about the
whereabouts of Jesse James' body is silly, if you know anything about
Mawmaw. For the 30 years she lived after Jesse died, Zee James made
sure that nobody stole Missouri's most infamous dead body. That's because she had him interred next to her rural Kearney, Missouri, house,
so she could chase off any body snatchers.

Her house still stands today off the back roads of Clay County.
It's a rough-hewn cabin in the middle of the woods. Hard to sneak up
on. For years, local folks presented a stage play in the front yard of the
house, recreating the Pinkerton attack on the homestead, and visitors

sat in a portable grandstand rigged right in the front yard. Jesse would have been skeptical of the spectacle, but Zee would have taken the money, I suspect. Indeed, decades before the reenactments began, Zee James charged a quarter apiece for tourists to view Jesse's grave, and she'd give each visitor a stone, supposedly chipped from his headstone, but just as likely retrieved from a nearby creek.

When Zee died, Jesse's body was moved to Mount Olivet Cemetery in Kearney, where he rests next to his wife, Zee James the younger. The original tombstone on Jesse's first grave has been chipped away by grave stone robbers, sometimes also called tourists.

So far, nobody has succeeded in stealing Jesse's body from its new resting place. A few years ago some scientists dug Jesse up, just to lay the rumors to rest. Turns out they are his bones, all right. And within minutes, people started chipping pieces off his new headstone. With such a carnival sideshow fascination with dead legends, it's no wonder Frank James requested cremation for his own body. He didn't want to end up in a circus sideshow. In an ironic twist, the ashes of Frank the bank robber hid in a bank vault until his wife died in 1944. Now both lie in the Hill Park Cemetery in Independence.

Frank always respected dead bodies. Some folks say he had a hand in the honorable return of one corpse. It happened after the Civil War Battle of Wilson's Creek near Springfield. During that battle, General Nathaniel Lyon became the first Union general killed in the War Between the States. Not particularly loved by his troops, Lyon's body was left on the battlefield when the Union withdrew to Springfield. The Confederates recovered the body and took it to a makeshift hospital and morgue. They cleaned General Lyon and prepared the body for burial. They sent a messenger to the Union forces, who agreed to accept the general's body. A teamster wagon caught up with the retreating Union forces and delivered the corpse. One of the teamsters was Frank James, so the story goes.

There are a million stories about the James Gang. But I know this one is true: My Dad and Frank James were invited to work at the same job. Not at the same time, of course. In his later years, Dad was drafted to become a doorkeeper at the Missouri Senate, a job he held until he died. In 1904, legislators invited Frank to become a doorkeeper at the Missouri House of Representatives. But Democrat leaders got cold feet at the last moment and withdrew their offer. Hell of a thing to do to a lifelong loyal Democrat. That made Frank mad. He never voted for a Democrat again.

I headed south into Clay County, Jesse's back yard, veering around Smithville Lake, a man-made beauty which has attracted hundreds of homes to its shores. I wonder what Mawmaw would think about all this settlement so close to her homestead on the outskirts of Kearney. She'd probably be more upset to learn that Jesse has been laid to rest three times now. But that's what happens to real-life legends who won't hire Pinkertons to guard them.

Personally, I think Jesse would appreciate the fact that today from the James homestead, he could ride two miles west after supper, hop on I-35 in a BMW and be in Northfield, Minnesota, by the time the bank opens. Better yet, he could fly to Northfield from the Roosterville Airport, minutes from his family's homestead.

If you believe all the stories about his whereabouts, Jesse is the only person who has been to more places in Missouri than I have. I'm okay with that.

The Best Place to Hide Fried Chicken

I don't know if Jesse James ever ate fried chicken. Historians don't seem to care much about that. But I care. And I found a spot in Jesse's back yard that I suspect he would've liked. Laid back. Unpretentious. And good.

The first thing Jesse would like about Harmer's Café is that it's as secluded as a hideout. At least it's secluded from major highways. You won't see a sign on I-29 directing you to tiny Edgerton, home of Harmer's, since interstate signs won't point to any town that sits two blacktops away from the highway. And you won't see any billboards touting Harmer's charms. It's the kind of place that relies entirely on word-of-mouth.

Mouth is the operative word. Harmer's eschews fancy visual cues. There's no mood music, no corporate brand. The restaurant's interior offers a refreshing ambiance that's, well, real. Real linoleum. Real vinyl. Real fake pictures on the walls. In this age of corporate color schemes and themey menus, plastic décor and cardboard taste, Harmer's hearkens back to the time when small town corner cafés had character. The booths, a victory of function over form, jut from the walls and point to randomly positioned four-top tables in the middle of the room. To paraphrase the Bard: the food's the thing.

Harmer's serves catfish on Fridays and Saturdays and fried chicken on Thursdays and Sundays. In between, main courses range from meatloaf to ham, served blue-plate style. Each side gets the loving attention you'd give your fiancée. For example, the green beans aren't just green beans. They snuggle with onions, brown sugar and bacon.

Because my body is a temple, I had the chicken fried steak with mashed potatoes, smothered in cream gravy. Stewed tomatoes added some color. For extra fortification, and upon recommendation, I punished a piece of chocolate cream pie. Satisfied, I pushed away from the table and paid cash, the customary currency of the small town café, although I hear Harmer's recently began accepting credit cards.

Taking one last look around, I caught a glimpse of the kitchen through the slit where the cooks pass food to the servers. A rush of gratitude compelled me to stride over and shout a thank-you through the hole in the wall. Cooks don't hear "thank you" enough. Just ask 'em. On my way out, I fished for a complimentary toothpick from the little metal dispenser on the counter. After lunch, a toothpick becomes more than a toothpick. It's a memory chip, an afternoon reminder of a satisfying meal.

As the Kansas City skyline jumped above the horizon, I could see the old Art Deco skyscrapers standing defiantly against their sleeker, newer sisters. Behind them is the unique silhouette of a penthouse restaurant shaped like a flying saucer atop the old Hyatt Regency Hotel. Even though the hotel has changed names, the flying saucer still sits atop the building, a constant reminder to me that this was the grisly scene of a skywalk collapse in the hotel's lobby back in 1981.

The collapse killed 114 people who had gathered for happy hour at a Friday tea dance to celebrate the birth of bebop in Kansas City. The huge crowd was jumpin' to the music, and the highest skywalk couldn't bear the weight. It gave way, pancaking dancers on two skywalks beneath, all crashing to the crowded dance floor below. I was driving through Kansas City on that day, and I remember seeing scores of ambulances and rescue engines screaming down I-70. I turned my radio to a news station and got sketchy details of the story. I could see the top of the hotel 20 blocks away. Its flying saucer looked normal. No smoke. No fire. But the lobby was a deadly gumbo of steel and concrete and flesh and blood.

Today I thought about a different Hyatt death story.

I heard about it from the lips of a good friend. Among the things Bob Smith does well, storytelling is at the top of the list. He swears this story is true. Bob's not dead. But for the purposes of this story, he became a dead guy.

Bob got mad at Kansas City's old Hyatt Regency Hotel. Earlier he had called the hotel and booked a room for the night. As the day progressed, he realized that his work was finished early, and he could drive home. So he called his assistant to have her cancel the room. But the hotel refused. The hotel's policy said that rooms must be canceled before 3 p.m. of the day of occupancy. Bob's assistant called at 3:05. So the room was his.

Fine. He went to the hotel lobby and calmly approached the desk clerk, a young man probably in his first job.

"Can you give me Bob Smith's room number, please?" Bob asked.

"Are you Bob Smith?"

"No," Bob lied.

"I'm sorry, sir, but the hotel can't give out information like that. I'll ring his room for you...."

"Well, that won't work," Bob said. "You see, Mr. Smith died last night, and I'm from the family. We've decided that since he had this room, and we couldn't cancel it, we'd just go ahead and have the visitation here instead of at the funeral home. You know, we'll save expenses. Oh, and the casket will be here in a few minutes. Can we get a couple of bellhops to help us get the casket on the elevator? And that marquee over there... we'll use that to announce the floor where Bob's body will be. Mourners will start arriving about 4:30."

The blood drained from the desk clerk's face. "Please, sir, tell me you're joking."

"I am," Bob said. "And please tell your management what I think of their cancellation policy."

Just a few blocks from there, in what some people call a rougher part of town, the sidewalks of 12th Street and Vine are worn thin by the heels of whores who strolled where Lieber and Stoller immortalized the song "Goin' to Kansas City." Down the street I stopped to take part in a ritual that's been happening every Saturday night since at least the Roaring '20s. Well, the ritual began only after Saturday night gave way to Sunday morning, after nightclubs—the Spinning

Wheel and Dante's Inferno, the Hi Hat and the Hey Hey—kicked the last patrons out the door. The musicians regrouped, climbing the creaking stairs to the second floor of a nondescript brick building on the fringe of 18th and Vine Streets, the epicenter of bebop. This building is its schoolhouse, where on early Sunday morning young wide-eyed cats would get a lesson, standing next to Count Basie and Charlie Parker and Big Joe Turner and Mary Lou Williams and Walter Page, who invented the walking bass.

It's the Musicians Mutual Federation, a union for black musicians, founded back in the days when African Americans were not admitted to white restaurants or white hotels or white country clubs or white Army barracks or white labor unions. Every Saturday night after the bars closed, every major jazz talent who played KC stopped at this address for the regular Saturday night jam. On this late Saturday night, I thought I'd take a turn at the piano. The McFarland brothers showed up with their trumpet and sax and tap shoes and talent, and joined some equally impressive young phenoms. I sat on my hands until 4 a.m., mesmerized, and never got up my courage to play.

I returned to my favorite home away from home, the stately old Raphael Hotel. Almost forgotten, it sits across a creek from the Plaza—the world's first shopping mall—and has sheltered shoppers in its cozy confines for the better part of a century. It got a makeover recently, and while the guest rooms got new upholstery and pillows and flat-screen TVs, they also kept the bathrooms with the postage stamp-sized white tile, and the boxy little elevator with the retractable scissor-gate door that yearns for its old friend, the elevator operator.

Trumanity, Saddles and Lasting Impressions

It's safe now.

Any time of day, folks drive between Kansas City and Nevada, Missouri, with little fear of being stopped to demonstrate their allegiance to one warlord or another. Shoot, there's hardly anybody hiding in the bushes anymore. And telephone poles have replaced bullets as the primary cause of death along these back roads.

Things have calmed down considerably since the 1850s and '60s, when people in Kansas and Missouri killed each other and kept score with scalps. Everybody hated everybody else. Nobody trusted anybody. And leaving Kansas City for a trip in any direction would agitate a succession of local ruffians, the first of which would likely convince you to turn back, if they didn't kill you on the spot. Tough crowd. After the Civil War, Missourians began their long journey toward civility. Commerce and people slowly crept back into the towns along the Kansas border. Remnants of families returned to their farms to bury burned bodies and rebuild their charred homesteads.

Today, my trip would be easy. Oh, Missourians still instinctively clutch for weapons at the mention of Kansas, but the modern weapons are footballs and basketballs, mostly. I must admit, when I left the comfort of the Raphael Hotel, that sweet old relic overlooking the Kansas City Plaza, I had no particular route in mind. I just wanted to explore some back roads on my way to the tin ceiling factory in Nevada, three hours south. And I had the luxury of time. The path of least resistance is Highway 71. A recent peacetime project turned this turbulent trail into a four-lane fast track, slicing down through the stack of counties bordering Jayhawk Nation. Leaving KC, my tires rejoiced on the 71 speedway. Nowadays along that route, the telephone poles go by fast.

I can't blame folks for being in a hurry. It happened to me once, too. So I continually remind myself to slow down and take my cue from gawkers and rubberneckers and Sunday drivers, who avoid such velocity. It traumatizes the neck muscles when your motor outpaces your curiosity. And if you want to absorb the history of this war-torn region, abandon the four lane highway.

So I took the back roads.

Early morning—well, late morning—first stop was a farm in Grandview. There, I stood in the nation's most talked-about kitchen, even though nobody eats there any more. Almost a century ago, a young farmer stood in the narrow covered breezeway between the hot stove and the farmhouse and uttered the second most famous phrase in the study of human conflict: "If you can't stand the heat, get out of the kitchen." Well, that's what my tour guide said. Turns out, when Harry Truman ran the farm, the breezeway and the oven weren't at that spot in the back of the farmhouse. But even though the current cooking area was added after Harry had left the farm, the old cookstove stands as a reminder to visitors that cooking and politics generate a fair amount of combustion. Never mind that Harry probably didn't originate that quip; he made it famous.

On this farm, Harry used some of the cooking skills his mother taught him to feed farmhands who worked the 600 acres that bordered the railroad tracks, tracks that snaked from nearby Grandview all the way to Kansas City, 17 miles away. This was Harry's second tour of duty on the farm. First time around as a young child, his mother taught him to be curious about the world around him.

This time around, his mother credits the farm as the place "where he got all his common sense." He became Grandview's postmaster, he established Grandview's Masonic Lodge, and he held Saturday evening jam sessions on the front porch.

Locals didn't think he'd survive as a farmer. And his culinary skills never transformed his slight frame into anything near a lumberjack's build, but that didn't stop him from hard labor. He couldn't see very well, either, but that didn't stop him from voracious reading. There's a pattern here.

During his farming years Harry overcame his deep shyness to pursue a young lady from Independence, so he'd often hop the Frisco and ride the rails to Kansas City's Union Station, where he'd switch to the Independence train.

Bess Wallace liked Harry, but her folks didn't think much of the relationship. After all, she was a Wallace, born to wealth and class. And he was a farmer. That didn't deter Harry. There's a pattern here.

* * *

Down the road, Belton shows off its collection of old railroad cars, right downtown. And an excursion train offers a short round trip for nostalgia buffs. I bought a ticket to ride the train, just like Harry Truman did, except his fare was a dime to ride the Frisco High Line all the way to Kansas City. My excursion was two miles each way, and cost about $2.25 per mile. What would Harry think? I suspect he'd bring the railroad to its knees. Still, it's nice to see somebody maintain a part of this old short line, and offer children a taste of transportation their great grandparents knew as a way of life.

I don't know whether Dale Carnegey ever rode the short line, but I bet he did. Riding a train is a great way to win friends and influence people. Another way to win friends and influence people is to change the spelling of your name to the predominant Carnegie, the one for which the concert hall is named, thanks to the millions of influential greenbacks behind Andrew Carnegie.

Dale called Belton his hometown, even though he was born up the road in Maryville. Early in his life, his parents moved the family to a farmhouse outside Belton, and it still stands. Dale is buried in the Belton Cemetery, where everybody is equally friendly and influential, except for the size of their monuments. His grave and the neighboring plots of his parents and daughter are simple markers atop door-sized slabs of granite. The granite slabs may be insurance against grave robbers. Early in my travels I began to notice a pattern of heavy cover over the graves of many of Missouri's rich and infamous.

She may not have been rich, but the lady buried in a nearby grave sure was infamous. This is the final resting place of the most fearsome woman ever to smash things with a hatchet. No, not Hatchet Molly. Not Lizzy Borden, either.

This six-foot battle ax waged all-out war against liquor. She first married an alcoholic, and that bad marriage steeled her resolve to destroy the tools that supplied liquor to men. Later she married a preacher and editor of the neighboring *Johnson County Democrat* newspaper. His last name and a slight change to her first name—oh, and her propensity for violence—would propel her to the forefront of the temperance movement.

She crusaded as Carry Nation, and she smashed whiskey barrels with sledgehammers, threw pool balls at barroom mirrors, and later employed a hatchet to smash up barrooms, to "carry a nation for Prohibition." Her intemperate temperance crusade lasted a decade, during which time she was beaten, bloodied, battered and arrested nearly three dozen times. Carry's crusade preceded American Prohibition by several years, but her efforts wrung the booze out of Missouri's public places in all but the most robust river towns.

She was sought by circus promoters and sideshows, but she traveled as a one-act revival, driving the demons out of married men, a few of whom came willingly to her crusades. While she did most of her damage in Kansas, a dry state at the time, with only a few establishments that served liquor "for medicinal purposes," her influence spilled over to Missouri, too. In 1906, less than a third of Missouri counties were dry. Three years after her death, 80 percent of the state was dry. Imbibers could buy a drink in only 23 of 114 counties. Almost all of those 23 holdout counties clung to rivers, those arteries that delivered the sternwheeling swift boats, too quick for Carry's hatchet. The boats delivered the demon rum and witches' brew and kept the old river ports steeped in a lifestyle that put the wild in the west.

I left the headstones of Carry and Carnegie, polar opposites in their approach to public relations, and headed for the wide open spaces. The back roads delivered a succession of towns whose very names hold the promise of good stories: Cleveland, Freeman, West Line. Oh, and Peculiar, a place with the motto, "The odds are with you." A sign downtown proudly proclaims the town's Civil War history: "In 1861-1864 while bloody battles raged throughout the southern states, nothing happened here." Nobody wanted to die for a Peculiar cause.

But a hundred years later, the town almost became famous. The owner of the Kansas City Athletics baseball team, an eccentric named Charley O. Finley, brought more innovation to stadium sports than any other person since Caligula: Colored jerseys. DayGlo orange baseballs. He installed a mechanical bunny rabbit under home plate that would pop up like a Jack in the Box to give the umpire fresh baseballs. And he threatened with regularity to move his team away from Kansas City. In one spat with the city, he vowed to move the team to Peculiar. The Peculiar A's. The name might've become a synonym for arsehole, but the move never materialized. Eventually, Charley huffed off to Oakland with his team, whose players cultivated handlebar mustaches and won pennants.

* * *

Within spitting distance of the Kansas state line, I stumbled onto a real find. I almost passed by an unimpressive metal building, except for the modest sign at the gravel drive entrance: Frontier Military Museum. The building resembles a small aircraft hangar. Avoiding the urge to judge this tin book by its cover, I pulled into the parking lot. Inside that simple metal building sits perhaps the greatest collection of military saddles in America.

Since Mark and Virginia Alley retired more than a decade ago from the aircraft industry in Wichita, they've focused on presenting their collection to the world. It's not where you think it would be. Not on the Smithsonian Mall. Not Texas or Tucson or anyplace known for riding tall in the saddle. It's not in Kansas City—or any city. It sits on the eastern edge of tiny Drexel, Missouri. Mark admits that the museum is out of the way. "But we love the area," he said. And after all, this was the frontier when many of his fifty saddles were enlisted.

Each saddle reflects the status of its rider, from the plebeian soldier's ride to the elaborate officer's saddle. I'd never thought about it much, really, that an officer sat on a leather Lexus, while a regular soldier perched on a stripped-down chassis. Rank be damned, the museum's caretakers ensure that every saddle tells a story, thanks to its supporting cast of characters including tack, boots, headgear, canteens, uniforms and firearms. A replica of the Drexel Mercantile Company displays frontier-style dry goods. Relics add perspective from several local Native American tribes: The Osage, Sac and Fox. Mark relishes in showing the displays and talking about the collection. It's nice to see somebody spend a big part of his retirement time and money showing people their past.

Thanking the Alleys for their pioneer spirit, I jumped back in my saddle, and spurred the horses under my hood ornament to take me down the trail. Minutes south of Merwin, I met up with a cowboy in a field. More precisely, Merwin Mike is a scarecrow-like dummy of a cowboy, riding up and down on the rocker arm of an oil well pump. Curious, I later Googled, "cowboy riding the rocker arm of an oil well pump," and I can say with some confidence that this sculpture is one of a kind. The visual conjures memories of rodeos, or the Wyoming license plate. But a real cowboy would point out that this art more closely resembles a tin horn on a teeter totter than a bronco buster. Still, in the middle of the prairie, artist Jerry Johnston earns his spurs. Since my first trip, Merwin Mike has migrated from the open prairie to Jerry's corral in downtown Merwin, population: 83... 84 if you count Merwin Mike.

* * *

The prairie? Today you see less of it. Most land has converted to cultivation. But the area remains rural, and remote. As Erifnus and I caromed between farms, fields and forest, locals kept talking about the mountains in southwest Cass County. Mountains? In the middle of the prairie? Amaroochie, they said. Turns out to be the Amarugia Highlands, sticking out like warts on the smooth landscape. Their altitude doesn't rival the Rockies or even the Ozarks, but from a flat start, Erifnus got a workout on her gears. And she got a view at the top.

The conservation area turns out to be a popular recreation spot. Who knew? This close to Kansas.

All this galloping flipped my switch to gourmet. I set my compass to take me from Amaroochie to Archie, home of a high school team called the Whirlwinds and the second most unique water tower in Missouri. Water towers generally are the first peek at a town's personality, visible from miles away. These small-town skyscrapers assume an infinite number of shapes, with only two requirements: hold water and become a billboard for the town's number one obsession. The Archie water tower is diamond-shaped, and the town's name cascades down the stalk. Under the shadow of the tower, I passed BJ's Rise 'N Shine Restaurant. The parking lot was packed. I glanced at my watch. It was 3 p.m. Curiosity propelled my car to the last available parking space, and I entered this roadside diner to find good food, like Piranha chili, and a counter covered with homemade pies. Ordering desserts here is a bittersweet process of elimination. The Pizookies® are fresh-baked cookies smothered in ice cream. The *beignets* are baked, not fried—the best beignets this side of Café du Monde.

I love small-town restaurants and their reasonable prices. Down the road in Adrian, Winfield's Restaurant served up a special of stuffed peppers, mashed potatoes and gravy with green beans and cherry cobbler for less than six bucks. I ate again. Then I found shelter for the night and regrouped for the next day.

✝ ✝ ✝

A statue stands on the courthouse grounds in Butler. That's not unusual, since statues seem to prefer such places. But this bronze likeness of a solitary soldier honors a turning point in the Civil War, a turning point that goes largely unnoticed. The Battle of Island Mound wasn't much more than a skirmish, although at least seven men were killed. This was the first Civil War battle involving African American soldiers. On the old Toothman Farm, where the 1st Kansas Colored Volunteer Infantry had built Fort Africa, federal troops repelled a larger Confederate force. The battle gets overlooked by just about everybody, save the most astute Civil War historians. But now the state plans a historic site. It's about time.

Under the neon sign at Sam's Hi-Way Hamburger, a line of kids waited at the service window to buy ice cream. My stomach wanted to stop for ice cream too, but my internal clock kept my foot to the gas pedal, since a stop would put me in line behind the better part of two little league teams.

On my way out of town, I stopped to see Linnie Crouch, a Butler legend. Well, I didn't see him. He's six feet under in Oak Hill Cemetery. I hope he lived an interesting life. Good, bad, I don't know. He died in 1898. But his fame extends beyond the grave, almost six inches. His plot sprouts the world's smallest tombstone, certified by *Ripley's Believe It or Not*. It's less than six inches square. He may or may not have been a Bushwhacker. But I'll bet he knew a few.

Driving down the highway, I did a double-take. Ahead, a garbage truck slowed to pick up a load. The sign on its side proclaimed, "Bitter White Trash." I looked again, closer this time, to read, "Better Rate Trash." Hey, my road is long, and the key to keeping my interest involves random sights, random thoughts and the ability to sort through trash.

Many Missourians are sensitive about the persistent belief that the state is overrun by white trash. It's a lasting scar that came from the shapers of popular opinion back during the years leading up to the Civil War. For political purposes during those prewar years, the abolitionist media portrayed Missourians as Pukes. The word was capitalized to formalize this subhuman culture, interested only in drinking whiskey, fighting and owning slaves. Missourians were almost universally described as illiterate and obnoxious, with vacant pig-like eyes and tobacco-stained teeth. Truth is, there were Pukes among Missouri's Civil War population. But like any other subclass of heathens, they were outnumbered by law-abiding citizens. They just shouted louder, shot more often, and burned and looted and raped their way into American lore. And with the help of the Union press, the whole state was branded with an image that persists today. Pukes. Bushwhackers. Hillbillies. Bitter white trash.

I didn't intend to pick up the scent of Bushwhackers and Jayhawkers and cavalries in blue and gray. But that's the allure of taking a random route and pinballing through frontier territory. I learned that while things have changed, much remains the same. Many western Missourians still hold to Southern sympathies. Documents in Missouri's "Bushwhacker Capital" of Nevada proclaim that "19 out of 20 Vernon Countians were Confederate sympathizers. Not counting

Bushwhackers, the county sent more men per capita to the Confederate army than any other in Missouri." That could explain why Union General Thomas Ewing issued his controversial *Order #11* in 1863. To flush out the Bushwhackers, Ewing burned four counties to the ground. Ewing's torching of Missouri's Kansas border wasn't the first act of eminent domain, but it's among the most heinous. His reign of terror punished the innocent as well as the guilty. There is still deep resentment among farm families in western Missouri who suffered in Ewing's effort to eradicate the Bushwhackers.

For a closer look at Bushwhackers, I pointed the mother ship toward Nevada, pronounced with a hard "a" (nuh VAY duh). Minutes later, I crossed the radar of another hard "a," just doing his job, and he handed me a warning ticket for speeding. Fitting, then, that my first stop downtown was the drafty old jail. It's a museum now, and I suspect local parents relish taking their miscreant teens to view the "cell room of medieval malevolence." They actually kept prisoners here until 1960. Its stone walls shout century-old hieroglyphics, haunting testament to time spent in Hell. Accentuating the spooky aura of the jail, somewhere outside its thick walls, the mother of all sledgehammers repeated its dramatic thud at half-minute intervals. I searched for the sound, conjuring images of anvils dropping into claw-foot bathtubs.

The dull pounding persisted, every 30 seconds, reverberating through downtown. I followed my ears around the business district, past the courthouse, a work of art under a red tile roof. I followed the sound, passing murals that leapt from brick walls like giant tattoos, telling vivid stories of the Katy Railroad and the Civil War.

I remembered what a waiter on the *Delta Queen* had told me: "When you enter Nevada, listen. You'll hear the sounds of old W.F. Norman."

And suddenly, there it was. Right in the middle of town. The W.F. Norman Sheet Metal Manufacturing Company sends its stamped tin ceiling art everywhere in America, to places as far-ranging as the wedding-cake ceilings of the *Delta Queen* to the ornate mouldings atop Washington, D.C.'s Willard Hotel, where President Grant and Sam Clemens smoked and drank.

I was fascinated. Right here is a uniquely American art form that flourishes only in this one red brick factory. This town owns the tin ceiling market, thanks to the perseverance of a company well into its second century of turning ordinary sheet metal into architectural ornaments.

The W.F. Norman Company stamps tin into original designs, based on customers' wishes. Even today, the company produces exact duplicates of mouldings and marquees, crestings and caryatids, to restore America's stately mansions.

At the edge of this tin ceiling factory, I stood outside an open window, not a jon boat's length from the ancient stamping apparatus. An iron-bottomed hunk of oak timbers, heavier than a Chevy Tahoe, raised slowly toward the ceiling, straining its giant hemp halter, and dropped like a guillotine on the unsuspecting sheet of tin. The tin was impressed. So was I.

The huge press offered a time-capsule trip to the Industrial Revolution, and with some adjustment I suspect this contraption could hammer a Humvee into gargoyles. Ropes as thick as Popeye's forearms raised and lowered the giant press, the same way it operated nearly two centuries ago.

Best anybody can tell, the press was built not long after Zebulon Pike explored the nearby Osage River. W.F. Norman bought the press in 1897, and began transforming copper and brass and bronze into balusters, finials and weather vanes. Many of the tin ceilings survive. In fact, next time you're downtown anywhere, walk into an old building and look up. Chances are, you're looking into an original tin sundae, stamped into a ceiling by this most unique company.

As I stood at the W.F. Norman factory, on the outside looking in, I realized it wasn't my high school history teacher, nor my unnatural attachment to my 1952 *World Book Encyclopedias* that launched me on a journey to see every square inch of Missouri.

It was a waiter aboard the *Delta Queen*.

Pontiacs and Prairies, Copernicus and Conflagration

So I set out to feel every crack in Missouri's pavement. As with all stories—and symphonies and carnal acts—it was an uneven ride. Although a dozen friends and a handful of reporters rode with me on segments, my only constant partner was my car. Racking up more miles on her odometer than the distance to the moon, my 1999 Pontiac Sunfire became Trigger and Lassie and Old Faithful all rolled into one. Her sleek lines suggest roadster, and she handles through twists and turns like a dancer. She understands her owner's commands, as I work through her 5-speed manual transmission to reach her comfort zone.

She has the spirit of a sports car with the gas mileage of a miser. Her flanks show the dings from parking lot encounters, and her roof is a quilt of dents from hail and scratches from hauling my favorite passport to nirvana: a canoe. Her interior transformed into a disheveled file cabinet, preserving an accurate record of our wake. She would star in a Pontiac commercial, if the Pontiac brand hadn't been put to death. Regardless, my Sunfire is a candidate for Best Pontiac Ever, the only car to cover every road in Missouri, so far as I know.

Every mile of every road in Missouri.

In a numbing display of inefficiency, my car traveled a quarter-million miles to cover the 33,685 miles of concrete and asphalt maintained by state-paid pothole fillers. To connect the dots, Erifnus carried me over thousands of miles of gravel and dirt, and water and mud, too. That car was as meaningful to my progress as the chariot that carried the Joads to *The Grapes of Wrath*, or the jalopy that delivered the Clampetts to Beverly Hills. To me and only me, Erifnus Caitnop is a family member.

I learned something new around every curve, every time. The entire trip defies linear progression, since my car and I functioned as one red blood cell circulating through the capillaries of the state. The heart of my journey is Columbia, in the left breast of Missouri as it stares back at you from the map. During scores of sorties spread over these dozen years, we gnawed away at the state like a lone termite eating your nestegg. Along the way, I've seen every slow curve sign and steep hill warning, every time and temperature sign in front of every bank, and thousands of prophecies on church marquees—all goading me to the end with a sense of urgency.

I guess I shouldn't be surprised that one highway map will not endure the trip across all its roads. Four maps disintegrated in my clutches, as they combined to guide me to the end of my journey. Each map, in turn, fell apart after constant opening and folding, tearing and tossing, spills and rain. As each successive map became more bandaged with tape, it struggled to show me the way, along trails followed by the Pahatsi, Daniel Boone, Bonnie and Clyde, Lewis and Clark, Zebulon Pike, Calamity Jane, and Frank James.

We left Nevada and headed as close to Kansas as I dared, happy that the air along this border is lead free, for the most part. We motored south toward Joplin on Highway 43, past a rusty old combine beside the road. Good-sized trees were growing out of the combine— so that nobody can steal it, I suppose.

Entering tiny Bronaugh, I could still summon the smell of that great fried chicken from Mar-Lon Café, even though it's been closed for 20 years. Back then, before genetic engineering changed chicken forever, the animals were real birds with natural, unaugmented breasts. Tasty, too. Folks would line up under the big brown awning to wait for a Sunday dinner table. Most of those folks are gone, victims not so much of bird fat as the sheer burden of living.

Nowadays, even though folks live longer lives, the chickens seem less tasty, as the scientists who engineer bird meat pump up the volume. You'd think that most folks in the Bible Belt would be angered by such genetic meddling. But most say nothing.

Meanwhile, along the back roads, I can sense a growing belief that Armageddon is at hand.

The message is unavoidable. It shouts from fencepost signs in hand-lettered earnest. It leaps off church marquees and covers the broad sides of barns. The end is near, the messages warn. On the face of it, they're right. Whether you believe or don't believe, whether your religion is based on resurrection or reincarnation or the Black Hole of Nothing, whether you believe in the Virgin Birth or 700 virgins in Heaven, whether you measure Creation in seven days or seven eons— whether any of that, for any living creature, the end is always near.

So I got busy.

I took every path. Along the way, the highways told me about routes and ruts, people and places, lost and found, Conception, Calamity, pride, prejudice, Success and Freedom, Elvis and Chester, Hoppy and Popeye, carp and crappie, hello, goodbye, come in, keep out, go to Hell, save your soul, cell towers, fire towers, water towers, wilderness, cleanliness, bathrooms, barrooms, Lithium, Licking, toads and spiders, Ethel & Elmer, crop dusters and liquor stores, Devils, assholes, noodlers, murderers, massacres, missionaries, squirrels and turtles, skunk and rabbit, Babbit, billboards, ziplines, trotlines, hemlines, whores and hemp, hooters, hellbenders, hillbillies, whiskey, barrels and murals, morels, Moses, Mexicans, Barkers, Berrys, robbers, Baldknobbers, barbecue, buffalo, beef, hogs, fish and chips and chicken. That about covers it.

When it comes to fish and chicken, Captain D must take a back seat to Bushwhacker Lake. On opening day of this modest 157-acre impoundment, one fisherman claimed he and his buddy snagged 200 bass in a six-hour frenzy of catch and release. If you ask me, I'll bet a couple of bass got really tired. But on this day, as we approached Bushwacker Lake, it looked calm, since the fish were all hiding under the water's surface, and no fishermen hovered above.

Meanwhile, the real stars of the local show, male prairie chickens, hadn't taken the stage to perform the greatest act this side of the Bolshoi Ballet. In a dramatic mating ritual, the birds display plumage worthy of Elton John or Dr. John and combine the moves of Baryshnikov with the bulbous chops of Dizzy Gillespie, busting onto their booming grounds like break dancers, spinning and jumping, inflating pumpkin-hued jowls to impress chicks or, more appropriately, hens. Nope, I didn't see anything like that on my drive by Bushwacker Lake. It was disappointingly calm. I had to get used to the idea that on my marathon journey, sometimes the show times aren't published, and I arrive during a long intermission.

Even though it doesn't look like it, the land along these back roads has undergone tremendous upheaval, having been converted from prairie to killing fields to farmland. Before Missourians made significant alterations to the landscape during the last century, both prairie chickens and prairies were common. Back before the Civil War, millions of bison owned 13 million acres of tallgrass prairie in Missouri. Great white hunters killed off every one of them, at the urging of General Philip Sheridan, the same guy who scorched the Shenandoah Valley to starve the Confederates into submission. He called the buffalo "the Indians' commissary." Son of a bitch. Two indiscriminate murder machines called Bushwhackers and Jayhawkers had already killed off almost everything else. The end was near back then, too. But the prairie grasses are resilient, with deep roots and long memories. The prairie grasses don't follow the Constitution or quote the Bible, but they do put down deep roots in their community.

I drove into Lamar, looking over my shoulder for Bushwhackers. But the mayhem has quieted since the Civil War and remained quiet when Lamar's most famous constable patrolled the streets. Of course, when he was constable, Wyatt Earp hadn't become famous yet. His fame would rise after Wyatt's wife died and he buried her here, and then left to tangle with Wild West attitudes in a succession of bordellos and gunfights.

Unlike Wyatt's house, which is gone, Harry Truman's birthplace is a wonderfully preserved little home on the prairie, but there are precious few places left where he ran or played or dined, since he left Lamar in his first year. His toys in Lamar were mostly rattles, his meals mostly mammary. Still, he was sensitive to the tragedy of this area. Harry left this spot as an unweaned pup, but he was raised along the Missouri-Kansas border, and he knew the scorching history of General Ewing's *Order #11.*

Ewing torched the entire region, burning farms and homes to the ground. Some historians believe that Truman established the Marshall Plan—a rare time in history that a conquering nation lent such a helping hand to the vanquished—because he remembered the resentment and economic depression in his burned-out backyard, a resentment that lasted long after the Civil War. The resentment simmers and festers today, in this region especially, and it wouldn't take much of a spark, I suspect, to ignite another conflagration.

Conflagration had recently visited the historic old Catholic church in the center of Lamar, consuming the interior with a fire so hungry that only the chapel's stone walls stand now. I left all these reminders of Hellfire and drove into the peaceful countryside.

As darkness fell along a remote stretch of Highway 126, I crested a hill to find a cow trotting loose along the road. I honked her into the ditch, wagged a shaming finger at her. Actually, I'd root for her if she wasn't in danger of becoming burger on somebody's bumper. A minute later I met the blazing lights of a highway patrol trooper rushing to secure the scene while the farmer prepared to guide the cow to safety.

I retreated to safety in a rustic cabin on the shore of one of America's greatest inland sailing spots, Stockton Lake. The hour was late, and my grateful frame unfolded into a brand new cabin that featured all the comforts that a fisherman or a sailor would want. Dry. Comfortable. Bed.

And coffee. Next morning we drove west to a tiny stone chapel near the center of Golden City. The chapel was bathed in sweet smoke wafting over a state championship barbecue cookoff in this town that swelled much larger than its thousand residents. Smokers and their stacks sat like riverboats, emblazoned with names like Full of Bull, Hog Tide, and Smoke This. The event is called the Rockin' Blues Festival, and its charcoal cookers survived the fires of damnation fanned by a few locals who worry that beer, bands and barbecue cause otherwise salvageable souls to dance with the Devil.

Down the road just beyond Kenoma, I passed the old Shapley place. At least I went near it. Never identified it. Nobody knows about it. Oh, some locals probably do. But nobody's erected a monument. They should. Here's the story:

On a farm outside tiny Nashville, Missouri, the Shapley twins were born back in 1885. Neither became a household name, but both were successful in their own ways. Horace eventually followed the family tradition to become a farmer, returning from the far West to keep the 100-year-old family farm humming. He went to college when he was 80 years old.

Meanwhile, his brother, Harlow, went to college much earlier, and later made a discovery that shook the foundations of belief unlike anything since Copernicus. Harlow's study of the speed of light illuminated the theory that Earth and its solar system are not in the center of the Universe. In fact, according to Harlow, we're nowhere near the center of the Universe, and the Universe is much bigger than anybody thought.

Copernicus proved that the sun is the center of the solar system. It was 1543, and Copernicus began his report by predicting his revelations would cause heartburn: "Perhaps there will be babblers who, although completely ignorant of mathematics, nevertheless take it upon themselves to pass judgment on mathematical questions and, badly distorting some passages of Scripture to their purpose, will dare find fault with my undertaking and censure it. I disregard them even to the extent as despising their criticism as unfounded." Even Copernicus's own printer censured his preface, replacing it with a cheap-shot disclaimer: "This work is not intended to be true."

Harlow Shapley's discovery was every bit as unsettling as the Copernican study. While some folks called him the "Organizer of Heaven," Harlow stepped into the great debate about the origin of man.

His life didn't start out that way. He was a reporter for the Joplin *Times* even before he finished high school. He had been rejected by Carthage High School and went instead to Carthage Academy. He applied to the University of Missouri in 1908 to study journalism, but the brand new journalism school wasn't ready to open, so he consulted the university's catalog and picked another pursuit: astronomy. It was just as well; he had misgivings about the newspaper business, where he watched a news story suppressed because it reflected negatively on an advertiser.

It's an early indication that he would later stand firm in his discoveries, even against popular opinion. He didn't attack religion any more than Copernicus did. But his discovery suggested that the Earth was not placed in the center of the Universe. He suggested that the Milky Way alone contains a hundred thousand million opportunities for life. He knew it would cause a great philosophical debate when his scientific discoveries collided with Genesis and miracles, mysticism and the supernatural. That was not his intent. He just discovered the size of the Milky Way and the fact that Sagittarius, not our sun, is at its center. He noted incorrectly that our sun is about 55,000 light years from the center of the Milky Way. In reality, our sun is only half that distance from the middle. Still, it's more than a Sunday drive away.

There is no monument in Nashville to Harlow Shapley. Not that I could find. Nor is there a Shapley bust in the state capitol's Hall of Famous Missourians.

I drove on, passing Mindenmines Mini Storage and Family Day Care, a unique blend of junk and children, I guess. My morning drive coursed through rural farmland and remnants of a vast prairie. Things appeared quiet, pastoral. So far this morning, I'd seen the seven key building blocks to the Universe: stars and storage, children and churches, blues, barbecue and beer.

Circling through the town of Liberal, I found a unique sign. In the noble effort to pick up roadside trash, there are 7,794 Adopt-A-Highway signs along these roads, but this one was special. A mile of Highway K is adopted for cleanup by the Liberal VFW. That warms my heart. The cleanup is noble enough. I'm just comforted to know there is a Liberal VFW.

Down the road, a different kind of comfort arises from the aftermath of one of the biggest tragedies to hit a Midwestern city since the Chicago Fire. Thanks to help from neighbors as far away as New Orleans—a city painfully aware of Heraclitus' proverb that you never step in the same river twice—the city of Joplin is rising from the rubble.

For too many good people in Joplin, the end came on May 22, 2011, 40 years and 17 days after an event immortalized as "The Joplin Tornado."

One day after a West Coast preacher's prediction for the end of the world came and went, the end came for everything in the path of an EF-5 tornado that thrashed through Joplin, leaving 162 people dead, killing countless pets, dashing schools and hospitals, crushing cars like stomping aluminum cans, pulverizing houses, disintegrating businesses, devouring keepsakes and photo albums and stained glass windows, busting eardrums, shattering every window and stoplight and skylight and porch light, stripping the life from every tree, and leaving tree trunks the size of tent poles.

On my last trip through Joplin a year before the devastating storm, I saw a vibrant city. Now, Joplin's history will forever be divided into "Before the Tornado" and "After the Tornado."

But the tornado could not erase Joplin's pride—or its ghosts: Bonnie and Clyde. Langston Hughes. Thomas Hart Benton. Dennis Weaver. Bob Cummings. And The Mick. I decided I'd eat lunch at the latter's legendary Holiday Inn, if I could find it.

I remember as a kid staying at the Mickey Mantle Holiday Inn and loitering outside the Dugout Lounge, fantasizing that The Mick might be there. Most people remember Mantle as a better-than-average member of the Joplin Miners baseball team. Some writers have suggested that he was a legendary party animal. He was pretty much uncooperative the only time I met him, years ago in Rolla. He was there to promote Bow Wow Dog Chow. I was an ad salesman for the local newspaper, and Bow Wow was one of my prospects. So I went to see The Mick.

Seizing an opportunity to launch my career as a sports reporter, I approached him to get a quote. He snapped, "Turn that tape recorder off. No interviews." I guess interviews weren't covered in his contract with Bow Wow Dog Chow. And I missed my best opportunity to capture any Mickisms.

He was proud of his restaurant at the Mickey Mantle Holiday Inn. Especially the fried chicken. "To get a better piece of chicken, you'd have to be a rooster," he used to brag. OK, so he was edgier than Yogi Berra.

Sadly, Mickey Mantle and his motel are both in life's rearview mirror.

Toasters and Lucifer, Scavengers and Carver

A witling would say it's a description of Hell: 4,000 toasters, no bread. But hey, if Richard Larrison ever used all his toasters at once, it might create Hell, or havoc, or at least a lot of heat, pulling enough electricity to cause a brownout in the tiny town of Skeeterville.

The city limit sign doesn't say Skeeterville anymore. Today it's called Fidelity. Fidelity's main drag isn't much longer than a two-lane bowling alley, tucked a mile south of I-44 on the road to the George Washington Carver birthplace.

In Larrison's parking lot an old farm windmill sprouts from the pavement, and clinging from the windmill, a tin cowboy offers a friendly wave. Behind the sign, Richard and Janet Larrison operate JR's Western Store. It's a nice store, with its dandy duds and new boot leather smell.

Attached to the store is The World's Largest Small Electric Appliance Museum, a labyrinth of ceiling-high display cases tastefully packed with waffle irons and mixers and coffee pots and toasters. Mostly toasters. In addition to 3.5 million watts worth of appliances, "I have 800 more to display when I make room," Richard says.

A friend in Joplin tipped me off about the museum. It turned out to be a revelation. A few years ago this was the site of a national convention called OcToasterFest. More than two dozen collectors converged on Fidelity to swap toaster tales—and toasters—and generally jam to toasterity.

The end is near. And if OcToasterFest is a harbinger, we're all toast.

I left there hungry. Traveling south we drew ever nearer to the Gates of Hell. Or maybe it's just the back entrance. Most locals offer a knowing smile when asked about the Hornet Spook Light. This mysterious Hellfire hovers about a dozen miles, as the raven flies, southwest of Fidelity. Near the tiny hamlet of Hornet, the Spook Light, aka

The Devil's Jack-O-Lantern, dances nightly, as it has since at least the Civil War. According to observers, this mysterious ball of light actually dances in Oklahoma, but the best spot for viewing sits along a road nicknamed The Devil's Promenade, just south of Joplin, west of Highway 43. There are many theories about the Spook Light's origin. Personally, I believe it's a wayward bouncing ball from the screen of an old TV show, "Sing Along with Mitch," that somehow caught the fire of eternal damnation.

The Spook Light show usually doesn't start until after 10 p.m., so in the high-noon heat my empty stomach guided me to a cooler spot on old Highway 71, just north of Neosho. There, the busy KC Southern railroad tracks parallel Shoal Creek as it meanders beside tall bluffs. Tucked under a towering overhang, a unique watering hole watches over the creek's shallow Tipton Ford. With a cave for a back wall, the Undercliff Grill & Bar is cool and inviting, in its campy cave *chic*. The locals keep coming back for the food. I know why. The French onion soup comes protected by a helmet of Gruyère cheese that could stand up a pitchfork. My eyes feasted on the décor: race cars and surf boards, airplanes and hornets nests, and classic cameos of Elvis, Marilyn and James Dean. In fact, a trip to the men's restroom turns into an adventure, just looking at the photos of Marilyn Monroe on the walls. Somebody said the greatest bathroom in the world is in Branson, at Shoji Tabuchi's theater. They haven't been to the Undercliff. I emerged from the bathroom shaken, but not stirred, as a freight train rumbled past the picture window.

Soon, owner Mike Winn's Dam Good Sandwich slid before me, a formidable stack of pastrami, ham and Provolone cheese grilled and served on focaccia bread, and slathered with slaw. I devoured the sandwich and the experience, said thanks to Mike and Melissa Winn—and to Marilyn—and returned to the road.

Minutes later, Erifnus and I rounded a curve and surprised a flock of vultures cleaning the carrion of some unidentifiable corpse. They dispersed reluctantly, just long enough to let us pass.

Vultures are derided as buzzards, and their Ichabod frames carry a negative stereotype. But turkey vultures show the observant human how to glide through life. They rest in the trees, and the hardest work they do is to flap their giant black wings and launch their big bird bodies into the air. Once airborne, they ride the thermal currents with little effort.

Their keen eyesight and sense of smell help locate their food, and then they perform the service they've been doing long before the first garbage truck or hockey wagon. They have no feathers on their faces or legs, which means they keep clean as they gorge themselves on rotting meat. They're a little too successful sometimes, to the point they eat so much that they get too heavy to fly. Then if they're approached by predators like coyotes, they projectile vomit, unleashing such a foul brew on their attackers that the predators retreat in disgust. And as most dog owners would attest, it's hard to gross out a canine. Not only that, but with the disgorging of the contents of their stomachs, the vultures can once again get airborne and fly away from attackers.

As we drive, Erifnus and I respect these great scavengers, and generally avoid their vomit.

We zeroed in on the shrine of my idol, perhaps the world's greatest scavenger, although few people know him as that.

George Carver was born outside tiny Diamond, Missouri, during the last shots of the Civil War. His childhood was turbulent. As an infant, he survived a kidnapping, and a bout with whooping cough which claimed his mother's life. As a kid, he showed a talent for art. The farm's owners, Moses and Susan Carver, sought education for George. They sent him to a childless black couple, Andrew and Mariah Watkins, who took him into their Neosho home, taught him values, nurtured his green thumb, and sent him on a path "with a satchel full of poverty and a burning zeal to know everything."

As a young teen, his application for art school was accepted by a Kansas college. But when he showed up for classes, they saw he was black, and would not admit him. After similar ordeals, George found an open door at Simpson College in Iowa and then at Iowa A&M, the precursor to Iowa State University, where he switched his focus from painting to plants.

His legacy transcends mere peanuts. He became the grandfather of green, no less influential than John Muir or Teddy Roosevelt or Rachel Carson. He became America's preeminent recycler, its patron saint of sustainable agriculture, and along the way its social conscience.

On the homestead where he was born sits the George Washington Carver National Monument, a scientific wonderland waiting for inquiring minds. In the middle of a restored prairie, it's packed with enough common sense to save the world, equal parts Carver science, Carver care and Carver lifestyle.

Jerry and Barbara Hixenbaugh are local volunteers with as deep a passion for Carver as any paid staffer. They proudly showed me the museum's new makeover, packed with more hands-on experiences than an oyster shucker.

It's understandable that in America's fast-food appetite for history, we know little more than peanuts about Carver. In too many instances, America's collective knowledge about our icons gets boiled down to the substance of a slogan. Whole lives get reduced to tombstone histories, not enough information to fill a movie trailer.

Yet Carver was a trailblazer in agriculture, education, ecology, and life. Sure, he developed 300 uses for the lowly regarded peanut, making paper and ink, gasoline and shampoo, insecticide and nitroglycerin. No, he didn't invent peanut butter. But he did develop 70 uses for pecans and 300 colored paints from clay. He made synthetic marble from wood pulp, paint from used motor oil, athlete's foot medicine from persimmons, paving bricks from cotton, and stamp glue from sweet potato starch.

Few people realize that Carver saved the world from the ravages of cotton. He introduced the peanut plant as a rotation crop to give southern fields a break from a continual cotton crop which, year after year, had depleted soils. By planting peanuts in rotation with cotton, the peanut plant actually introduced nutrients back into the soil. Just as important, Carver's idea to rotate the peanut crop with cotton dealt a blow to the boll weevil's devastating grip on cotton country.

Jerry and Barbara showed me the trails young George Carver walked every morning. It was on these morning walks that he would "collect my floral beauties, and put them in my little garden I had hidden in the brush not far from the house, as it was considered foolishness in the neighborhood to waste time on flowers."

Personally, I see another Carver indulgence that elevates him to greatness. He made it a lifelong practice to demonstrate creative uses for things people normally throw in the garbage. As such, Carver became America's foremost recycler.

He believed that nothing around the house should be discarded if it could be used. "America has got to turn its attention in those directions to save what we have," he said. He warned that destroying usable items was a lack of vision. "And where there is no vision," he said, "people perish."

Damn, George, I fear the end is near.

"Everything on Earth has a purpose," he told students. And Carver practiced what he preached. To illustrate this idea, he recounts one of his first days after leaving his alma mater. He had accepted the invitation by Booker T. Washington to become the new director of agriculture studies at Tuskegee Institute in Alabama. "I went to the trash pile at Tuskegee Institute and started my lab with bottles, old fruit jars and any other thing I found I could use." From that trash, he built on a concept that guided his every move: "Nature produces no waste." Amen, say the vultures.

I stayed longer than I planned at the Carver site. It was dark when I left, and I thought about heading to Hornet to say hello to the Devil and his Spook Light. Instead, I started the three-hour journey to my own bed and to a home-cooked meal. I drove past Pepsin, named for chewing gum, maybe, and Parshley, named for a strong vegetable, I suppose, and Motley and Sarcoxie, the latter a town that takes its name from the old Shawnee Indian chief Sarcoxie, the rising sun.

We had driven almost 1,900 miles the past three days, crisscrossing southwest Missouri. In the darkness, we headed in the general direction of home.

Soldiers, Saints and Sinners

Ahead over the horizon, the nighttime clouds reflected the glow of a gaggle of neon lights that represent safety and danger, all wrapped together in a tawdry collection of delights.

Tired of sleepdriving, I found shelter for the night in St. Robert, the incarnation of an ancient Roman outpost. Beneath an old relic of a water tower reminiscent of the Tin Man turned topsy-turvy, the town makes no attempt to hide its warts, offering wine, women and song—pretty much in that order—to its most celebrated residents, the soldiers at Ft. Leonard Wood.

Leonard Wood is one of those names that survives only in certain circles: veterans, historians and the Moro people of Indonesia. Historians are aware of Wood's long and mostly distinguished career. Army veterans remember his name because it's plastered over the entrance to a military base and tattooed into the memories of a million soldiers who trained there before marching off to war. But for at least three decades, Leonard Wood, an army surgeon, was a major player on the national stage.

His early career was propelled by his personal diary documenting the chase and capture of Geronimo. During that campaign he was awarded the Medal of Honor. That fame probably helped him become personal doctor to Presidents McKinley and Garfield. Teddy Roosevelt launched the next chapters in his career. Wood served with Teddy's Rough Riders, then he became military governor of Cuba, and later territorial governor of the Philippines. He was the only surgeon to become the U.S. Army chief of staff.

It was a monumental career, with one tragic flaw: He presided over the massacre of 600 Filipino men, women and children of the Moros, an Islamic sect that resisted American control of the southern Philippines. In the battle of Bud Dajo, the Moros were holed up in a volcanic crater. Leonard Wood's superior firepower slaughtered the mostly unarmed Moros. At first, President Roosevelt praised the victory, but when the details became known, many Americans were horrified. Mark Twain called the event a disgrace and termed Leonard Wood's troops "Christian butchers." Despite this ugly chapter in his otherwise distinguished career, Leonard Wood was nominated by his friend Teddy to become a major general, a step toward his ultimate position as Army chief of staff.

Fort Leonard Wood itself demonstrates the discipline you'd expect from a school that cranks out military police officers and crime scene investigators—and engineers, adept at road building. It's fitting, then, that St. Robert sits on the edge of rugged hills and steep ravines, the most difficult passage along our nation's most celebrated road. A perfectly preserved stretch of original Route 66, lips and all, cascades from town toward the confluence of two rivers.

Sunset Village sits along the way. It's a retirement complex that's aging gracefully along with its residents. Just downhill, Big Louie's stage supports a titillating lineup of naked ladies. This road is a metaphor for the wages of sin, especially for a patron of age: the walk downhill from Sunset Village to Big Louie's is easy, the return home is rough.

Avoiding the wages of sin and the expenses of nightlife, I motored straight to the local Fairfield Inn. Next morning, Erifnus rolled me downhill on concrete ribbon that's older than most of the residents of Sunset Village. As we passed, the octogenarians were finishing their second cup of coffee, and the strippers were still sleeping.

Further downhill, a wide spot in the road offers an overlook, a panoramic view of Devil's Elbow, a riverbend that's the mother of all logjams. Through the trees, in the steep valley below, the hairpin riverbend was just out of sight. But I knew the story. Around the time of the Civil War, new railroads cut through this rugged region, and a rough and tumble breed of lumberjacks called tie hackers cut down all of Missouri's forests to make railroad ties. Near Arlington, at the bottom of this deep valley, loggers attempted to shove billions of logs downriver. But they couldn't squeeze enough log rafts through this tight bend fast enough for a hungry sawmill that needed to produce 3,000 cross ties for each mile of track. The bend was punctuated by a giant boulder that wouldn't budge. It was put there by the Devil, the loggers believed. Logs piled up in the bend like early-bird shoppers on Black Friday. The loggers named the bend Devil's Elbow.

At the bottom of the hill, old Route 66 rolls past the town of Devil's Elbow, where not much has changed in a hundred years. Oh, Miller's Market has changed to Allmon's Market and changed again to Sheldon's Market, but the market continues to do what it's done for my entire lifetime: sell everything you need to survive, and serve as the post office, too. We crossed the 90-year-old truss bridge that was the first Route 66 bridge across the Piney River, then traced along the Piney to view an engineering marvel called Hooker's Cut. Half a century ago, engineers blasted a deep slice through a mountain, at the time the deepest roadcut in the world. They laid four lanes through this gnarly area for the first time— the last section of Route 66 to become four-lane. The new passage helped cross-country travelers make better time across this rugged valley. The name Hooker comes from a town nearby, not from the whores who chase the servicemen up on the knob.

I paid my respects to the Hooker Church and Hooker graveyard, the old Hooker High School and John L. Hooker, the woodsman whose name is used for these icons. And I paid respects to John Lee Hooker, too, for no other reason beyond power of suggestion, before turning my attention back to the little side road—the very first Route 66—and the Elbow Inn.

The Elbow Inn doesn't disappoint thrill seekers. It's a hideaway bar in every sense of the word. When we rolled to its door, a thundershower was beating down on the low slung structure made mostly of cedar logs with mud chinks, its back wall standing just a couple of feet above the swollen Big Piney River. It was still before lunch, and the neon beer signs were switched off. A dog with a pit bull jawline and a defensive attitude greeted my car door. I sat frozen for a moment, undecided about dipping my leg out of the car to troll for jaws. Lightning flashed, and the dog retreated off into the shelter of the woods across the road. He knew he couldn't bite thunder. I dashed through sheets of rain to the front door.

The Elbow Inn Bar and BBQ has been cranking out good times in one fashion or another since 1929, when folks called it the Munger Moss. Back then, there weren't nearly as many motorcycles. Today, it's a waypoint for every Harley rider who enters the Ozarks, and a watering hole for half the soldiers who ever set foot in Ft. Leonard Wood, a short cab ride up the hill. The inn lures customers from as far away as Sweden. Most women walk into the bar wearing their brassieres; the tavern's ceiling bears proof that a couple hundred women left without them.

I walked in and let my eyes adjust to the dim light that managed to penetrate through rain-spattered windowpanes. A voice greeted me from beside the thick shellac that preserves the rust and cream-colored wood of a classic cedar-top bar. "Can I help you?"

"You open?" I opened.

"Kitchen's closed, but the bar's open." Terry Robertson is the perfect typecast for this historic bar. He's a retired game warden who knows the area and its history, and he loves to visit with wayfarers. Two locals, long in the tooth, sat at the bar.

"Great place," I offered, looking up at the low ceiling covered with a unique décor: dollar bills papered the ceiling, and hanging from that ceiling was a rainbow coalition of brassieres, liberated from the shoulders of women who got swept up in the moment. It's not the first time dollar bills have been this close to bras, but it is the first time I realized why the father of our country has that *Mona Lisa* look on his face. Like a fly on the ceiling, his thousand eyes peered into the hundreds of lacy cups just inches from his face.

In short order, three old historians at the bar were telling me about the place. This tavern sits on the original Mother Road, now an appendage to the newer Route 66 that was carved through Hooker's Cut. Now, even Hooker's Cut has been bypassed by Route 66's granddaughter, I-44.

The door swung open and two middle-aged men walked in. "You open?"

"Kitchen's closed, but the bar's open," Terry replied.

"Great! A round for everybody," one of the men said. Terry obliged, pulling an unholy alliance of Miller Lites and Busch cans from the cooler, abstaining himself, as all good bartenders do before noon. The two men explained that they were from Chicago, a fact verified by their Ditkaesque accents. They were driving an old Ford Econoline van, and their goal was to drive the Mother Road from pier (Navy) to shining pier (Santa Monica). They knew about this roadhouse, and within minutes, every member in this group was adding to the story of the Elbow Inn's connection to the Windy City.

Al Capone used to send his henchmen down here to hide. A guy named Bud Medina was a regular here, they say, especially after his role as triggerman at the St. Valentine's Day Massacre in a Chicago warehouse. The name doesn't show up in any history that I could find. But it probably was an alias. According to everybody at the bar, a whole rogue's gallery of mobsters used to hang out here, in the middle of nowhere, while their trails in St. Louis and Chicago slowly iced over.

Lightning flashed, thunder crashed, and the rain beat down harder on the old roof. I kept glancing at George Washington, who kept looking at the brassieres.

I first visited this bar a dozen years ago, before Terry had quit busting poachers and started bussing tables. Back then, I entered to find a gaggle of locals drinking and arguing about religion and politics and the weather and everything but the military, in deference to the GIs who sat at the bar and who might any day get orders to ship out to Afghanistan. As I walked in, the discussion around the table got more intense. A guy named Vance seemed to have the edge. Maybe it was because of his radio voice, or his extensive travel experience, or his ability to think on his feet. But everybody at the table knew that his greatest gift was bullshit. The crowd at the table looked at me, causing Vance to turn around. "J.R.! Come on in and grab a buttload of vinyl!" I did.

Vance lives on the banks of the Gasconade River near Jerome. Or he did. But usually he's on the road. He's a gypsy shooter. No, he doesn't shoot vagabonds. He travels throughout the world with a video camera that costs more than his house, and films for the likes of CBS and *National Geographic, The Great Chefs of Europe* and *America's Most Wanted.* I told the group I was doing some traveling too—every mile on the Missouri highway map. They laughed and shook their heads. "Why would anybody do that?" they all agreed. Vance, the gypsy shooter, knew why.

Over the next two hours, we debated religion, politics, sex, drugs, rock 'n' roll, beer, barbecue and yard sales. When it was time to go, Vance said he'd catch up with me and film some of the countryside as I drove. Fat chance. His phone would ring any minute, and he'd be off with his camera to Marrakesh or Ketchikan. Full of barbecued ribs and bullshit, I bade *adieu* with an Eisenhowerism: "Beware the military-industrial complex."

But that encounter with Vance and the gang was years ago. Time has been kind to the Elbow Inn; so have the brassieres, and the girls who left them behind, and the guys who watched them do it, and the river, lapping at the tavern's back door, sparing the inn from its swollen rage.

I thanked the bartender, offered best wishes to the Windy City wanderers, and walked out into the storm. The pit bull was nowhere in sight, still hiding from the thunder, and I jumped in the car to follow this ancient path that snaked up the hill, across the interstate, to a place called Trail of Tears grotto, built, from the looks of it, shortly after the last Cherokee passed through.

The builder used 10,000 native stones, each the size of your liver, to construct an archway and columns and a wishing well and walls and water wheels, in a painstaking process that would keep idle hands from doing any Devil's work.

Rocks are the world's original building blocks. Assuming that the number of rock structures on Earth might loosely correlate to the number of human beings who ever lived, a total of 112.459 billion rock walls, towers, homes, bridges, fireplaces, churches, bowling alleys and tombstones have been built, all of them in various stages of crumbling back into Earth's crust. But among all the rock monuments over the history of the world, nothing quite matches this one.

Beneath the mystic stone archway hangs an upside-down crescent moon with the words Trail of Tears. Near the entrance, a life-size concrete statue of a one-armed man in a suit sits on a stone throne in a position that suggests he might be using the toilet, except that his statue pants are up around his concrete waist, and there's no stone toilet paper dispenser at his side. There's no sign explaining anything about this guy or the whereabouts of his other arm or anything about these rock monuments. If this is a statue of the guy who built this grotto, it must've been painstaking for him to stack these rocks with only one arm. Maybe he had help, or maybe he had two arms when he stacked these stones, or maybe somebody else built the grotto after he died. Or maybe he's not dead. There was a serious lack of information at the site. So I did some digging.

"Who stacked the stones?" I asked around town. And I began to get a composite picture of the life of Larry Baggett. Larry had two arms, and so did the statue when he built it. He began building the monument in the 1970s to honor the Cherokees who walked across this spot 175 years ago. Larry apparently had a mystic side and kept in contact with nature—and the spirits of the Cherokees who visited him. But Larry died a few years back, and his stone monuments began to crumble. His statue arm fell off. Or maybe some asshole hacked it off, since the arm originally raised in a friendly wave. Whatever the fate of the statue's arm, its friendly wave has been replaced by a PRIVATE PROPERTY sign. So Erifnus and I drove on down the hill to the river.

Around the bend, a huge bluff is cut in layers like a wedding cake to keep the crumbly limestone cliffs from tumbling into the Gasconade River. Even with the gash in Mother Nature's face, it's a pretty spot, ruined only by the KEEP OUT signs along the private riverfront drives. The road bends through Jerome and past high bluffs overlooking the Gasconade. Looking up, I could see a system of connected caves peeking out from the bluff's face. The caves are called the Rifle Holes, not because they were made by rifles, but because some imaginative pioneers thought that Indian snipers sat in the caves on these towering bluffs to shoot people below. There's no proof that happened, but it makes for a scary story.

Highway 28 snakes up toward Dixon through steep hills to a ridge that's no wider than the backbone of the Devil himself. Through the trees the road affords breathtaking views of the broad Gasconade River valley. Closer to the road, a church marquee reminded me of my urgency: "In the last days, terrible times shall occur." Seconds later I skidded in for some petrol at a rural roadside mom'n'pop, and filled Erifnus with her liquor. I wondered what might happen if all the gasoline in this gas station's holding tanks spilled into the ground and entered the silent spring. It would seep downhill and poison the wishing well at Larry Baggett's place, that's for sure. Refueled, I followed my imaginary oil spill back downhill. Erifnus slinked back onto I-44 where she made some easy miles, heading east, her hood in the shade, the setting sun battering my eyes through the rearview mirror.

* * *

We followed the Arlington road five miles to find out that Arlington is the official definition of a dead end. Seems that way. It used to be a pretty little resort town, tucked against the tight bluffs of the Gasconade River, serving both a railroad and a highway. But the highway took a new route and railroad passenger service dried up. As time passed the old resort patrons died off. An old brick building still stands, with a cornerstone that says, "E.M. Pillman, built in 1912." An old frame boarding house sits next door. Another house perches a block away on a knoll overlooking the river and the tracks.

A roadblock prevented us from driving along the tracks, down a narrow dirt road to a campground, closed for some reason, maybe the threat of flooding, maybe the economy, maybe lack of interest. A sign along the tracks spells the town's name. Only railroad engineers see it anymore, and maybe an occasional drifter in an open boxcar.

The old buildings wait for a makeover. They wait for new visitors who will discover this little river burg, and make it a favorite vacation spot again. It's not likely to happen. When the new interstate supplanted Route 66, access to Arlington became limited, only reachable from interchanges three miles away in either direction. That's not so bad for folks who like seclusion and solitude. Only one problem: Arlington's south boundary is framed by two imposing superhighway bridges, one eastbound, one westbound, both slicing like concrete contrails across the beautiful view upriver.

It was dark when we emerged out of that valley, headed to my own bed a hundred miles away.

The Ugly Truth

I-70 sucks. Oh, the road is okay. The pain and suffering comes from uncooperative drivers. It reminds me of something my grandpappy told me once. He said, "Son, get outta my way!" Those words hang with me, especially as Erifnus and I attempt to share the road with drivers who suffer from stubbornness or unawareness. Especially today.

Driving east past Oak Grove, we moved into the left lane to get around slow traffic. No luck. The passing lane had become a mobile dam, the driver ahead of us had no interest in yielding to our superior speed. It was then that Erifnus reminded me of the road-clearing tactic graciously supplied by the highway department. When a car edges to the shoulder stripe on an interstate, its tires hit a corrugated rumble strip that makes them roar like a foghorn. The rumble strip alerts dialers and texters and sleepy drivers that they're running off the road.

Erifnus likes it for a different purpose. If we're stuck behind a car in the passing lane, whether it's a lane hog or a cellular hellcat, Erifnus instinctively edges toward the shoulder stripe, where the tires play the corrugated highway strip like a tympani. The noise annoys cell phone talkers, who oblige grudgingly and get out of the way so they can once again hear their phone conversation. The noise even unnerves most left lane hogs, who eventually relinquish the lane because they're unsure of my next move. Hey, I'm not a speed demon, and I've only rarely been described as dangerous. I observe the rules, mostly. One of those rules instructs drivers to stay in the right lane except to pass.

Even without the senseless idiots in the passing lane, this is the busiest, most dangerous highway in the state. It's also the only strip of Missouri that most cross-country travelers experience. From the perspective of these long-distance trekkers, they can't get through Missouri fast enough.

They see clutter that stains the roadside, making the trip an ugly experience. Billboards shout at the eyes like a field of dandelions, while fast food franchises dangle comfort colors designed to appeal to a majority within each vehicle. The interstate's shoulders bear roadsigns with the familiar tattoos of gas stations and convenience stores and drive-thru restaurants, each offering the same things dressed in different packages. And for the sake of convenience and consistency, most travelers rely on these comfortable colorful tattoos.

Too bad.

Just off the interstate, in any direction, the classic roadside eateries await.

We had to do a bit of extra driving to find Bates City Barbecue. It's well-hidden, no gleaming arches or scallop sign sitting atop a towering mast beside the business. Not even a pink piggy. I left the exit ramp, drove around the corner and down the street, made two more turns, and looked for the dump. In the great tradition of dives with good food, this place earns a Confessional Medal of Honor. In previous incarnations, the building could've been a warehouse or a maintenance shed. Crossing through the door, the interior was dark and thick with the smell of hot grease permeated with barbecue smoke. That sweet smell of a hickory forest fire is a signal that the pig parts weren't parboiled or rushed through the smoker.

The homemade sign behind the counter offered a homemade menu of homemade fixins, like crunchy coleslaw and potato salad, for those folks whose bodies are temples. I had fries and a smoked pork sandwich that made me understand why this place has a branch in Kansas City, where people brag about serious barbecue.

Living near Bates City would be lush, I concluded. On my way out of town, two signs assured me the area has the key ingredients to life: One sign marks the entrance to the Ballerina Mobile Home Country Club. The other sign, just down the road, offers "Eggs" in big hand-painted letters, guaranteeing they're fresh from the layers. On the same sign, the farmer offers "horse poop for garden." There you have it, life's essential building blocks: eggs and poop, a country club for trailers and ballerinas... and barbecue.

The next exit requires a commitment. It's a rare diversion, damn near unique in the land of interstates: an exit ramp whose corresponding entrance back onto the interstate is three miles away. So the Odessa exit offers two choices: Turn right and visit the outlet mall, or turn left and drive through town before you can reenter the superhighway. It takes only five minutes to traverse the entire town, stop signs and all. But for the modern interstate traveler, wired for rapid returns, a five minute entrance ramp is tantamount to the road through Hell.

Back on the interstate, Erifnus rolled only a dozen miles before somebody's finger yanked us off the road. The finger is attached to a half-billboard-size wooden sign shaped like a giant gloved fist pointing to Higginsville.

The town lives up to its finger.

Halfway around a downtown bypass, we found an old low-slung roadside shack remarkable from the outside only for its redness. Its legal name is Red Shanty Liquor Bait & Barbeque. Ken and Annette Dittmer bought the shop a couple of years ago, when it sold only booze and bait. They added the BBQ.

"What's your best seller?" I asked Ken, as he led me to a spacious sunlit dining area added to the back of the building.

"We sell liquor, of course," he said. "And we still sell some bait... had a guy in this morning. But the restaurant is taking off."

I can see why. The meats are slow-smoked to perfection. And you surround your entrée with sides like deep-fried green beans or MC's smoked pit beans. MC is a creative cook, one of Ken's secret weapons in the war against dull highway food.

I asked Ken about another menu item, the Frog Pollard, a whole hog sausage sandwich with pickles and white bread. "It's named after a local guy who became a legend around these parts," Ken said. "Frog Pollard got his name when he was a kid. He kept jumping out of his bedroom window to escape, so his aunt nicknamed him Frog." He grew up to be a great chef and an even better humanitarian, volunteering to help folks like him—minority and poor—to survive. He died a few years back, but his name lives on, at least on this menu. When I asked for a doggy bag for my leftover Memphis Classic pulled pork sandwich slathered with slaw, the server packed the leftover in a most unique container. It's a cardboard beer flat, slit on the sides to fold neatly in the middle, making a perfect doggy bag. "It's green," Ken said proudly. Green indeed.

Only a few miles north, along Highway 13, I found The Shrine of Our Lady of the Two Ugly Utility Poles Standing Side by Side in Our Front Yard. That's my name for it anyway. It's the world's best attempt to divert your attention from the unfortunate mass of warts and boils standing between the homeowner's picture window and the highway: a pair of power poles with transformers and heavy transmission lines, stabilized with heavy guywires. Somehow, a concrete statue of the Madonna at the base of this industrial utility offers peace to the people who live under its shadow. I doubt if the shrine adds to the value of the property. But for folks who drive by and notice, it's a reminder that the end is near.

* * *

Branching off onto one of the 4,100 roads that awaited me, I took a patchwork route back south to the evil efficiency of I-70. Even along its most distressing stretches, cross-country travelers have no idea the number of stories that wait within minutes of this motorway. The countryside is loaded with original icons that every American recognizes, from man's best friend to Iran's worst enemy. You wouldn't know it from the interstate signs. In fact, one highway sign discourages travelers from leaving the main highway. It's a source of frustration for locals around Aullville, an hour east of Kansas City.

Like a silent conductor, the big green highway sign along I-70 announced we were approaching Aullville. "No services," the same sign warned. That message spurred my recollection of a comment years ago from an Aullville resident. He was upset because the sign discouraged traffic to his town. I asked him if greater Aullville offered any services for interstate travelers.

"Well, not at the exit."

Aullville itself sits two miles off the interstate. Assuming that the collective temperament of interstate traffic trends toward immediate fulfillment, if not gratification, it's hard to argue that the "no services" sign is misleading. With no such warning, impatient drivers would reach the top of the exit ramp and face an uncertain choice between Aull or nothing.

We rose to the challenge. Erifnus coasted up the Aullville exit ramp to the stop sign. There, I surveyed land around the interchange that wasn't so desolate as it was pastoral. Rather refreshing, I thought, this panoramic view from the crown of a hill along this crowded highway. We turned north on Route T, and drove a couple miles. Just short of the banks of Devil's Creek, a tributary of the Black River, we rolled through Aullville. If tiny Aullville, population 86, doesn't provide for most of the basic needs of an agrarian community and its visitors, neighboring Higginsville can.

We motored four miles farther away from the interstate, the back way into Higginsville, past the Central Christian Church and the Republican Cemetery—no relation that I could detect, short of proximity to each other. We passed a flagpole flying the historically correct version of the Missouri Confederate battle flag—not the ubiquitous Battle Flag of the Army of Northern Virginia (the X). The flag reminded me that Higginsville is the final resting place for hundreds of Confederate soldiers.

Minutes later, I was strolling through that cemetery on the grounds of the old Confederate Soldiers Home of Missouri. The home had housed more than 1,600 veterans and their families since 1891, when the vast majority of Civil War veterans officially got old, until nearly 60 later years when it closed in the 1950s. The home is gone, but the cemetery protects the soldiers in their big sleep.

Walking down the rows of tombstones, I spied the marker. His name startled me at first, although I knew his remains were interred on these grounds. Well, at least part of William Quantrill is buried here. As *de facto* king of the Bushwhackers, Quantrill was a role model for young Jesse James, and directed the burning of Lawrence, Kansas.

Quantrill's body has yet to be reunited with itself. Hunted like the Devil during the Civil War, he finally was tracked down and shot to pieces in Kentucky. His mother asked that he be exhumed from his Kentucky grave, and re-interred in his home town of Dover, Ohio. Most of his body parts made it to Dover. But skulduggery diverted his head and five bones to a dank corner of a museum at the University of Kansas... in Lawrence.

Knowing this, a couple of bold Missourians, members of the Sons of the Confederacy, convinced Kansans in 1992 to give up his skull and five bones. The skull went back to Dover, Ohio, and is buried in a baby's coffin on top of Quantrill's semi-official grave. The other five bones ended up in the Confederate Cemetery in Higginsville. Fair and square. No thievery. But just for insurance, the Sons of the Confederacy poured a slab of concrete over the casket to keep it from wandering off.

I backed away slowly.

World Peace

We crossed Highway 50 near a waypoint that's guided locals for my whole life. It's called the Silo Tree, a mulberry tree that grew up in an old abandoned grain silo. It's fitting that an old silo, host to ten billion seeds over its lifetime, would finally let one sprout in its belly.

There were other silos around here, for a different purpose. Sprawling beside the little town of Knob Noster, Whiteman Air Force Base was the nerve center for America's 1960s defense system: 150 Minuteman Missile silos dug into the countryside and pointed at Russia and Cuba. Of course, that meant that for the better part of my life, there were Russian nukes pointed at Knob Noster's little cluster of silos. I've since learned that in Uzbekistan there's a town named Nukus. Nukus. That's what we were prepared to do to them, and they us.

I grew up about an hour from here during the '50s and '60s, a dead child walking, trained in grade school to drop to the floor, duck under my desk and cover my head with my hands, so that I could survive a nuclear bomb.

From what I remember, the warheads were decommissioned after I left the area for college. Today the missiles are long gone. But the silos remain. They're female silos, each with internal plumbing that plunges into the earth's skin, so the only thing visible is a cyclone fence surrounding what looks like a concrete parking lot the size of an average filling station. Clearly visible are the warning signs: U.S. Government Property. No Trespassing. Anyway, there are still 150 of these silos dotting the landscape. I don't know if any of them have a current or future purpose. Wine storage or tornado shelters, or maybe a rural annex to a county jail. I heard a guy turned one silo into subterranean condos, a self-sufficient underground city that can withstand World War III. It's enough for me that these silos stand empty and dormant, monuments to the fact that we dodged some big bullets, and survived the end of the world. So far.

Driving past these icons of war and death and destruction, I'm not paranoid. But I do try to minimize the risk. I realize that out here on the road, I'm much more likely to be blindsided by a careless driver or a deer bounding across the highway than by a nuclear warhead. That's why I always carry a little extra insurance, my Ozark air bag.

When I'm dead and gone, I'll be comfortable in anonymity. Certainly my daughters won't remember me as an inventor, although I'm proud of a pair of my creations. One invention, the high-pressure cigar washer never became a big seller.

But necessity offered me the opportunity to co-invent the Ozark air bag. Twenty years ago a buddy and I came up with the idea late one night as we sat in an empty bar, both of us intent on relieving the world's sternums from steering wheel implants. It's our contribution to safety, an add-on feature for cars built before airbag technology dipped down into the everyday lives of poor people. A lot of folks own older cars built before airbags became standard equipment.

The Ozark air bag is a by-product of the supercenter, where buying big really saves. In this case, it saves lives. Buy an 18-roll package of toilet paper. The package sits snugly in a driver's lap, and fits comfortably under the chin, between the arms. Being safety-minded, and lacking a factory-installed air bag at the time, I experimented with the concept, and the Ozark air bag was born.

Erifnus has implants, airbags of her own, and she has never had to test them. She's grateful. Nevertheless, in consideration of her advancing age, I picked up a little extra insurance at the dollar store, where the clerk looked puzzled when I told her I was going to wear a bag of toilet paper on my chest.

* * *

To learn the value of a culture, check their barbecue. At Perry Foster's Bar B-Q, on the edge of Warrensburg, the lesson went far beyond smoked meat....

The credit card machine kept disconnecting. I didn't have cash or my checkbook. "No problem," said Perry Foster, "mail me a check."

Perry Foster's Bar-B-Q embodies all that is good about humankind: Trust and harmony and world peace. Oh, and taste. My dinner was a combo sandwich, generously endowed with smoked ham, brisket, chicken and burnt ends slathered with sauce, accompanied by a steering-wheel-size platter of homemade seasoned french fries. Perry and his cook laughed when I approached the sandwich with a knife and fork. "Your hands! Use your hands," the cook coached me. "Eating barbecue ain't pretty. It's just good."

Good? No, great.

A great barbecue joint goes beyond great food. Several hundred photos adorn the walls of Perry Foster's. Among visages of former Kansas City Chiefs players and cheerleaders and Hank Williams' child, Perry pointed to his favorite picture: "That's the commander of Whiteman," he said, "flanked by the two top generals in the Russian Air Force." All three were smiling. When the Russian generals returned to Moscow and reported the highlights of their American experience—which probably included peeking into empty missile silos—their favorite stop was Perry's.

World peace.

I sat back down, and finished exactly half my sandwich. Perry wrapped the rest, including the french fries, which I devoured the next day when I got home. But first, I sent him a check.

Trust.

Downtown Warrensburg has another monument to trust. It's a statue of Old Drum. My dogs are convinced that every time I walk out our front door, I'm headed to sniff out Old Drum, the central character in the story about man's best friend. Our dogs, Baskin and Queenie, are Yorkshire Terriers. Together they weigh 11 pounds on the hoof, only a fraction of the statue dog's size. But they share that canine trait the statue celebrates: Loyalty.

Old Drum was a victim who unwittingly strayed into controversy, which evolved into a court case, *Burden v. Hornsby*. It wasn't poetry. Hornsby got tired of dogs straying onto his property. So he enlisted his nephew to shoot the beast of Burden, Old Drum, for trespassing. When Burden and his attorney entered the courtroom to sue Hornsby for the loss of his dog, most everybody thought the shooter should pay. The plaintiff's story so moved the initial jury that they awarded the grieving dog owner four times the $50 he sought, in 1870 dollars.

More lasting is the attorney's speech. George Graham Vest's whole testament—only 68 words longer than Lincoln's *Gettysburg Address*—produced the most famous sentiment in the history of interspecies friendship: "The one absolutely unselfish friend that a man can have in this selfish world, the one that never deserts him and the one that never proves ungrateful or treacherous is his dog." Those words adorn the statue honoring man's best friend, standing faithfully on the grounds of the Johnson County Courthouse, on the Warrensburg town square. Good dog.

All dogs will go to heaven, where they will grow opposable thumbs so they can spay or neuter you when you arrive. Count on it.

Bleach on the Streets

"Sedville will shine tonight, Sedville will shine.
"When the sun goes down and the moon comes up,
"Sedville will shine."

The old high school fight song rang true as we rolled into Sedalia. The sun was down, the moon was up, and Sedalia was prepared to let its Brylcreem shine, and revel in its ducktails and its sideburns, its Bel Airs and Deuce Coupes, its 'Vettes and Goats, its Challengers and Chargers and Mustangs. As we rolled into Sedalia under a full moon, we happened upon a smoky shroud that hung around the mother of all classic car rallies. The highway had an unnatural sheen, and the smoky smell alternated between engine exhaust and Clorox.

It was on Highway 65, along the edge of the Missouri State Fairgrounds, but this was no state fair. A giant car rally spilled onto the road in a nocturnal parade. Must've been a thousand hot rods on the highway, so we pulled into a parking lot to watch the procession. It was a massive chain of hood ornaments and hubcaps, hardtops and tops down around high-gloss candy colored quarterpanels, with enough chrome to sink a barge, enough leather to dress a battalion of masochists. The tail lights represented every character in the Morse code, the tailfins illuminated by headlamps shining through white smoke coming not from the tailpipes, but from the tires. The smell of bleach wafted up into my nostrils, as I joined the three-deep crowd lining the road.

At regular 30-yard intervals, uniformed highway patrol troopers kept onlookers on the curb. But with a laser focus that rivals a cat watching a bird, the troopers fixed their eyes on the cars' front bumpers and their fat rear tires. Cops watched for drivers and their crews smuggling small containers of bleach to the path in front of the car, and when they thought the cops weren't looking, they'd dump the bleach on the asphalt. Then the drivers would roll forward onto the slick bleach, and spin their tires in screeching burnouts.

In defense of the hot rodders, each burnout is a science experiment: the chemical reaction from blending rubber, asphalt and bleach at 8,000 RPMs makes a cloud as white as Santa's beard. The cloud gives gifts, too, as it wafts into waiting lungs and eyes, depositing microscopic particles of blasphubber. The cops had to catch the perps in the act of pouring bleach on the street to make arrests or write tickets. I didn't see any arrests, which is probably a good thing, since such action could touch off a riot.

It was a carnival atmosphere, with happy crowds watching hot rodders do what they do best: Parade like peacocks in souped-up penis extensions.

Sedalia is the perfect place to stage a car rally. Every driver will agree that for a town of 20,000 people, this is the longest city in the history of western civilization. You can eat lunch on one end of town, and only hope to make it to the other side by dinner. Especially if there's a road rally on the streets.

Lust for the classic automobile is alive and rumbling in Sedalia. So is the love of railroads, which get credit for building this town, back when it was called Sedville, named after a girl named Sed, I guess. Railroads still deliver passengers in and out of Sedalia, the way they have since cowboy days, when massive cattle drives terminated at the rail heads in town, as documented by Rowdy Yates in "Rawhide." As a kid I watched Rowdy drive his cattle to Sedalia every Friday night on CBS. Turns out, some of that history is true. For cowboys and railroad passengers, bawdy houses sprung up like Viagra commercials. There were so many whorehouses in Sedalia that one St. Louis newspaper called the town the "Sodom and Gomorrah" of its time. Rowdy, indeed.

Even with intermittent half-hearted attempts to rout out the vice, a row of bawdy houses remained on the other side of the tracks until I was past puberty. Scott Joplin used to play piano in at least one of them. Some folks trace the origin of "Staggerlee" to this sporting ground. And one place survived right up until a few years ago. The whores at Nat's frolicked with the railroad folks mainly, and college and high school boys from miles around. At least that's what I've heard. Nat's is gone now. The end is near.

But on this moonlit evening, I stood on the curb with a thousand people, having fun learning new things about '57 Chevys and sideburns and Elvis. After the car show peeled off into the distance, I headed down the highway to one of my favorite spots.

Back in 1947, a round drive-in restaurant popped up in an old auto dealer showroom on the busiest corner in Sedalia. Lyman Kueper knew this intersection guaranteed his restaurant would stay busy. Two major highways.

So the Wheel Inn opened for business, serving its famous guber-burger—it would have been known elsewhere as goober-burger—a sandwich that would make Elvis salivate. The burger gets a topping of peanut butter, spread thick like protein relish. As uber as the guber was, the restaurant was a treat. Round and glass, with red round stools at a horseshoe shaped counter on a ketchup 'n' cream colored checkerboard linoleum floor, you couldn't help but grow a ducktail and let your sideburns get a little longer. And I always stopped to eat there on my way through town.

But the two major highways eventually strangled the drive in, when the highway department needed to widen the turn lanes at the intersection. So after decades on that busy corner, the last owners closed the Wheel Inn. They auctioned off most of their stuff to a throng of faithful guber eaters. The restaurant's hardware and furnishings left in a hundred different hands, and an icon dissolved into legend... almost. It turns out that a former Wheel Inn carhop got permission to use the name and the recipes and reopen the restaurant down the road.

So I drove down Highway 65 to get my guber. I was a bit surprised that there weren't more customers, with the car rally headquartered across the street on the sprawling grounds of the Missouri State Fair. As I got good and gubered up, I looked out the big picture window, across the highway where the State Fair rages every summer, and immersed my mind into campy, corny, carny nostalgia.

This state fair has all the necessary ingredients: The smell of hot grease along foody row, the smell of hot grease in the grandstands, the smell of hot grease along the million-dollar midway. Best of all, the mix of people is inspirational. Last time I went, I watched a carny barker lure a young couple into a tent to see the Amazing Angel Snake Woman. "No arms or legs!" he cried. "She has the head of a beautiful woman, the body of an ugly snake." I waited until the couple came back out of the tent, bent over laughing. "It was a carny slut in a potato sack." Ah, there's a sucker born every minute....

Down the midway was a ride called "Pirates of the Sea." I bypassed the ride, knowing that soon I'd come face to face with my nemesis, "Pirates of the Beer Stand."

On my walks through the fair, I've seen a lot of freak shows. But according to locals, the biggest freak show spilled out of the fairgrounds and into the neighborhoods of Sedalia back in the summer of '74. It was an innocent little event called the Ozark Music Festival. State officials thought they were leasing the fairgrounds for a bluegrass concert. Indeed, the Earl Scruggs Revue was there, and Leo Kottke, too. So were a quarter-million other folks, and the event turned into one of the three seminal music festivals during the Age of Aquarius. Promoted by Wolfman Jack and advertised in *Rolling Stone*, the lineup included The Eagles, Lynyrd Skynard, Marshall Tucker, BTO, REO, America and Bob Seger. At the bottom of the promotional poster was an obscure name in small type: Bruce Springsteen.

The festival promoters assured the town that only 50,000 tickets would be sold. Crowds grew to 300,000 by some estimates, swamping not only the State Fairgrounds, but the town itself, with people piss-ing, puking and passing out in front yards. It was too much to bear, even for a city built on the slick foundation of brothelism.

Now 35 years later, acting on a tip, I drove around the fields near the fairgrounds, looking for a remnant of the festival, a shack with the words "Bruno's Whorehouse" scrawled on the side. Somebody said it's been converted to a duck blind, but I couldn't find it.

No matter, Sedville still has that shine.

Byrds, Billiard Balls and Billionaires

Otterville might or might not have otters. But it does have a spot in history, thanks to the ubiquitous Jesse James. On the night of July 7, 1876, the James gang stole a lantern to flag down a Missouri Pacific train in the deep Rocky Cut pass near Otterville. They stopped the engine, jumped from the bluffs onto the top of the train, got $15,000 from the two safes on board and used the money to finance their trip to Northfield, Minnesota. They shoulda gone to Hawaii.

I rolled into Tipton, home of two great icons. One is visible. The other is six feet under. His name is Harold Eugene Clark, and the epitaph on his headstone reads, "No other." Fans of the seminal rock 'n' roll band the Byrds know what that means.

Gene Clark was born here in 1944. He moved away with his fam-ily to Kansas City when he was a kid and sang with the New Christy Minstrels. Eventually he wound up co-founding the Byrds, and sing-ing with the likes of Bob Dylan.

As worldly as he'd become, Gene knew that when he died, he wanted to be buried where he started. He's been in the Tipton Cemetery since 1991. Gene Clark is big in Europe, still. And he's big in Tipton. But elsewhere in America, most of the attention heaped on the name Clark is for Dick. Oh, Tipton had a concert once, in Gene's honor. I imagine Gene's bones enjoyed the concert, since it's my belief that dead bodies can hear. At least the middle ear's percussive instruments—its hammer and anvil and stirrup—continue to vibrate when it thunders. If a tree falls...

Tipton's most visible icon is everybody's favorite water tower, a perfect sphere painted like an 8-ball. It used to preside over a pool table company. When the company vacated, the 8-ball was painted over for a time, but now the ball is back.

I caromed through Tipton and banked right, feeling good about driving through Fortuna, and the back roads through Latham, where I paused to watch an Amish softball game. It was a community event, coeducational, everybody in uniform—not softball uniforms, of course, but the traditional dress of the Amish. It appeared that some of the players would have difficulty running in bulky workwear, but as I watched, I realized that the game itself was secondary to the camaraderie. Maybe one or two participants had the mindset of a take-no-prisoners little league parent, but I didn't see it.

I raced a train to California, the small town with a state named after it. OK, that's a lie, since the state name California is the fifth-oldest surviving name of a place in the United States, according to something I read somewhere once. The other four are St. Augustine, Jamestown, Santa Fe and Pizza Hut. The Missouri town of California wasn't named after the state, either. Locals say a guy named California Wilson promised to give his neighbors a couple of gallons of whiskey if they'd name the town after him. So for a while the town was called Wilson, Missouri, until the neighbors sobered up and realized what they'd done.

The train I raced to California was the afternoon Amtrak headed for St. Louis. I didn't race it as much as matched its pace toward the east, as we moved side by side at 60 mph. An engine, two passenger cars and a café. The train was packed, the faces at the windows looked happy. I was happy, too, since the sounds of trains have provided the background music from my earliest memory. I can still hear the faint call of a steam whistle, growing ever closer with each throaty blast, giving way to the rhythmic clacking of steel wheels, a cadence that lulled me to sleep as a child.

But as I grew older and learned to drive, I learned about the train's only flaw. It can follow only the same rigid path, back and forth. Erifnus and I drive every path. That's why trains will never supplant cars, even when gasoline reaches $10 per gallon. Cars are here to stay. Trains, not so much. I don't like that, but I understand.

I beat the Amtrak to downtown California where the main drag crosses the railroad tracks, and watched the train roar through the intersection. There's no rush quite like being close to six billion tons of hurtling steel. The heart always beats faster at a railroad crossing, when you're sitting in a car and a train approaches, and you know that you could gun the engine and try to beat the train in a deadly game of chicken. I didn't. Never have, in a car anyway. Matter of fact, I haven't challenged a train like that since I was nine years old.

Back then, I was brave. One night, I'd just finished playing a little league baseball game at Frisco Park in Rolla. My path home took me over the railroad tracks. Walking straight out of center field with my back to home plate, I left the secure glow of the ballfield lights and entered the realm of long shadows and dark images.

Approaching the rail bed, I climbed the ten-foot bank to the rails. A freight train stood stopped on the tracks, presenting a mile-long barrier. No way around it. No way over it. I'd have to duck under it, as I'd done a dozen times before. Just as I approached the rails, the train lurched into motion. It jolted loudly, as all trains do when they start moving, a churning succession of metal clashes passed through each coupling like loud metal knuckles popping, and the train began to crawl at the pace of a chess game. I picked my opening, dived onto the tracks behind the front wheels of a boxcar, and easily reached the other side, beating the slow rolling back wheels with ten feet to spare. I went home but I didn't tell Mom. If you're reading this passage to your toddlers, tell them not to try this. But please understand that your children, as they grow and experiment with life, will do stupid shit like this, and they'll never tell you. That's just the nature of things.

The train that hurtled through California was gone in seconds, and the bells and flashing lights stood at ease. Erifnus crossed the tracks and we passed the court house, and circled north past Potato Chip Lane and Berger Branch and a town named Bacon. Food cues are big in this rural area, but none bigger than the biggest burger on the block, Burger's Smokehouse, a world-famous producer of country cured hams, the kind you give to special friends for the holidays. In almost every case I know, Burger hams are met with more delight than fruitcakes or zucchinis and are not passed on to the next gift recipient in line, but consumed like cherished aphrodisiacs. I turned south through McGirk and meandered to the end of a blacktop near Dynamite Ridge. I watered the "State Maintenance Ends" sign and Erifnus turned around. A train could do none of those things.

Steering south, Versailles soon appeared in our windshield, and we did a lap around its gorgeous courthouse, and I whispered an apology as we left the businesses along its town square and pulled into a Walmart parking lot.

I try to avoid Walmart as much as possible, except, of course, when I need something. Then I'll go there and buy it, because like everybody else, I'm sensitive to price. It torments my soul that every dime I spend there is another nail in the coffin of competition, a poke in the eye to small-town main street. The Versailles Walmart is the ultimate irony because this one is locally owned. Sort of.

It's the hometown of exactly one-half the founders of Walmart. Most everybody knows the story of Sam Walton. His co-founder, brother Bud, set up shop here, first acquiring a local Ben Franklin's dime store. The Walmart ideas came later. Today the local Ben Franklin's is gone.

Bud and Audrey Walton made Versailles their home. He died years ago. Audrey remains, and maintains a mostly low key demeanor. Even as the de facto queen of Morgan County, she definitely doesn't display the flamboyance of the European gentry for which Versailles is named. But when the community center receives an anonymous financial boost or the town's children get a new playground, everybody figures they know the secret donor.

Around here she's jes' folks, and the locals call her Audie. What they call their town causes a smile.

Versailles (vur SALES) has little in common with the French palace with the same name (vur SIGH). The local mispronunciation is the town's most famous feature, perhaps the most repeated phonetic butchery in Missouri.

Speaking of butcheries, down the road in Stover, we stopped at a country market called the Split Rail, which calls itself cleaner, leaner, greener because it has natural, additive-free meats and lots of great Amish products. After a pork cheddar bratwurst and homemade ice cream, I probably wasn't leaner, but the store was greener. I left with some natural peanut butter with dandelion jelly. I was glad to find the jelly, because at home every time I try to make dandelion jelly, it tastes like RoundUp.

Down the road is a roundup with frightening implications if you're an aspiring boar or bull. It's the Olean Testicle Festival. Like Versailles, Olean isn't pronounced the way it looks (oh lee ANN). You already know how to say testicle, even though you may snicker. Don't. This is serious business. Especially for the barrows and steers and hokies who donate your meal. And it's serious business for the 157 residents of Olean, when the town swells to 20,000 nut-cuttin', ball-bustin' party goers.

A dozen years ago the state tourism guide's editors balked at Olean's first request to buy an ad for the Testicle Festival. The state events guide has strict rules. No profanity, of course. Most of the stuff is G-rated. So, for example, the state doesn't advertise the annual Beat Me in St. Louis meeting of sadists and masochists. Seriously, there is a Beat Me in St. Louis convention every year, "A fun, educational pan-sexual event for the entire BDSM community." I've never been there, wouldn't know what to wear.

But the testicle festival? "If people get the wrong idea, it's their fault," said one tourism official. The state printed the ad. Now deep fried-nut lovers come from all over the nation.

Erifnus rolled into a parking spot a mile from town and I walked down the road that's the only entrance to Olean, past hundreds of sleek Harleys and their photogenic owners with their leathers and braided hair and beer bellies and stretch marks and tattoos positioned perilously close to cleavage. Downhill from The Hut, Olean's gathering spot, is ground zero, an open park pavilion surrounded by a field filled with folks popping testicle tots.

Well, the nuts were all cut and fried by the time I arrived. The crowds were going full-tilt, balls to the wall, swilling beer and swinging to live music, pausing to gorge themselves on the main course. By late afternoon, the vendors sold out of bull fries and turkey fries and hog fries. But there was plenty of beer.

During past festivals, some of Olean's residents got a little tired of looking out into their front yards to see people projectile vomiting animal genitalia. So organizers decided to move the Testicle Festival a dozen miles down the road to a spot below Bagnell Dam at the Lake of the Ozarks. That change of venue lasted one year, because attendees and promoters alike yelped as if they'd been castrated. Like the inbred turkeys whose fries they ate, the festival goers couldn't adapt to the new feedlot. The very next year, the Testicle Festival moved back home.

* * *

I plunged south through Eugene, past the Narrow Road Baptist Church, over the ghostly old abandoned Rock Island Railroad tunnel that burrows beneath the town for a third of a mile, until I reached the turnoff to Mary's Home. The village is on a dead-end blacktop. But the community is vibrant, even if it's off the beaten path.

That's the way Russell and Debbie Stansbury like it. The family has lived on the edge of Mary's Home for a generation now, raising four kids in this tiny town with no stoplights. A solitary general store sits at the only 4-way stop sign, on a sharp bend in the road. Across the street, the Catholic church is the center of the community. And the town still hangs on to a post office for now. The general store forms the central business district. It's called the Corner Market, itself a time-honored structure, with two stories outside and a thousand stories inside, with one gas pump in front and barely enough of a dirt shoulder for a car to fill'erup and not be on the right-of-way.

Jason and Jessica Parr bought the place a couple of years ago, and they've turned it into a happenin' spot. It's a grocery store, restaurant, bar and feed store, a place to meet everybody who lives within 40 miles. Inside, they serve Busch Beer on tap and support live music on weekends. I stopped in to look around and had a beer with Russell.

"This is the kind of place," Russell says, "that everybody will be having a good time, and word will come that somebody got a tractor stuck in the mud. Everybody will go to help the neighbor in distress." Then, of course, they all come back to the tavern to celebrate getting unstuck. Life is good in Mary's Home.

It's common along these back roads to see messages opposing abortion and promoting prayer in schools. But just outside Osage Bluff I noticed a hand-painted sign that said "Lord for sale." I hit the brakes and backed up to re-read its message: "Land for sale." My mistake. The Lord doesn't ask for money. Only humans do that.

Entering Wardsville, I read another sign with a clear message: "This stretch of highway is adopted by the American Sign Language Club." That should give comfort to folks who want to make sure sign language is spoken in American. But the next sign caused some confusion. It's one of four city limit signs in Wardsville, and the signs can't agree on the number of residents. Two signs say the population is 976. The other two report 1,506 inhabitants. Maybe the highway department is only halfway done updating the population on the city limit signs. That's okay. Highway crews have higher priorities, like filling more and more potholes, with less and less money.

Towering, Taking and Mining

The famous philosopher Yogi Berra and I share at least one thing in common. We both married ladies from Salem. So we've spent a fair amount of time there, on the golf course, munching tacos at Stephens Drive-In, dining in Ozark elegance at the Tower Inn. Never at the same time, of course. Truth is, I've never met Yogi. I just hear the stories.

Speaking of stories, the Tower Inn had ten of 'em. Built back in the '60s, the hotel was the tallest building between Springfield and Cape Girardeau, that I know of. And even in the Ozark folds, drivers coming to Salem from every direction could see the Tower from miles away, its dark tin skin rising above the hills. Atop its roof a radio tower punched a hole in the sky. On the tenth floor, the elevator door opened up to a nightclub full of patrons drinking and dancing and opening the windows to watch their vomit spill a hundred feet to the parking lot below.

Across the hall from the bar were two opulent suites, almost presidential, considering the remoteness of this outpost on the rim of civilization. One suite featured Chinese furnishings, fragile silk tapestries and graceful wood carvings. The other offered a Spanish motif with leather saddles, iron furniture framed in dark wood, and decorative ox yokes on the walls. It could endure more abuse than the delicate Chinese room, and thus was the favored spot for freewheeling drunken toga parties, where sometimes people ended up wearing the ox yokes for photos or bondage or both.

So far as I know, nobody ever jumped from a Tower Inn window, although the Spanish suite lost its television set late one night. The TV just flew out the window and smashed on the pavement below. Kinda like spontaneous combustion, I guess. Some witnesses know what happened. They're not talking.

Tragedy struck three decades ago when the hotel's elevator crushed a repairman to death. I heard that a local preacher said the poor repairman was probably going to Hell. For the life of me, I can't believe a preacher could say something like that. Maybe the preacher thought the repairman was doing the Devil's business, fixing that elevator that delivered sinners to barrooms and hotel rooms. But even after the repairman's death and the preacher's warning, plenty of folks stepped into that elevator for a ride to the tenth floor, to dip into sin.

That's all changed, since they lopped off the hotel's top six stories. They just lopped 'em off. I guess the building had fire code issues, or maybe the insurance liability got to be too steep. But considering the Salem Fire Department probably didn't have a ladder truck capable of reaching much past half way up the side of the building, I guess the lopping-off is logical. I was lucky I didn't perish, all those nights I spent on the top floor, windows open, bouncing rock 'n' roll anthems off the Baptist church a mile away. Most of all, I'll miss the view from the top of the Tower. You could see halfway to the mining camps at Boss and Bunker and Bixby. And since Salem was upwind of the mines, you didn't have to worry about snorting too much lead dust.

The first time I ever drove down to Salem, it was like taking a long driveway to a different world, along a path cut through a forest so thick the road looked like Moses' path through the Red Sea. That was almost 40 years ago, and the slow creep of civilization has changed the landscape. More and more, felled forestland makes room for parking lots and fast food billboards.

But the bigger change is the road itself. Between Rolla and Salem, old Route 72 is retired now. I watched them replace it over a period of years. Building roads is a painful process for everybody: the builders and their crews who wrestle stumps and level hills and smooth out valleys; the commuters who cuss the flagmen as they wait impatiently to move through construction bottlenecks; the landowners, who for years have dreaded the day when their front yards would be circumcised and trimmed in concrete. Landowners mutter about the unfairness of eminent domain and scream at their elected officials about the nightmare of taking private property. But most folks support the benefit of newer, straighter, safer highways as long as the roads are not in their front yards.

I see a cost that goes beyond money and lost land and bigger carbon footprints. Old roads have character, like old wooden roller coasters. Scary, but memorable. New highways are safe. Boring, but safe.

Much of old Route 72 was chopped, ground up, and used as landfill for other projects. Old bridges were dismantled and sold for scrap or reconstructed as spans over streams in remote parts of the world. A few stretches of the old road remain, and I can see sections of the old road as I pass. It looks narrow and winding and dangerous. The old road offered damn few safe spots to pass slower cars. Faster drivers needed the skills of a race car driver to blast past slowpokes in the face of cars cresting the next hill. ...

Nowadays along this shiny new straightaway, I must keep a tight rein on my car, because even at her advanced age, Erifnus likes to stretch out and run at top speed through that sleek course. Patrol cars like that road, too, for the same reason, with a different outcome. But if time is money, every commuter reaps an extra reward. Even staying within the speed limit, the 30-minute drive to Rolla is shortened to 25 minutes, saving commuters 25 hours a year. A free day. But so far, nobody in Salem or Rolla has organized a freedom day to honor the project and its benefits of time and safety. They're too busy fighting taxes. Ah, the forest for the trees...

Even as civilization spreads, Salem is still an island in a sea of dense forest. The town offers what an island offers: shelter, entertainment and food. We pulled into the McDonald's, not to eat, but to use the restroom facilities. In my quest to conquer all the roads in Missouri, I relied on supply depots along the way to refuel my car and me. The golden arches were strewn strategically in our path, with bathrooms nearly as consistent as their burgers. I'll eat a filet o' fish now and then. But more than anything, I appreciate their plumbing.

Here's a rule of thumb. If a Midwest town has a population more than 500 people, you'll likely find a Casey's General Store. Put another zero on a town's population, and you'll get golden arches, or some similar monument to consistency, convenience, and landfills.

Salem scores in the above categories, including the landfill. Although its population barely eclipses 5,000 souls, it's a center of commerce in the Ozarks. But while the town has always wrestled with its Jekyll and Hyde identity as part sleepy town, part commercial hub, and while critics consider the area third-world by some standards, Salem has evolved. Years ago, you'd see a constant column of black smoke rising south of town from a giant mountain of smoldering vehicle tires. They finally put the fire out, and I assume the tires have been properly recycled into asphalt or crappie beds.

One day back in the '70s, I watched big black helicopters invade Salem. They swooped out of the sky and landed right on the parking lot in front of the Tower Inn. Rich white men in Brooks Brothers suits climbed out. Townsfolk soon learned that these rich men were the board of directors for a big mining company, then-owner of the lead and zinc mines around Boss and Bunker and Bixby. The directors were touring their domain, and offered living proof that, indeed, corporations are people. But they're neither neighbors nor friends. They don't live around here, among the miners.

This invasion 40 years ago by black helicopters also vindicated a vocal minority of local conspiracy theorists who have predicted for years that Big Brother would swoop down and take away our rights and send covert signals using the backs of highway signs. I never subscribed to the black helicopter theory, but this corporate copter landing in the Tower Inn parking lot gave fuel to the conspiracy. Only one problem: the copters were from big corporations, not big government. That distinction goes right over the flat heads of fearmongers. Landing in their midst, Big Brother is disguised as a corporate citizen. A job creator, if you want a job in a lead mine.

Some folks who lived downwind of the mines became incapable of knowing simple things, like their own zip code. Maybe it was natural, or maybe it was plumbum poisoning. For more information on this subject, study the fall of the Roman Empire. Lead plates. Lead goblets. And the ancient Romans didn't know their zip code either.

Anyway, the helicopters left without firing a shot, and life pretty much never changed in Salem, except now the Tower Inn is gone, and they put out the tire fire. And the town has lost some of its rugged innocence to a new Burger King that competes with the McDonald's. It has a nice bathroom too. As for future invasions, long before the trilateral commission lands helicopters to round up all the guns along Highway 19, the road will be littered with crap and albescent trash. Pogo knows: The end is near.

I found refuge in a Holiday Inn Express, almost in the shadow of the shrinking Tower Inn. The new motel has new amenities: a nice hot tub and, most important, a great location from which to launch my search, because I'm a miner, too. Unlike the lead miners who live around here and disappear underground to find heavy metal, I'm a strip miner.

So I tied my running shoes and headed out on the strip. One of the richest deposits of curb ore in the state lies along one mile of Highway 32 between the shell of the Tower Inn and the shell of an old Walmart on the edge of town. Along this road's shoulders I've discovered hundreds of little round slugs of copper and nickel, all stamped with dates and pictures on them, and enough iron and steel to replace the rivets on the USS *Constitution*. Today I found a quarter, two dimes, a nickel and six pennies, four face-up. My superstitious friends avoid the pennies if Honest Abe is facing the dirt. Ben Franklin didn't care which way a penny faced. And since Old Ben didn't die picking up pennies, I pick 'em up too. I also found a lug nut, two washers, a gas cap, and a sheared bolt that once helped hold the Tower Inn together.

I found something else, hiding in plain sight in the Salem Cemetery, which stretches along the roadside, with graves as old as the early 1800s. Amid the gravestones is one mausoleum built in the distinct "early sod quonset kiln" style. It takes the shape of an old charcoal kiln, as tall as a man, rounded like a quonset hut with stone walls on front and back, its curved hump packed with sod so it forms a grass roof. The rusted iron door on the back wall was locked. In front a headstone supplied by the Woodmen of the World said this:

Edwin N. Pendergrass
October 22, 1845—April 22, 1907
"Gone spiritually"

In the hundred years Edwin Pendergrass has laid beneath this berm, shaded by a giant oak tree, ten thousand people may have stood here and wondered what the hell is a Woodman of the World. Maybe

Edwin helped cut down the forests to hack ties for the railroads. Or he might've been an environmentalist. The truth is less romantic, since the Woodmen of the World is a fraternal organization based in Omaha. The group's primary function is to offer insurance to its members.

The Woodmen of the World provided something else, too: elaborate gravesites for many policyholders when they died. Most of their headstones were carved in the shape of tree stumps, like the one in the Hannibal cemetery. But soon after Edwin Pendergrass got his monument, Woodmen of the World quit building these memorials to its fallen brethren because more and more cemeteries began favoring headstones with their faces even with the ground. Two-dimensional hallowed ground is so much easier to mow.

So I'll never know whether Edwin favored the forests, or rooted for the railroads. The bigger question is why he ended up "Gone spiritually."

I always hate leaving Salem. It's my favorite hideaway, damn near exotic in its remoteness, a cross between God's country and the Wild West, on the leeward side of lead dust. But it's a crossroads, and I knew I would be back.

Forward and Backward

Ava is a palindrome. It looks the same coming from any direction.

The water tower sits atop a hill off the center of town, shouting "Ava Bears" from its steel sides. This garden spot in the middle of the Mark Twain Forest missed a fun opportunity to call the school team the Ava Gardeners.

Three designated scenic highways meet just outside town, so it's easy to circumvent Ava's heart, where several things are refreshingly off center. The courthouse is on the edge of the town square, not in the middle. And French's Highway House Café isn't on the main highway anymore. The café didn't move. It's been there nearly five decades. When the highway bypass rerouted traffic, owner Doris French was unfazed.

I met Doris when I walked into the restaurant before the dinner hour, carrying my steno notebook and my map. She eyed me warily, thinking I might be a salesman. "May I help you?"

"You bet! I'm here to eat."

Her face showed relief. "Well, come on in and sit anywhere you like." I looked around at the tables, cozy in their tall wooden booths that offered intimate family dining. I picked a corner booth near the counter in front of the kitchen service window. The booth spoke history from its dark wood panels and comfortable cushions only slightly firmer than grandma's feather bed. Doris brought me a menu. I ordered the special. In the quiet before the supper rush, she took time to tell me about the place.

"I raised four kids in this restaurant," she said. "Becky and Cynthia and Cody and Rodney came here every day after school, and sat right there in that back booth." She pointed. "I had one rule: We met for supper every day at 5, right here. And when they left home it made a big empty spot that no one could fill."

Her cook brought me the biggest blue plate special I've ever had in my life: a slab of country ham surrounded by an Ozark mountain of mashed potatoes and gravy and hominy and homemade apple salad and hot homemade sliced bread. Dad would be proud.

I ate. Doris talked.

She told me her husband had worked for years with the U.S. Forest Service, at its headquarters compound on old Highway 5 on the south edge of town. Those old rock buildings were built when space wasn't at a premium, and trees were royalty. "He worked on all the trails around here," she said. "The Glade Top…"

"Bear country," I volunteered through a mouthful of mashed potatoes. The Glade Top Trail is tattooed in my memory because of a sign at the entrance to the trail: "Watch for bears."

She continued. "He helped build the motorcycle trail at Chadwick. And the horse trail at Hercules. And the parks around Wolf Junction."

She still has a cabin on Bull Shoals Lake down around Protem, where they planned to retire. But he died a few years ago, and Doris keeps serving up blue plate specials to hungry customers, and hosts the weekly gathering of her Kiwanis Club. After nearly 50 years in the grind of restaurant life, Doris hasn't lost the twinkle in her eye or her love of watching the eyes of satisfied customers. And I get the feeling that if she retired from the grind of operating a restaurant, she just might not know what to do.

"Dessert?" she asked. The big meal left me no room for such indulgence. She gave me an old restaurant placemat that showed the area trails, and a program from the recent Fox Trotter Heritage Days, with its seed-spittin' contest and a husband calling contest and a rolling pin toss.

I left the cowboys behind, crossed the picturesque persistence of Bryant Creek and descended into the vigorous hydrology along the east edge of Douglas County.

Next to an old general store, Topaz Mill perches on the upper North Fork of the White River. The mill has been restored to its 115-year-old glory. Nearly two centuries ago, Henry Schoolcraft, the first explorer to write about the Ozarks, stumbled onto this spring.

As most area bats know, it's not far from Topaz to Hell. Hell Roaring Spring eventually adds waters to the flow beneath the Twin Bridges, launching spot for a million great floats on the pristine North Fork. Hell Roaring Spring is just another example how the Devil contributes to tourism and the local economy.

* * *

Twisting Erifnus' radio knobs, I found KKOZ radio, which calls itself the "best radio in the Ozarks," and I couldn't disagree. It certainly is the most dependable, as I drove into the deep cracks around Tater Cave Mountain, Caney Mountain and Long Bald. At the end of one trail, I found Romance. With no intention of making time, I retreated from this little village with the amorous appellation and felt my way up curvaceous Highway 95.

Soon, from a mountaintop, I spied the Mountain Grove water tower, a mammoth aerial gland that spills a bit of character about its town and watches over the folks it waters. Just past the tower, I turned west and took the back roads to Hartville.

Painted olive green, Hartville's water tower earns style points as it sticks out from the old red brick buildings like a garnish on the swizzle stick in a giant bloody Mary. I know that image isn't the town's intent. But, hey, I've seen every water tower in this state, and each offers a first impression. This one's a garnish atop a tasty little town.

Residents of tiny Hartville probably feel insulated from the world, hiding at the mouth of the Gasconade River, tucked amid layers of thickly-forested hills that unfold in every direction. But the little capital of Wright County couldn't always hide from conflict. Seven generations ago, when Union and Confederate forces finally clashed on the hilltop in downtown Hartville, a battle raged all day. Union troops rebuffed several Confederate charges. The battle was a draw, although both sides limped away from the little town claiming victory.

The conflict was minor in the grand scheme of the Civil War. But don't tell that to the 19 killed and more than 150 wounded. No doubt the troops needed comfort after the battle. Too bad the comfort food of Mom's Family Café didn't come along for nearly a sesquicentury. In my view, anything named after mom makes it a compelling magnet. And while I've seen plenty of tributes to mom, including the National Mother's Shrine—a rotating statue of the Virgin Mary in the backyard of a Catholic Church in Laurie, Missouri—I'm particularly fond of shrines to moms that serve good food. Welcomed by the café's official dress code, jeans and T-shirts, I felt right at home on Rolla Street right next to Bullfrog's Pawn, bathed in the aroma of beans and the promise of frog legs. No bloody Marys, though. Or beer.

Between bites, I learned that Mom was Betty Vanderstine, who always dreamed of owning a little home-cookin' place like this. She died in 2004, and her son opened the restaurant a year later as a tribute to her memory.

It's more than a tribute, when you think about it. In the general category of tributes to loved ones, gravestones are most common, of course. And a yellowed newspaper obituary stuck in a Bible. A few folks become immortalized in song or verse. Lately, many survivors have enlisted in the Adopt-A-Highway program, which affords them a 2x4 sign to remind passers by of their dearly departed loved one. But to build a restaurant in honor of mom is a real commitment. Long hours, daily. Hot kitchens. A slew of unanticipated headaches. Forget flowers. This is something mothers can relate to. Betty would be proud.

But dammit to Hell, nothing lasts forever, and crossing through Hartville a few months later, I noted with sadness that Mom's is closed, with that small-business synonym for a Grim Reaper's scythe—a real estate sign—sitting in the window.

Just down the road from Hartville, Baker Creek Heirloom Seed Company ships a billion seeds all over the world from a place called Bakersville, a replica pioneer town. A big billboard lured us into Bakersville to look around, where we came face-to-face with a real live Sultan. This sultan is a chicken, with a crown of feathers worthy of a king. But in these parts the Sultan is safe, since the proprietor is a vegetarian. It makes sense that Jeremiah Gettle eats only vegetables. That's what he sells, the vegetable seeds anyway. He personally scours the world for rare varieties of vegetables, in places like Belize and Siam, and he sells them through a catalog that has mushroomed into big business. His seeds propagate in gardens from Monticello to Sonoma, Williamsburg to Disneyworld.

Jeremiah and Emilee Gettle are still young. But their teenaged heirloom-seed empire is blossoming, thanks to a burgeoning market of folks who want better taste and better nutrition. Bakersville is booming, too, with a new grand barn built by Amish neighbors, and regular festivals featuring musical groups that have a propensity to yodel. Presentations get dusted with a fair amount of agro-political chatter, promoting libertarian and bioconservative political views: "Save the Earth." "Watch out for genetically altered Frankenfoods and the big corporations that support them." Stuff like that.

Among Gettle's hundreds of pure varieties of open-pollinated vegetable seeds, I have my eye on a few intriguing members of the *lycopersicon lycopersicum* species (You say tomato). How can a garden do without a tomato called the Tartar of Mongolistan? Or maybe I'll try the Sub-Arctic Plenty (World's Earliest), or Joe Thieneman's Australian Heart. For sure, every Italian food lover should grow a meaty tomato called Amish Paste.

The Amish are prevalent in this area. Hard-working, decent people who make great neighbors and produce top-notch products, most notably furniture and food. And buildings and honesty... They're a fine fit for Bakersville, which looks a bit like *Little House on the Prairie*.

It set the mood to launch me into my next discovery, down the road just outside Mansfield. It's a modest homestead called Rocky Ridge, the home of Laura Ingalls Wilder. Even with this famous icon as a magnet for tourists, Mansfield suffers from an affliction common to small towns. Granted, it was late afternoon when I stopped downtown at a local museum. On the door, next to the "No public restroom" warning was a "Closed" sign. I understand the struggle to keep small-town museum doors open. Limited budgets. A short list of volunteers. And it's a tribute to the town that they offer a museum.

But I was annoyed by the "No public restroom" sign. Maybe they didn't have a bathroom. Or maybe it was out of order. I simply object to the wording of the sign, which offers no alternative for folks in need. The sign might as well say, "Go to Hell." In Mansfield, England, the sheriff of Nottingham used to lock transgressors in stocks and pillories, and for a whole afternoon the offender would have to hold her bladder. Withholding a potty from the needy is just a mental pillory.

I don't mean to pick on Mansfield, a neat little town. The "No bathroom for you" sign is repeated in lots of tourist spots, where proprietors forget the most basic rule of tourism: Think like a tourist. Hint: If you must put up a sign, maybe it should point to an available bathroom. Find one. Build one. But don't kick travelers where it hurts.

On the outskirts of town across from the accessible bathrooms at the Rocky Ridge parking lot, Laura Ingalls Wilder unlocked the minds of little girls and their mothers. Her books are heirlooms from the frontier, points of view from the female perspective. The publishing of such sentiments was rare back when Laura was a kid.

In her late 20s, Laura's family purchased 40 acres outside Mansfield and named the land Rocky Ridge. They built a modest log cabin, planted apple trees and eventually started a dairy and poultry farm. After years writing columns for the *Missouri Ruralist Magazine*, Laura began her *Little House* memoirs, collaborating with her daughter, Rose Wilder Lane. By that time the log cabin had grown to an impressive ten room farmhouse, which today is a museum and National Historic Landmark.

Laura is buried in Mansfield Cemetery. I paid my respects and dipped south. Along Route U, Dyer Cemetery offered the opportunity to mutter a pun.

Eminent Domain

The definition of the word eminence is "a high or lofty place, superior in rank and achievement." Well, in terms of topography, Eminence isn't high or lofty. It nestles in a steep valley and straddles the banks of one of Missouri's most glorious rivers, the Jack's Fork. But there are many things eminent in this community, not the least of which is a weekly publication with my second-favorite newspaper name: *The Current Wave*.

If there was an eminent ruler of this domain, it was Captain Jack. At the Ozark Orchard Restaurant, between sumptuous bites of home-made onion rings and fish soup, I learned the legend of Captain Jack, who poled his jon boat up the river that bears his name. Or at least I learned one legend. There are many. They all start in Ohio with a young Shawnee Indian boy who stowed away on a packet steamer down the Ohio River in 1811. As the boat reached the Mississippi and started south, the New Madrid Earthquake turned the waters back-ward and wrecked the steamer, pinning the captain in the wreckage. The boy, nicknamed Jack, freed the captain, and for the kid's bravery the skipper gave his captain's cap to Jack.

After a career on the Ohio and Mississippi rivers, Captain Jack settled along the river that eventually took his name: the Jack's Fork. Jack became a fixture on the river. Apparently, over the decades, he never once took off that cap. He could be seen day and night, summer and winter, poling his jon boat up and down the river. He was a bit mysterious, but he looked official in his captain's hat.

Jack died years later in a freak accident when a Ferris wheel broke free and rolled across two counties, before hitting a whiskey still, which exploded, killing Jack and the only other rider who managed to hang on, a girl named Jill. That's one legend, anyway.

Just across Highway 19 from my favorite Ozark outpost—the rustic River's Edge Resort—Dean's Barbecue sits as close as it can to the Jack's Fork River without getting a floodwater douche. Good thing. Dean's is the quintessential hillbilly shack. Some places, most notably around Branson, recreate hillbilly culture, using quaint sym-bols made to look authentic. Dean's is the real deal, the most rustic restaurant in this town of 48 dozen people. It's a low-slung timber shack, steeped in wood smoke and Ozark culture. Customers sit on rough-hewn benches, surrounded by log walls with few windows, no frills, just good barbecue experience washed down with their favorite nectar from an old fruit jar.

My first dip into Dean's was stealthy. A small group of us sneaked into the place right under the noses of thousands of horse-trail riders camped across the road. Dean was gone the day we ate there. A sign said the restaurant was closed, but smoke poured from the smoker, and we pounded on the door until the cook let us in. "Shhhh," the cook said, "Don't let the horse people know I'm feeding you. I don't have enough barbecue." Nothing against the horses or their riders. But Dean's is a tiny place, with a limited number of slabs coming off the smoker. It wouldn't survive a stampede. We were finger-lickin' lucky.

I've recently learned that Dean's is closed now. The end is near.

I spent the afternoon on the river looking for Captain Jack's hat. No luck. I headed north. Jason's Place was nearby, and I stopped for nourishment and shelter. Jason's is nothin' fancy. A cinder block kitchen with a screened-in pavilion dining room, it's built for folks dressed in river rags and swimwear, in transit to and from the Current River. After stuffing myself on homemade rolls and salad and fried chicken and pie, I pitched my pup tent. Thunderstorms flashed in the distance. The sun settled into the Ozarks hills, replaced by the light of a campfire.

Thunder and lightning crept closer. I retired to my tent and drifted off to sleep. The first strong gusts of a thunderstorm awakened me and with seconds to spare, I jumped out of my tent and ran to the cinder block shelter, joining other campers who made it to safety in the nick of time. We watched through the screen as the wind thrashed my tent, turning it into a low twisting green pennant. The storm intensified, tearing big trees out of the ground as we scrambled into the kitchen to find an interior storeroom within strong walls. It was the beginning of a storm that continued a hundred miles east and plunged whole neighborhoods of St. Louis into powerless darkness for weeks.

Next morning, I stuck my wet shredded tent and gear into Erifnus' trunk and we limped back onto Highway 19.

On the road toward Salem, the Ozark contours still define the course. There are no roadcuts through hills, no straightaways. Tracts of virgin pine forest hug the roadway as it twists and undulates across these remote Ozark folds. Danger lurks along these hairpin turns.

Around one tight bend, I came upon a dump truck that had entered a curve too fast, crashed and overturned, spilling its cargo. The truck was a support vehicle for the highway department's striper, the rig that paints the center lines. The dump truck crash unleashed 2,000 gallons of bright yellow reflective paint, which splayed against the bluff like a Jackson Pollack painting. That spill probably represented 2,000 miles of yellow center line.

One Blob, Two Kings, Hillbilly Heaven and the Klan

Crossing the Missouri River on Highway 47, my windshield framed the blufftop burg of Washington. The town is a postcard, a weekend in itself, promising the two most important ingredients to save a marriage: beer and shopping. Solid old German brick architecture has stood for nearly 200 years and will last 200 more. Doors open to shoppers who love antiques and art. Indeed, it's home to one of America's foremost artists: Gary Lucy soon will stand with George Caleb Bingham and Thomas Hart Benton as Missouri's world-renowned masters.

Sandy Lucy is as talented in business as her husband is with a paintbrush. She negotiates the marketing and sales of his paintings from their gallery in a historic old building on Main Street. Sandy and Gary escorted me upstairs to see his inspiration: His studio occupies two back rooms of the couple's living quarters on a high bluff over-looking the same Missouri River that stars in his canvases. Most of his themes hail a time when this river was the main street. The scenes depict Lewis and Clark shoving off from St. Charles and steamboats crowding busy river quays. My favorite Lucy painting shows a lonely riverboat advancing slowly through darkness, while two crew members hold torches at the ship's bow, looking for deadly snags in the water.

The view from Gary's studio would inspire anybody. As nifty as the studio is, one malignant blob dominates the room: The growing mass is a signal that Gary wastes nothing. Rather, he turns waste into art. At the center of his easels and half-completed canvases and pal-ettes is a sculpture of a bird with more colors in its plumage than the toucan son of the NBC peacock. The sculpture grows each time he finishes a painting, and strategically loads the extra paint blobs from his palette onto the bird. "I've been building this bird for years." I have no doubt that Sandy could sell it in a heartbeat. Not a chance. This sentimental centerpiece will continue to grow right where it sits. With good fortune, and good health, the bird will outgrow the doorway to the outside world.

Washington's riverfront is the blueprint for any community's con-nection to a river. A row of historic brick buildings with patio cafés and art shops overlooks a vibrant marina, the only place you can fuel your boat for miles in either direction. Even the Amtrak station is a relic from the golden age of steam.

An overnight in the historic Schwegmann House reintroduced me to an old childhood comfort: A dozen freight trains passed in the night, within bowling distance from my bed. Some folks might be unsettled by the rumbling and the hoarse whistles, a thousand ten-ton wheels sending vibrations across the street to shake the old home's solid brick walls. I dreamed old dreams of my youth, a time when steam engines were losing out to diesels, clacking along the rails in a rhythmic surety that only mile-long chains of boxcars can offer. Next morning, invigorated by my trip back in time, I ate a leisurely breakfast in the courtyard, drank enough coffee to fill a ditch and pointed Erifnus toward roads unmet.

* * *

Erifnus Caitnop's wheels took me north, back to I-70. Cars that think they're Cadillacs have an unstoppable gravitation toward Elvis, and Erifnus is no exception. She traces her recycled steel frame back to a '58 Cadillac bumper, the one that looks like Barbarella's bra. We headed to the Elvis Is Alive Museum in Wright City. Even by Elvis standards, this place gets a gold star for tacky. Make that past tense: When we arrived, Elvis had left the building, and it was converted to a storefront church. Elvis is dead.

There's a giant 20-foot plywood cutout of Elvis that still towers over the little building, but Elvis has been whitewashed. The church painted over this plywood hunk of burnin' love, and placed a Golgotha-sized cross across his shoulders. So the King of Rock 'n' Roll has morphed into the Prince of Peace. Despite the whitewash I could see the unmistakable outline of Elvis in his pompadour and high-collared jumpsuit, leaning into the microphone he held in his hand.

I'm not sure why the museum closed. Maybe the people who own the Elvis brand threatened to shut down this renegade museum, with its aging Elvis memorabilia. Regardless, Erifnus was crushed, and sputtered her disappointment. Life's lessons are hard. In such a situation, I'd normally console myself with comfort food at nearby Ruiz Mexican Restaurant, one of my favorite stops to refuel. Ruiz predates the proliferation of the Tex-Mex craze that swept this area over the past 20 years. Still, at the restaurant's heart, it's all Tex-Mex. Confident that Ruiz would be there the next time I pass by, I searched for something new.

Hidden from the interstate along the main drag in Wright City, the sign over Hillbilly Heaven sticks out like buck teeth. It's the local watering hole. Like the best hideaway bars, the storefront looks like a brick mortuary. No windows. That's not so much to hide what's inside as it is to keep patrons from exiting the bar through plate glass, a sure sign that society has evolved somewhat. Inside I looked around. It's a big place, with pool tables and an electronic monstrosity from which a DJ presides over a dance floor. It was early, 11 a.m. Nobody was dancing. The place still smelled like yesterday's sticky beer spills, saturated with stale cigarette smoke. The morning patrons, hunters and third-shifters just getting off work, sat at the bar medicating.

Hillbilly Heaven's motto is "Thank you for stopping in to sit a spell," which has a familiar hillbilly ring to it. Mary, the server, told me that a guy named Dano just bought the place, so now it's Dano's Hillbilly Heaven. Dano had the good sense not to ruin the essence of the name. For ten bucks, Mary fed me catfish with hush puppies and tasty potato puffs, pickled beets and vinegar-based slaw.

Hillbilly Heaven needs a billboard on I-70. Everybody else has one. Seriously. An endless succession of billboards, arranged like a trail of dominoes, announces everything you need: fried foods to fortify your arteries, chiropractors to fix your bad back, attorneys for your fender bender or your next divorce. The whole effect of this billboard jungle allows drivers to enter a giant living phone book. It's *Alice in Wonderland* meets the Yellow Pages. "Got a bra problem?" a billboard for Ann's Bra Shop asks in double-D letters. Nearby, Baue Funeral Home urges drivers to be safe and alert because "We can wait for your business." And of course, sprinkled among these comforting messages are the signs that warn the end is near.

If the end comes, folks in Wright City will hear about it immediately, judging from the town's water tower, affixed with so many whistles and antennas and appendages it looks like a calliope.

An unmistakable boldness emerges along the roadsides as the population becomes more dense: The Adopt-A-Highway signs seem to grow more eccentric. Harpooners of the Sea Unicorn is a gaggle of Sir Arthur Conan Doyle groupies based in St. Charles. Their name, borrowed from a boat in a Sherlock Holmes novel, explains their deep-seated need to spear trash. Nearby, Remains Inc, a women's clothing recycler in St. Louis, resurrects refuse. Keep an eye out for members of

Greater St. Louis NORML, the local chapter of the National Organization for Reform of Marijuana Laws. When members pick up trash, they carry two bags, one for trash and the other filled with cheddar cheesy doodles.

Some prosecutors might want to eradicate NORML's pot-smoking trash busters. But that spat pales in comparison to controversy over the Adopt-A-Highway sign sponsored by the Knights of the Ku Klux Klan. The KKK staked their claim on a section of major highway, bolstered by their right to freedom of speech. After members of the anti-Klan community continually knocked down the sign, MoDOT grew weary of replacing it at taxpayer expense. The Klan was eventually disqualified from the site for not fulfilling their obligations under the agreement. I personally suspect they were disqualified because they picked up only white trash.

Slick

Most people do what I do when they drive: hurry to their destination. But sometimes they're forced to stop.

Heading west on I-44, we hit a late-spring snowstorm that quickly turned the roads into a luge run. So we retreated to a town called Traveler's Repose to let the snowstorm pass. Well, that was the name of the town nearly two centuries ago when a wayside inn by that name flourished. But the wayside inn is long gone. Now the town is called St. Clair, and it sits beneath twin water towers, one labeled hot and the other cold. As we sought shelter from the storm, I uncovered a gem, one of the reasons an aimless driver keeps driving. I found the warm comfort of Lewis Café.

Lewis Café doesn't look like much from the outside. It sits on Main Street in downtown St. Clair under an old 1930s-looking awning in an old 1930s-looking beige brick building. But in the restaurant world, the homely facade means there's a good chance to find home cooking inside. As soon as I entered, I knew Lewis Café was a keeper. Hardwood floors. Chrome-plated chairs with vinyl seats pushed up to tables that had local business ads laminated inside. Real pictures on the walls.

And I was right about the home cooking. The onion rings are homemade. The coconut cream pie is homemade. The chili is homemade. The beef is home grown. I was at home on the road, a rare feeling. I counted the booths. Seven. Across from booth row, seven squatty stools stood at the low counter. The place radiated good vibes. Daniel, the server, was the owner's son. He was enthusiastic, with no hint of preacher's kid attitude. More important, when he said that today's blue plate special was outstanding, I believed him.

Virgil Lewis started this café in 1938. Back then, Lewis Café featured the same seven booths, same seven stools at the counter, same dedication to homemade pies and home-grown beef.

I ordered the special, a country fried chicken breast smothered in homemade gravy and surrounded by peas. Daniel recommended homemade poppy seed dressing for my salad. Outside the storefront window, the snow came down in flakes the size of Frisbees. It made the restaurant even cozier. An elderly couple came in from the blizzard and took a seat. The woman was distressed by the weather, and further distressed by her dead cell phone. She couldn't call her destination to report their travels had been interrupted. I loaned her my cell phone.

Daniel arrived with my meal, and I ate as the snow piled up outside. When I finished, I asked Daniel for directions to the St. Clair Historical Museum.

"Easy," he said. "Go down Main Street one block and make a right. Can't miss it."

Sure enough, I saw the big painted museum sign above the door of an old house on the corner. Through the falling snow I could read the museum's business hours: "Open 1—4 p.m. Saturdays and Sundays." I was in luck. It was 2 p.m. Saturday. So I pulled to the shoulder and stepped out into four inches of fresh snow. As I walked to the museum entrance, I noticed that my tracks were the first upon the front porch. I tried the door. It was unlocked. So I entered.

"Hello?"

No answer. The lights were turned off, and it was apparent that no curator was present. That's understandable. Who would expect a visitor to a small-town museum on a snowy afternoon like this?

I fumbled around in the darkened room for a light switch as a staccato beep began to register in my ears, soft at first but getting louder with each successive beep. The burglar alarm! I hesitated, and considered looking around the museum for a bit while waiting for the police to show up. I'd just explain to the cops that I came to see the museum, that the sign said it was open.

Then I envisioned handcuffs and delays and fingerprints and lengthy explanations and 18 coats of paint on the iron bars across the front of the cold confines of a rural jail cell I'd be sharing with some sobering-up wife beater. So I calmly exited the house, shut the door behind me, and waited for the cops. Nobody showed up, even though I could see the police station from the porch. The beeping intensified, blaring from a loudspeaker above the museum's old farmhouse door. I slowly walked toward Erifnus, allowing plenty of time for the authorities to respond to the alarm.

But nobody showed up. I scraped an inch of new snow off Erifnus' windshield, climbed in the cockpit and backed onto a side street. I took my time turning Erifnus around, leisurely driving back up to the main street, and looked for a policeman. But nobody. They must've been busy attending to a dozen fender benders on the slick streets. I drove around town, taking pictures of an old Frisco caboose and the old International Shoe Company, a big empty brick building that dominates the eastern end of downtown. We circled back to the museum. The alarm was turned off. Nobody was around. We made tracks out of town.

Bourbon and Burgers and Bobs

Spring snowstorms can howl, but they can't last. The snow stopped falling, the sun peeked through the clouds, and the roads started clearing. I left downtown, and taking a cue from two uncles who were back-door Baptists, I took the back way to Bourbon.

The Civil War was looming when the town was formed, and workers on the new railroad to Rolla weren't shy about seeking their rations of whiskey. The Irish rail workers drank whiskey as a matter of custom, and when a new style of mash called bourbon came down the rails in 1860, the local general store kept a barrel on the front porch for easy access. The barrel was labeled Bourbon, and the workers fell into the habit of saying that after work, they were headed for Bourbon. The name stuck, and locals claim this is the only American town named after Bourbon whiskey. The town's most prominent nameplate stays true to the theme, with the word Bourbon painted in giant letters on the side of a water tower with a tin-man top and a bulbous bottom.

With an abiding love for the foods that help make bulbous bottoms, I stopped at the Circle Inn Malt Shop on old Route 66. For 37 years this old diner has defied the bright plastic hamburger chains with an effective defense: It serves great burgers, and the locals love it. I ordered a malt and visited with Elizabeth while she made it. It was mid afternoon and I was the only other person in the joint besides a man at the end of the counter.

"That's Bob," she said. "He's the owner." We exchanged nods.

Owning a restaurant is hard. Long hours. Hot kitchens and unpredictable customers. Bob looks like he's been a restaurant owner for a long time. He's low key with an "I've seen it all" look in his eyes.

Bob had just remodeled the place, but he hadn't disturbed that '50s feel. New black-and-white floor tiles competed with the artwork. A hand-painted map of Route 66 from Chicago to Los Angeles splayed over two walls in the back dining room. "A local artist did that," Elizabeth volunteered. "He did these, too," she nodded toward two portraits of the diner.

"May I borrow your facilities?" I asked.

"Right there," she pointed with her elbow as she kept her hands on the milkshake machine.

When I walked out of the tiny windowless bathroom, she asked me what I thought of the picture on the bathroom wall. "Didn't notice it," I said, sticking my head back into the bathroom and turning on the light. I hadn't seen the picture since the door hid it when I walked in and I'd done my business with my back to it. Sure enough, covering the back wall was a delightful full-size painting of a window looking out on Route 66, with classic cars and old gas pumps. The painting and everything else at this little diner oozes the warm feeling you get when you think nostalgic.

My stop at the Circle Inn was just the beginning of an afternoon of kicks on Route 66.

* * *

The Route 66 Fudge Shop has closed its storefront. Oh, the owner still makes candy, but she does it in her own home kitchen now. Further down the highway I found one of her signature candy bars. It's called the "World's Largest Rocker" candy bar, a fitting tribute to Meat Loaf, I thought. But the truth was even stranger....

The candy bar sat for sale on a shelf that's only a couple of cattails from a giant rocking chair. The chair sits on the edge of the parking lot beside the Fanning US 66 Outpost and General Store on old Route 66.

I'd never thought much about big rockers. But in 20 minutes at this general store, I learned about the competition. West Amana, Iowa, says they have the world's largest rocking chair, an 11-foot walnut beauty with a cane back. Texas Hill Country boasts the world's largest cedar rocker, topping 25 feet. But at 42 feet, the Fanning rocker will give you a nosebleed, not so much from sitting in its rarified air, but from falling off it. By far, it's the world's biggest.

The chair got even closer to the heavens when owners Dan and Carolyn Sanazaro had the measurements verified by a priest, to lend credibility to its application to the *Guinness Book of World Records*. If this chair is the world's biggest, it might also be the ugliest. It's a straight-backed metal monster with lawn-chair arms and a billboard back. On each of its front legs at eye level, signs warn "Please don't climb." Unlike the graceful Amana chair and the rustic Texas cedar rocker, the Fanning rocker style is best described as "modern-American campfire gear," although it doesn't fold to fit in your trunk. Because its metal frame might attract lightning during thunderstorms, the chair also qualifies as the world's biggest electric chair.

Despite its lack of living room aesthetics, the chair is a favorite of plumbers, welders, ironworkers, sheet metal workers, sign painters and scaffold jockeys everywhere. And tourists, of course. The locals embrace their world's largest rocker, even convincing the fire department—every once in awhile—to hoist folks up to the chair seat for keepsake photos.

Fanning's general store is a hunter's paradise. Yeah, you can hunt souvenirs among the shelves, but in the back of the store, I watched four archers sharpen their bow-hunting skills at an indoor archery range, under the watchful eye of a giant moose head on the wall. The moose also watches people buy Route 66 Route Beer and Route 66 Red Wine.

"Where's Bob's?" I asked the young lady at the counter. She knew what I meant.

"Well, you take a left out of the lot," she motioned, "and when you come to the first county road, take it to Bob's. Can't miss the signs."

I thanked her and followed her directions to the county road. Sure enough, Bob's Gasoline Alley jumped out at me, since it's well-marked with about 200 vintage gasoline signs.

During its long history, Bob's Gasoline Alley has cast a shadow on both the Mother Road and her modern offspring. The place stands apart from every other fuel plaza along I-44, because it displays every old gasoline sign ever made. But it doesn't sell gas. Bob's is part gathering place, all museum. In a succession of fast food billboards that pretty much look the way their products taste, flashy and fructose, Bob's shouts out like an oasis.

I met Bob Mullen in the parking lot. He looked apprehensive. He was expecting an anniversary party of "maybe 60 cars" any minute. But he still took the time to show me around.

Bob's made it a lifetime obsession to collect just about everything that has anything to do with the roadside industry. The hundreds of old gasoline signs warmed my eyeballs with familiar logos from the past: Zephyr and Cities Service, Gulf and Skelly and Champlin DX. Old Campbell's 66 signs feature those wild-eyed camels that are Humpin' to Please. Bob has five dozen old gasoline pumps with logos from Hudson and Signal and brands I never knew. From the interstate your eyes are drawn to Bob's teasers, towering petrol signs you can't miss, unless you're texting, dialing, eating or shaving while driving.

But inside Bob's three museum buildings, guarded by a pasture full of animals including ostriches and exotic turkeys, the views get even better. Caroming from one building to the next, I saw an endless collection of clocks and advertising thermometer signs, old die-cast model cars and metal pedal-cars like I rode when I was a kid, old ice chests and chesty 1950's mannequins dressed like carhops. Every square inch of Bob's buildings wear memorabilia, including the stairs, which display a perfect set of Burma Shave signs that make you wiser as you climb higher. The best part of this museum is that it's not junky. Bob presents his collections with taste.

I kissed the mannequins goodbye, left the signs behind and headed north, crossing the Mother Road's offspring, I-44. The uncrooked lines of I-44 represent the corrected smile of Route 66 after billions of dollars of asphalt orthodontistry.

Erifnus took a victory lap through Champion City and persisted through Strain to Japan, pronounced JAYpan, wouldn't you know, in local Missouri dialect. It's home of the Church of the Holy Martyrs of Japan, given its name decades before World War II. But even after the Japanese war machine attacked Pearl Harbor, the locals and diocese had the courage to resist changing the name. They thus avoided punishing the good Jesuit and Franciscan martyrs who gave their lives for their cause: The 26 martyrs, who were Japanese, Spanish and Portuguese priests and lay brothers, were crucified in 1597 during a three-century attempt to wipe out Christianity in Japan. Inside this little Missouri country church is a painting showing the crucifixion of the martyrs on a hill overlooking Nagasaki. But the mass crucifixion didn't eradicate this insurgent religion, and Christians continued to worship, often in secret, until eventually they were wiped out. By an atomic bomb.

We passed Rosebud, a town that locals say was named by the Rock Island Railroad because "those engineers gotta know where they're stoppin'." During America's prolific railroad building era, numerous new towns sprung up daily, and sometimes the name bank got depleted. So, like just-hatched baby chicks, railroaders often imprinted on the first thing they saw when they stepped off a locomotive, and that's what they'd name the town. Here, the first things railroaders saw were wild budding rose bushes. Hence, Rosebud. It's fortunate that they didn't see horse turds or buzzard vomit.

The Lazy Way Out

Some folks hike the Ozark Trail from just south of St. Louis all the way to Arkansas. If you don't have that much energy, take Highway 21.

My journey started with a surprise at Whitehaven, Ulysses Grant's St. Louis homestead. Whitehaven is not white. It's painted a bright spring green, the color favored by young girls yearning to be noticed. That's not the only surprise. On my last visit, archaeologists had just unearthed evidence that there were slaves on the property, maybe owned by Grant's wife's family, nobody was quite sure. Grant himself may never have owned slaves. From Grant's front lawn, it's an easy mortar shot to the beginning of Highway 21. And Grant's Farm sets the tone, the first of dozens of historic and geological delights along the undulating 200-mile drive south to the Arkansas border.

Starting down the highway, I got discouraged. The brand new concrete ribbon of road sliced smartly through bluffs and bridged the valleys, but the highway department is powerless to hide the junk alongside the pavement. The roadside looked like reality TV, in a Granny Clampett kind of way. Realizing it was time for an attitude adjustment, I gave myself a stern lecture. After all, life is life, and crap is a by-product. I can't fret about the ravages of civilization along the roadside. I must look for the positive. With that in mind, I viewed discarded beer cans as valuable curb ore. Old junk refrigerators became yard art. Abandoned automobile tires were nothing more than safe houses, nurseries for baby mosquitoes, away from abortive killer pesticides. Ugly is only skin deep, and some of life's best-kept secrets lie just a scratch beyond the ugly distractions.

We rolled across an ancient hillscape that bore intermittent man-made monuments to American culture. A drive-in theater waits for darkness, when it can cast its spell. Just down the road sits another giant rocking chair, this one with a graceful, inviting shape to lure Lily Tomlin.

Minutes into the drive, I entered the land of Moses. Most people are aware Moses never made it to the Promised Land, a detail that disturbs more than a few Texans. Technically, Moses Austin made it to Texas, but he didn't stay. In 1821, Moses was the first person to get permission from the governor of Spanish Texas to establish an Anglo-American colony there, leading a group of 300 families from Potosi to San Antonio de Bexar. He returned to Missouri and died soon after.

His remains rest in a cemetery in the middle of downtown Potosi. Encased beneath a slab of concrete the size of a carport, Moses has resisted body snatchers so far. Lone Star historians say Texas made overtures to remove Moses from a "neglected cemetery" and repatriate him with his son, Steve, in Austin.

Potosi historians are a bit more blunt. They tattle on Texas undertaker Thurlow Weed, who they say drove a hearse to Potosi in the early 1930s and started chipping away at Moses' tomb. The marshal and a posse of enraged citizens sent Weed tumbling back to Texas, bearing no pall. Texas historians say there was no posse and that Weed returned to Texas with a Potosi City Council resolution opposing the move.

In 1938, both parties agree, the governor of Texas made one more attempt to get Moses. Texans say the Lone Star secretary of state came to make one last plea for the body, but instead came away recommending that Moses rest in peace in Potosi. Local tales persist that the Texas official came to apologize. But regardless of the purpose of this final attempt, Potosi is the only American town to repel a Lone Star invasion.

Moses is the grandfather of Texas, not Missouri. But among his Missouri accomplishments, he donated land for this Washington County seat of government. Named for a Bolivian silver mining town, Potosi is a South American Indian word for "place of much noise," a harbinger to the Moses grave dispute. Backwards, the word Potosi comes close to spelling isotope, appropriate for the region's heavy metal mining. In the realm of heavy metal, Moses Austin was a rock star. He established the first reverberatory smelter west of the Mississippi. And like most rock stars, his rise and fall was mercurial. A bank failure and recession in 1819 forced him to close his lead mining business, and he turned his attention to "the Texas Venture."

Dipping into the land of Moses' bones, I neither saw nor smelt, nor heard heavy metal, but heavy woods stretched in every direction over these foothills to the St. Francois Mountains. Route 47 snakes down to join Highway 21, and like two old friends, they share a path for five twisting miles. The trail could be named Memory Highway, because every two miles or so, an Adopt-A-Highway sign declares "In Loving Memory of [YOUR NAME HERE]." The most intriguing dedication is "In Memory of Beef." Well, then. Suffice it to say that this road has delivered more than one species to glory. It's just another indication that the end is near.

As I left Potosi through a light mist, I drove down a path with a pine forest veneer and a hardwoods core. Route F dances along the edge of the Mark Twain Forest, weaving through miles of woods and few signs of civilization. I passed another grave, the plot of a close friend who died too young. It's the grave of Vance, the friend I saw not long ago at the Elbow Inn. His life as a gypsy cameraman ended abruptly, cold turkey, after a long descent into the bottom of a vodka bottle. He quit drinking on New Year's Day of the new millennium. Fifteen days later, the cure killed him, and he died of the violent side effects dealt by delirium tremors.

Yet his work for *National Geographic* and *The Great Chefs of Europe* stand as a goal for me. His exploits took him around the world, and his work is preserved in celluloid. Vance and I filmed hundreds of Missouri small towns, always including the city limit signs: Tightwad. Freedom. Success.

Now he's buried in this little country cemetery, against his wishes. It's not anybody's fault that he ended up buried and not cremated and scattered to the winds, as he wanted. He just never made a living will. As I drove past, I saluted him but didn't stop. Some dark night, when I know my time is nigh, I'll return with a shovel to free him from his stainless steel sarcophagus, and we'll go to a spot in the woods near the river, and I'll set fire to his bones and scatter the ashes throughout his beloved Ozarks. He'd like that. It's a tragedy that he was too full of life and vodka to stop and sign a living will. He just didn't think that the end was near.

With death on my mind, I steered clear of Mineral Point, home of a maximum security prison where a dozen years ago I watched a man die. His name was Frank J. Guinan, convicted by a jury and sentenced to death for murdering a fellow inmate who was wooing Frankie's punk. Guinan and another inmate each took half a pair of scissors, entered the victim's cell and repeatedly stabbed his eyes out.

As chief of staff for an acting governor, I volunteered to witness the execution. For days before the event, I couldn't sleep and suffered nightmares during the little time I dozed. The October night was foggy and cool when I arrived at the prison. Guards admitted me into the prison through the strictest protocol I'd ever endured, tougher than any TSA checkpoint.

Escorted to a waiting room, I was surprised to see the news director of the statewide Missourinet radio network. He had come to witness this execution, he said, because he asks his reporters to witness these executions, and he believed he should bear the burden, too. Even though we'd known each other for 30 years, went to the same church camp and played softball together, on this night we sat in silence.

When midnight approached, guards led us to a room with a small set of bleachers facing a window with drawn curtains. At the appointed time the curtains opened, revealing a clinical scene, almost antiseptic. Frankie was strapped to a gurney, and he fixed his eyes on two women who sat at a window like ours on the other side of the execution chamber. Through their window, they mouthed, "I love you." He raised his head once, then lay back as the indicator lights on the wall changed from green to yellow to red. He was dead. I left the prison, passed the white hearse at the loading dock and drove home in the fog. Haven't been back since.

I knew about his crime, of course. But I didn't know what had made him into a killer. Later, I studied the few existing bits of his biography, all tragic: Early on, Frankie became alcoholic. He endured a steady diet of lead pipe beatings and pistol whippings, bookends to his multiple suicide attempts. He traded his 6th-grade education for reform schools and prison for more than half his life. Jailed for burglary, he was an easy mark, hobbled by organic brain damage, raped by older inmates. His conscious hours were clouded by the toxic inmate speed-brew known as "chicken dust." He led a tortured life. And regardless of your view of capital punishment—or the afterlife—his existence was Hell. Death was escape.

Tears, Charm, Chaos and Upheaval

Erifnus weaved back onto Highway 21. At Route C, a pair of memorials share the same corner. One sign notes the spot of an old college, long gone. Next to that marker is a sign with a headline in an alphabet I couldn't recite. The Cherokee language survives only in pockets of this nation. But storytellers repeat the Trail of Tears tragedy in the land's newer, more dominant language. On this sign, both languages mark this spot on the trail where in 1838, thousands of Native American families passed on a forced march westward. Descendants of this area's European settlers tell stories about how their ancestors prepared baskets of food for a whole people, suffering as they marched toward Andrew Jackson's Promised Land.

And as they walked, the Cherokees listened for the *Nunnehi*, the invisible spirits that might help them through this tragedy.

Nearing Caledonia, we passed a sign declaring, "I buy old glass milk bottles." In these hardscrabble hills, folks gotta make a living somehow. Yet this sign is a poster for the success of Caledonia, which is booming even in a deep recession. With a city limit sign that confesses 158 souls, Caledonia could have become little more than a wide spot in the road. From smack dab in the middle of town visitors can almost see the city limit signs from every direction.

Thankfully, the town avoided becoming one of those nagging little speed trap havens that rise and fall along rural byways, with constables justifying their existence by trading speeding tickets for cash. Caledonia has 35 mph speed limits, but it relies on its stop signs. They're everywhere. No, not those red octagonal stop signs. These signs shout.

Antiques! Home cookin'! Come on inside!

Next to historic old Village Mercantile, across from the world's smallest former Phillips 66 Station, sits Caledonia BBQ. Owner Rich Jenkins is proud of his slow-cooked ribs. He should be. The aroma hangs around town like perfume, and the ribs don't disappoint. Rich explained Caledonia's economy over the past year or so: "It took off. Business is getting better. We're staying open on Sundays 'til 8. We used to close at 5, but there's so much traffic coming through town from Johnson's Shut-Ins, headed back to St. Louis, we couldn't afford to close early."

I walked into an open door in a historic old stone building. The light was on, and I'd seen a lady scurrying around inside. Mary Lou Akers welcomed me without stopping her scurrying. I asked her to tell me about Caledonia. She said she moved to the area with her husband years ago. She's proud of this town, and she stays here even after he died. On this day, she was setting the tables for a meeting in the old Masonic Lodge.

"The oldest continuous operating lodge west of the Mississippi," she said. "Caledonia has the highest number of buildings per capita on the Historic Register." That translates into five residents for every historic building.

I thanked Mary Lou, and started for the door. She told me one more thing: Caledonia's community betterment chairman is named John Robinson. I knew I liked this place.

The Arcadia Valley's pastoral serenity is framed by rugged beauty. But that beauty has come with a heavy price. The land has known cataclysm.

* * *

The most devastating topographical rearrangement—with the most beautiful result—occurred during the Precambrian Period when the Earth's stuffing, molten rock, thrust through the Earth's skin. Mountains erupted onto the landscape in a shower of volcanic ash, dust and hot gases. Today, you witness the by-products of 1.5 billion years of upheaval and erosion, nature's handiwork. From a distance, you really can't tell how old these mountains are. It's when you get up close that you see their craggy countenances and deep wrinkles. They hold the wisdom of the ages in their weathered faces, because they're among the oldest mountains in North America. For millions of years, these mountaintops were islands in a vast sea, looking much like the Virgin Islands do today, but without sailboats and rum punch.

These awesome geologic convulsions produced formations that hint at Mother Nature's humor and timing. At Elephant Rocks, a garden of granite, she threw a changeup that delivered the world's first bat and ball, predating Abner Doubleday by 1.5 billion years. Up the road, Pickle Springs demonstrates what a little wind and water can do to a crack, given enough time. Nearby, the steep terrain grew a giant patch of pines on its back. Those pines at Hawn State Park form a rare virgin forest, somehow missed by railroad tie hackers.

The Black River smashes into a shut-ins at Millstream Gardens, where boulders resembling igneous chessmen try in vain to stop the water. Aggravated, the water churns a frothy white and beckons brave kayakers to test their skills. And everywhere throughout the region, hundreds of springs continue to pump forth their pure, liquid benefit.

Up the road, Taum Sauk Mountain waited patiently for the Ozark Trail to drape across its shoulders. The trail switchbacks to the summit and down the other side. Tucked into the St. Francois Range, Taum Sauk Mountain is Missouri's tallest peak. Tall is relative, of course. You might be looking out your window at something taller than Tom Sauk. Still, it took Erifnus twenty minutes to climb along its curvy back to the summit.

The mountain bears the name of a legendary Piankasaw Tribe chief. Piankasaw legend says that the Great Spirit heaved a lightning bolt, splitting the mountain and creating a waterfall to wash away the blood of Taum Sauk's daughter, who jumped off the mountain to her death after her tribe had thrown her Osage lover off the mountain. Tough times.

Although Taum Sauk's peak used to rise nearly 2,000 feet above the valley floor, erosion has slowly filled the valley, and cut that drop in half. Still, the mountain stands tall among its sisters, Proffit Mountain, Wildcat Mountain and Church Mountain.

Descending the mountain and angling up through Ironton, I happened upon the second cataclysmic event. It was the most ingenious escape during the Civil War. Early in the war, Confederate General Sterling Price's Missouri Militia surrounded a Union munitions storage depot named Fort Davidson. The Battle of Pilot Knob began when Confederate forces hurled a series of cannon fusillades from Shepherd Mountain onto Fort Davidson. Rebel soldiers charged the fort, and Union troops repelled the invaders away from the small earthen ramparts. Dozens of soldiers died in close fighting during the daylong battle. Vastly outnumbered and surrounded by Confederates, the Union soldiers hunkered down to defend their fort until nightfall. As the sun set beyond the smoke, the fighting stopped, and the Confederates set up camp in three spots, a mile or so from the besieged fort.

The Rebels were content to wait until dawn to slaughter the Feds.

Knowing they would face massacre the next day, Union leaders averted further bloodshed by fashioning an escape worthy of Houdini: Deep in the night, Union General Ewing ordered his troops to wrap their wagon wheels with tents and muffle their horses' hooves with their coats. Under cover of darkness the Union troops slithered between the rebel encampments and off to safety in St. Louis. The Southern camps, hearing the muffled sounds, thought the Union must be fellow Confederates, heading to another camp for the night. The Confederates awoke to begin bombardment of... an abandoned fort. A pair of Union soldiers stayed behind and blew up the munitions before the Confederates could capture them.

That night, I slept in the cozy Fort Davidson Motel in the valley between Shepherd Mountain and Pilot Knob and had some silly recurring dream about sneaking out of town in the middle of the night with my socks pulled over my shoes.

A few years back, a third cataclysm—a manmade tsunami—hit Johnson's Shut-Ins, Missouri's favorite state park. The flood was every bit as turbulent as the Johnstown Flood, but because of timing and luck, nobody died.

Before the flood, a summer afternoon at Johnson's Shut-Ins would have made you forget about manmade water parks. It contains some of the most hair-raising chutes that water can push a human body through without killing. The rushing water is entirely natural, with no chlorine. And the ride is free.

But two leap years ago, a calamitous chain of events caused a mountaintop dam to overflow and break, spilling two billion gallons of water down Proffit Mountain, a peak on whose back Union Electric Company had built a giant reservoir. The torrent ripped through the park, sending a wall of water, boulders and trees that vaporized campgrounds. The flood would have killed hundreds of campers. But it happened on December 16th, when the campground was empty.

The flood did unhinge the park superintendent's house, and dashed it against canyon walls. The superintendent and his family were found next morning, hugging two treetops that had withstood the raging water. All five family members were plucked to safety, suffering from shock and hypothermia, but alive. It's damn near a miracle that the youngest child, a five-year-old, hung on to a tree limb through the night.

I'm just thankful that Jesse James wasn't alive to hear what happened. It might've sent him over the edge.

The Road by Gads Hill Leads to Ellsinore

Dropping into the deep valley that shelters Ellington, I found the newspaper office, a good source for knowledge, and asked the editor to direct me to her favorite restaurant. "Well, there's Don's," Monica said, "and Spooner's out by the highway. Or you can sit down with some pretty good home-style cooking at Hall's, at the end of the street." She pointed in the direction I had just come from.

"Oh, the old bank building? I saw all the cars...."

"No, that's the senior center. They have some good food, too."

They must, I thought, with a parking lot that full. I thanked Monica and headed straight to the senior center. It's the most satisfying meal decision I'd made in a long time. I knew the routine, having eaten hundreds of meals at senior centers with Dad. No matter where you are, the best meal deal in town is at the senior center. It's a balanced meal. The price is right, even for a patron who doesn't qualify as a senior citizen. But the value goes way beyond price. The best thing about the senior center is the company you keep. So I walked into the dining room ready to fill up on more than food.

The food is home cooked, with the same number of dishes your grandma shoved in front of you. I walked through the cafeteria line, and friendly servers heaped my plate with chicken livers and onions, peaches and cottage cheese, salad, mashed potatoes and gravy, carrots, and milk and tea for less than five dollars.

From experience, I knew to honor the seating chart. The seating chart is not posted on the wall, it's not at the cash register or in the manager's office. It's in the habits of the seniors who come here every day at the same time, and sit with the same friends in the same chairs at the same table. I've been conditioned to heed the warning, sometimes shouted in unison: "Don't sit there, that's Mabel's spot!"

I chose a seat next to senior center manager Peggy Richards and her aunt Ruby Ruble. Ruby retired from Brown Shoe Company about 15 years ago.

"And then Brown pulled up stakes and left," she says. "I had warned them they couldn't run the company without me." She laughed. "Now I volunteer here at the senior center. Been doing it for 13 years. You know, I've never heard of a volunteer getting fired." She laughed again, an infectious laugh that made lunch taste all the better.

Other seniors were eager to tell me about Ellington, stuff you might not hear at the Reynolds County Museum down the street. Robert, an affable chap at a table within earshot, told me about the industry in town. Boats and saws, mainly, reflecting the predominant natural resources surrounding the town. Blazer Boat company makes jon boats. Down the road, Ernie's Boat Sales takes blank jon boats and turns them into custom aquatic hot rods. Baker Industries makes state-of-the-art band saws for the timber industry.

According to the folks at the senior center, if you're going to Lake Wappapello, don't miss Bullwinkle's. "You'll find out about the airplane," Robert laughed.

I thanked Ruby and Robert and the rest, and left the warm security of the senior center for the surprises of the road, including the airplane at Bullwinkle's, whatever that might be.

But nobody mentioned the scene of the crime. Odd, since this one historic robbery links the area to the world's greatest thespians. Here's the story:

The bandit played his part like a trouper, quoting Shakespeare to his intended victims:

"I am joined with no foot-land-rakers, no long-staff sixpenny strikers, none of these mad mustachio purple-hued malt-worms, but with nobility and tranquility, burgomasters and great oneyers, such as can hold in, such as will strike sooner than speak, and speak sooner than drink, and drink sooner than pray, and yet, zounds, I lie, for they pray continually to their saint, the commonwealth, or rather not pray to her but prey on her, for they ride up and down on her and make her their boots."

Frank James knew his lines. Upon boarding a railroad car at Gads Hill, Missouri, he quoted what must have been one of his favorite passages from Shakespeare, announcing to startled passengers his justification for his gang's intent to rob them. But just the rich, mind you. Not the working poor, with calloused hands. No women. No children.

In *Henry IV Part I*, the Bard describes that fat-kidneyed rascal Falstaff and a gang of highwaymen on the "Road by Gads-Hill." The well-read Frank James might have favored that scene because it fit his disdain for fusty fat cats who rode the rails.

So why not stage a train robbery at Gads Hill, Missouri, conveniently located in the middle of nowhere?

That's one theory, anyway. Since the bandits' faces hid behind bandannas, witnesses and historians can't be sure who quoted *Henry IV* during the robbery. Nor can they be sure what specific lines were quoted. That's okay. Nobody is quite sure who wrote the play, either.

Even though locals at the Ellington senior center told me about everything but that robbery, Erifnus knew we'd find it. We motored across Route K and then south down Route 49, twisting and undulating through remote rugged wilderness, to survey the scene of the crime. Erifnus was almost to the blue granite shut-ins of Lon Sanders Canyon when we came to that spot where the words of William Shakespeare and Frank James intersect. Oh, and Charles Dickens, too.

Gads Hill is barely a wide spot along a road that rolls beside the tracks of the St. Louis & Iron Mountain Southern Railroad. Some say the town is named for Charles Dickens' English estate, Gads Hill Place. Maybe so. But Frank James knew that long before Dickens, the Bard said the Road by Gads Hill was a hangout for highwaymen who robbed travelers.

Often as not, trains didn't stop in 1870s Gads Hill, Missouri. They just slowed to snag the mail sack from a trackside saloon. But on this afternoon, the southbound Little Rock Express planned to stop and discharge a passenger, even as the James Gang prepared to force it to stop.

Sarah Bernhardt would've chuckled, the way the robbers played the passengers, including Frank's soliloquy about robbing nobility. At the conclusion of the plunder, one of the outlaws—likely Frank, if you ask me—handed over a written statement describing the robbery, muttering that newspapers had misreported details in some of the outlaws' earlier exploits. Frank was a contemporary of Sarah Bernhardt, the hottest act in show business at the time and a capable self-publicist. Frank probably watched the success of Sarah Bernhardt's self-promotion. It worked for Sarah; Frank could do it too.

So Frank wrote the first-ever robbers' press release, which he handed to the startled conductor. It described the outlaws' appearance and mischaracterized the general direction of their escape, thus forever casting doubt on the veracity of billions of subsequent news releases. Evidence suggests the gang escaped by heading west following the Black River, then the Current River. Eventually, Frank's younger brother Jesse made it back to his betrothed, and they used his share of the loot to honeymoon on the Texas Riviera.

Nowadays, there's not much at Gads Hill. A sign marks the spot where the outlaws stopped the train. The old saloon is gone, and a succession of local watering holes have come and gone, including a pub owned by a St. Louis publicist. Somewhere, Sarah Bernhardt is smiling.

I whistled past Graveyard Hollow, and Erifnus danced across Deer Run and Doe Run and Dickens Valley State Forest, another clue that somebody around here had an affinity for Boz Dickens, the Sparkler of Albion.

And Frank James? Since he never got to be a House of Representatives doorkeeper, Capitol visitors never got to hear Frank's version of the Road by Gads Hill.

In another part of the forest, up Highway 49, geologist sleuth Jerry Vineyard explored a sinkhole called The Gulf. It's not very far off the road, so I took a look. Viewing the sinkhole from its rim, it's an impressive hole, just big enough to drop a double-wide trailer into it from the sky. But the hole is tiny compared to the underwater cave beneath the opening. The cave contains a subterranean lake that's 200-feet deep and two football fields long, extending like a giant pelican's beak. From the rim of the sinkhole, it's a four story descent to reach the surface of the water, and if the James Gang ever stopped here to bathe, they truly were fearless.

* * *

Down Route A, deep in the woods, I killed somebody.

A part of my soul perishes every time an animal darts in front of my car, and I feel the bump beneath a tire. Squirrels and birds are common victims. An occasional rabbit. Raccoons and possums at night. Lately I've been dodging armadillos. And I had a scrape with a giant snapping turtle in Callaway County. But I never hit a box turtle, until now.

All animals are sacred. Coyotes and cattle. Foxes and hens. Birds and worms. Even water moccasins. But of the creatures I spy along the road, I have a special affinity for box turtles. Their armor is a blessing and a curse. It protects them from furry, feathery predators. But their heavy shells make them slow and vulnerable on the highway. Box turtles are shy, docile herbivores, like the cow whose shoulder you ate for lunch. But box turtles outlive domestic cattle 40-fold. They outlive most humans. They've seen more hailstorms than any of us—and survived. The primary predator beyond their egg stage is man. But as prey, terrapins die for a useless reason: Happenstance. The wrong place at the wrong time. Needless slaughter with no benefit for any member of the food chain. Even the vultures complain there are too many bits of shell in their food.

It was October, and autumn leaves lay in thick patches along the road, thick enough to obscure a turtle. This one's amber belly stayed disguised among the oak leaves as it lay on its back, flipped from an earlier encounter with a vehicle. Only at the last instant did I see its legs, pointing upward, grasping for a grip it couldn't get. As I heard the crunch, I knew immediately what we'd done. We stopped and returned to the spot.

The animal was obliterated. At least my strike was swift and complete. I couldn't be sure how long he'd been lying in the road, helpless to turn upright. I took his shattered carcass to the side of the road, where a coyote or a vulture would dine on its delicacy. It was the best I could do.

We circled north past the Pine Hill Drive-In Theater and Panther Hill, where the James Gang had stopped to sort through the loot they'd just stolen at Gads Hill, as evidenced by a search posse's discovery of burned mailbags and charred mail the next day. A northern course brought me to the loneliness of Buzzard Hill, and lonely roads in the backwoods brought me to the old Redford general store, long barren of provisions.

In the time it took Frank and Jesse James to get from Panther Hill to Maggard's cabin on the Current River, I motored around Reynolds and Corricon and Henpeck Creek, down through the ancient orchards near Fruit City and Alamode.

We passed a sign that said Chapel Hill Cemetary (sic). Imagine any English teacher buried there, eternally damned to lie under a misspelled word. Then again, maybe the sign was painted by one of her students, in which case she shares some of the blame.

Some of her students would remember Hamlet. He lived in Elsinore. The students also would know about the local Ellsinore, a tiny hamlet in Missouri. One of Ellsinore, Missouri's central characters trod the boards in a life worthy of a Shakespeare play. Ellsinore, Missouri's, central character was a man named Mel Carnahan. He was my boss for a while, until he fired me. But we remained friends through his years as Missouri governor up until his untimely death in a plane crash, which also killed his son, Randy, and his chief-of-staff, Chris Sifford. Mel's remains are buried at Ellsinore Cemetery.

Down the road, the kilns of Ellsinore stood silent and spooky. Back in the days when Mel and his brother operated them, they made charcoal. Before the kilns were closed by stricter air-quality standards, the town was bathed in the sweet smoky odor of a barbecue pit, or as Mel was fond of saying, "Smells like money." For years after they shut down, those crumbling concrete curvatures bubbled out of the ground like surfacing storm cellars with rusted superstructures. Gaping doors allowed a glimpse into the blackened interior, cool for many years, eerie and foreboding, like the catacombs or the ghastly chambers at Bergen-Belsen.

Those kilns are gone now, but even deeper in the woods, other ghastly contraptions lurk. In the world of wood processing, chip mills are the agents of deforestation. The chip mills use industrial strength wood chippers—think "Fargo" on steroids— that can grind a clear-cut forest into sawdust in a matter of hours. The Devil may lurk there, too, basking in the chips.

The local churches stand strong against the threat. I'm not sure they see the threat from the chip mills, but they routinely rally against the Devil. Down the road from Ellsinore's Shakespearean spookiness, in neighboring Oregon County, a sign points to Shilo Baptist Church, Skeet and Trap Range. Nearby, Peace Valley's Victory Chapel and the Church of the Bretheren maintain a vigil. I saw the Full Gospel Tabernacle. Contrary to rumor, there's no Half Gospel Tabernacle, or

90-percent Gospel, 10-percent Fried Chicken Tabernacle. I'm content with the Shilo Baptist Church, Skeet and Trap Range. What else does a body really need? But I digress.

Erifnus set a course toward the sunset.

Cabool is named for Kabul, Afghanistan, but don't bring that up among the local patriots. They might prefer the story that it's named for an Indian chief. Back in 1881, the British had just pulled out of Kabul at the end of their second of four wars there. About the same time, a railroad builder arrived in southern Missouri from a railroad project in Afghanistan. He thought the area looked like Kabul. It is a ruggedly beautiful area. No poppy fields, though, that I could see.

I headed west along Highway 60 toward Springfield and lost my race with the setting sun. I stopped at a KFC in Mountain Grove, because I knew it was a fast buffet, a dine-and-dash.

Inside the KFC I filled my flimsy Styrofoam plate with too much hominy and beets, mashed potatoes and gravy and a chicken part, and found a plastic seat. In the next booth, a talkative man spat little bits of chewed chicken as he talked loudly to himself. His rugged face betrayed a hard life, 65 years maybe. His thick black hair behaved under its Brylcreem sheen. He wore a dull cowboy shirt tucked into industrial pants that cuffed over a scuffy pair of black cowboy boots. He was upset the government wouldn't let him drive a truck anymore.

At first I'd nod when his eye caught mine as he talked. At one point, I answered him in a simple "hmmm" of acknowledgment. I was there to eat, and I just wanted him to remain stable as I inhaled my beets. He kept talking, directly to me by this point. He told me he was forced to retire after he suffered a stroke. "They won't let me drive any more," he spat, as he leaned over the back of his booth into my space. "I hate this town. I wanna get on the road again."

Depressed and splattered with chicken bits, I wished him well, said goodbye and got on the road. I hope he finds contentment, and something to occupy his time. But I really hope I don't meet him out there on the highway.

In the darkness, I followed a silver Suburban for two hours. Visible through its back window was a video screen playing to backseat passengers, so as I drove along Route 60 to Springfield, I watched "Finding Nemo" on a small-screen, rolling drive-in. Wish I'd known their cell number, so I could have connected to the soundtrack. Alas, I drove on in the darkness, chasing Nemo on the silent screen.

Pushing westward through the night, I approached Diggins, just west of Seymour. Diggins used to be called Cut Throat. I'm not sure why, but leading out of Diggins is a highway that's a carnival midway of redneck culture on the skids.

Near the beginning of the road, the first thing I encountered was a magnificent 12-foot wooden monster truck with wood tires as big as Boss Hog. Instead of a treehouse or a clubhouse, Daddy built his kid a giant wooden monster truck. There must be a thousand board feet of lumber in this playtime pickup. What fun! Trojan horsepower. Across the road is an abandoned church building, now inhabited by a family who keeps their motorcycles on the porch and a big Confederate stars-and-bars flag flying on the church flagpole out front. People along this road must believe that the way to Heaven is through ornamental refrigerators and washing machines, because several front yards feature shrines to that great appliance center in the sky.

Junk cars? Heck, this road goes one better with a full-size tow truck in one front yard. All those observations were made on a previous trip, in the daylight. Maybe the elements along the road have changed since my last visit, and some other road has risen to the coveted title of Most Redneck Road, proudly displaying a deeper collection of old washers and Pintos, monster pickups and rebel flags. Maybe. Things change, and it's hard to keep track of 4,000 two-lane soap oprys.

Besides, on this trip toward the lights of Springfield, it was dark. So I kept driving. When it gets dark, Erifnus sprints like a gazelle. She senses I want to get to my overnight accommodations. Her radio strained to pull in a crackling AM station, playing a country song I didn't recognize. Through the crackle, I swear I heard the DJ identify the artist as Red Rotten and His Wall of Gas.

Red's and Leong's, Anton and the King

We made it into Springfield for the night, and I checked in to the University Plaza Hotel. I thought about a giant hamburger from Red's Giant Hamburg. Alas, Red's is only a memory, gone for a dozen years now. Sheldon "Red" Chaney, the Charlie O. Finley of fast food, opened America's very first drive-thru hamburger joint on old

Route 66 on the west side of town.

It was also America's first green restaurant, with a blue ceiling and a green floor to imitate an outdoor picnic... except the walls were papered in patrons' Polaroids. Red looked like Buddy Holly if Buddy had lived to be 70. And like Buddy, Red was in tune with his times. Long before fast-food supersizers came along, the Redburger came in five sizes: Junior, Giant, Senior, Jumbo and Sooper.

A big white '55 Buick sat out front with a hand-stenciled sign on its rooftop that said Red's. Next to the Buick, Red erected a semi-giant wooden sign that was giant for its time but not giant by today's gargantuan sky-poking interstate standards. The sign was shaped like a two-word crossword puzzle: Giant (across) and Hamburg (down). The words intersected at the letter "a." The sign would've been taller if Red woulda called the sandwich a hamburger. Instead, he called it a Hamburg. That's what Jack Kerouac called it too.

Sadly, the city razed the place after Red died, despite the joint's historic significance. Now, folks are clamoring for a historic marker.

It's okay. Honorable burger joints always fall where they stand. And even though they're gone, they all leave a little grease spot behind. I drove slowly past the hallowed ground of Red's.

Despite its reputation as the buckle on the Bible Belt, Springfield is a town with international flavor and a unique cultural balance. The community seems to have slightly more Chinese restaurants than Bible schools. Some locals worry the Chinese are taking over America. At least in the battle for the gut, the Chinese got a foothold long ago, about the same time Springfield started consuming tons of Chinese take-out.

Springfield is a proud town, and locals seem especially proud of one Springfield invention that strikes a perfect Chinese-American balance. I set out to try this local creation, called cashew chicken. It's the ideal marriage of Chinese cooking and hillbilly taste, something David Leong must've realized when he created the dish back in the '50s. Punt the wok. Forget stir-fry and go deep-fried. Leong's invention guaranteed his kitchens had a good run for longer than the life expectancy of a truck driver on a fried chicken diet.

On an earlier trip through Springfield, to find the best cashew chicken in the home town of its creator, I followed a tip and went to Canton Inn on Sunshine Street. As I walked through the door, I dodged a patron who muttered as he left, something about paying for refills. Hey, some things are sacred, and around here, it's God and country, guns and bass boats, fried food and free refills.

Like almost all the six trillion Chinese restaurants around Springfield, this one was locally owned. A high percentage of these operations open for business in the shells of failed franchises, abandoned burger huts and taco stands. The Canton Inn used to be a Waffle House or a Dunkin' Donuts, so the tiny diner fills up fast. I filled up fast, too, in the shadow of that other Springfield shrine, the world headquarters of Bass Pro Shops. Nobody's figured out how to deep-fry a bass boat yet, but if it happens, Springfield will be ground zero.

Next morning, 19 minutes at Burger King changed my life.

I was running behind. Miles of untraveled road awaited to unfold north of Springfield, and it was already nearing lunch time. I wanted to stop at the legendary Anton's Coffee Shop, looming ahead in my windshield. The experience at Anton's begins at first sight: Towering tree-like beside the tiny coffee shop, the marquee sign stands in the unmistakable shape of an ice cream cone, a subliminal cue to start the salivary juices. But ice cream was the former tenant, maybe a Dairy Queen or a Dairy Belle or a Dairy Doodle, I don't know. Now the whitewashed sign simply says "Anton's Coffee Shop" in bright red letters.

Anton is there every day. Day after day, year after year, he pitches in with his busy staff at all points in the process: greeting and seating, building a billion varieties of omelets, busing tables, sitting and chatting with regulars, and taking cash. Anton belongs to a dwindling breed that doesn't take credit cards. Or maybe the breed is growing. Since I had no cash, I kept driving.

My stomach lurched toward every restaurant my eyes reported. In a decision protested by both eyes and stomach, Erifnus swerved into a Burger King parking lot and parked next to a car with a canine prisoner inside. The car impounded a small lapdog, barking through a two-inch crack its owners had left in the driver-side window.

With absolutely no sense of adventure, I entered the Burger King and approached the counter, where an age-seasoned couple stood at the counter, employing all of their options before ordering their meal. They were excruciatingly particular. The attendant, a man about 35 years old who wore the look of hard life on his face and ink-scarred arms, showed the patience of a watchmaker as he guided the couple through the entire menu. The elderly man finally decided on his fare.

"Whopper. Burn it. No pickles, no onions, no ketchup, extra mustard, no mayonnaise."

When the woman made similar requests, I chuckled out loud. "I wish I'd brought a camera," I told the trio. "This is a perfect Burger King commercial."

They looked startled. The lady began to apologize for delaying me while they made their painstaking order.

"No, no, this is great," I stopped her. "You know, 'Have it Your Way,'" I repeated the old jingle.

They chuckled too, to humor me I guess, in case I was unstable and might resort to murder-suicide. After all, they'd strayed from the protection of their dog, left to defend their car.

I ordered something simple and sat down to eat. A young Burger King employee limped past, on custodial duty. He moved with some difficulty and appeared only marginally responsive when I greeted him cheerfully. He went about his chores slowly, deliberately. I raised my sandwich to peel back the wrapper. That's when I saw a middle-aged couple sit down at a table next to me. They held hands and prayed before they ate. I hoped their prayers included one for the young man who struggled with his chores and one for the hard-life counter attendant who struggled one day at a time.

Finishing my meal, I rose to refill my drink and leave. I held the door open for the elderly couple as we left. The lady turned to me and agonized, "I wish we had let you order first."

"Not at all," I reassured her. "I wouldn't have missed that moment for the world." They got into their car, and at long last the dog was reunited with his best friends. That sweet reunion between man and dog reassured me about the key to life.

As we pulled out of the parking lot, sharpened for another adventure, I watched the young custodian struggle to raise his arm, to squeegee the windows clean.

Erifnus merged into traffic, and we headed back toward wilderness, along a veneer of shops and houses and billboards and trailers and trash and blue signs declaring that for the next 2.2 miles, somebody's gonna pick up all this shit.

Tango and TB and Unexpected Joy

Mount Vernon is a town of many layers, named for the homestead of the Father of Our Country, and gathered around one of the prettiest courthouses in the Midwest. From earliest memory, I've associated Mount Vernon with the a tuberculosis sanitorium. It turns out, there are three tuberculosis sanitoriums in Mount Vernon. One here, another in Mount Vernon, Illinois, and a third in Mount Vernon, Ohio. Talk about contagious.

Sometimes you catch something really good. And in Mount Vernon, I got a triple treat. Just west of town, Williams Cemetery is the final resting place of James Marion Woods (1838-1910), whose headstone indicates he was a soldier. But it says nothing about his more enduring legacy as the original shepherd of Mutton Hollow, the model for Harold Bell Wright's *Shepherd of the Hills*.

Back in town, the courthouse grounds feel the fun of many local events. But on this day I discovered the coolest, campiest combination of events ever in the western part of the northeast sector of the southwest corner of the state. The Not So Square Arts Festival features outside-the-box performers like the Not So Shakespeare in the Park Players, a Celtic jazz band, genuine Samoan hip-hop, dueling pianos, Native American storytelling and a tango demonstration. What a melting pot of hoot!

A tango demonstration? Just off the square, a hundred or so of the world's top tango dancers have assembled for the past few years at the Meet in the Middle Tango Festival. I'll never sit willingly through an episode of "Dancing With The Stars," but this event is nothing short of a movie scene on a movie set: the deep elegance of a hardwood dance floor gleaming in the soft light of chandeliers hanging from an original tin ceiling, and the grace of the Argentine tango, the dance and the music. Inspiration pours out of this setting, called Murray's Vintage Venue, a classic ballroom lovingly restored to its 1893 grandeur, inside and out. Tango upstairs, stained-glass studio downstairs.

Zipping down Highway 60, I resisted driving 360 mph, as suggested by a car dealer in Republic whose TV ad claims that the trip from Springfield to Republic is just one minute at that speed. Call Carl Edwards.

Anyway, too many stoplights along Route 60 impede such speed. Good thing. Prudent driving allowed me to slow down and soak in the charming character of Billings, a town with a proud claim to greatness. From each direction on Highway 60, signs proclaim Leon Rauch hails from here. Leon left Billings to sing with Bob Wills and His Texas Playboys. So in a sense, Billings gave us the voice of western swing. Just off the highway, Billings' main street extends for two blocks, looking kinda Western and swingy, a quaint two-block shopping hotspot.

I patted Erifnus on the dashboard. She can't go 360 mph, but she could break a hundred, no sweat. That's all the speed she'd ever need, and then some. We drove the speed limit north to find food. In the distance a jet landed at Springfield International Airport. Within minutes I passed rural Bird Field Airport. If I had a choice, and could pick my landing spot, I'd take Bird Field. Nothing against the big airport. But we all yearn to end up somewhere with an enchanting name, and Bird Field ranks right up there with Love Field and Sky Harbor and Idlewild. Who wouldn't want to land at Leonardo da Vinci International or John Lennon International? The truly great airport names are in the former Yugoslavia: Alexander the Great Airport in Macedonia and Constantine the Great Airport in Serbia.

But on this day, as I drive through the middle of the Ozarks, Bird Field flies high in my imagination. It sits patient as a glacier along with two nearby farm airfields, nameless as far as I can see. All three would be willing to help troubled travelers touch down, even though they're small private fields, because that's the spirit of the airways.

As Erifnus pushed on, past these grass airstrips that dot the countryside, I recalled the story about one man's last request. One day a pilot friend took off with a passenger, a newly widowed lady, and an urn containing the ashes of her husband. At 2,000 feet, the February air was frigid. The woman opened the airplane's cabin door to fulfill her husband's wish to be sprinkled across his beloved Ozarks. She held the urn through the gap in the open door, and slowly poured his ashes out the side of the airplane, a sprinkle here, a sprinkle there. Finally, the pilot encouraged her to finish the ceremony. "Hurry up and dump him out," the pilot pleaded. "I'm freezing my ass off." His passenger tipped up the bottom of the urn, and her soul mate scattered to the winds. She shut the door, and the pilot landed the plane. On the rural grass strip airport, a lone attendant approached the plane to help tie down the wings. He looked quizzically at the wet gray ash caked on the side of the plane, and swiped his finger across it, giving it a taste. "Y'all musta flown over a brush fire," he said. The pilot said nothing. The widow fainted.

That's why when I die, my ashes will only leave the mantel once a year, and strap into Erifnus for a tour of new roads, and avoid the dreaded asterisk in the record books. I really don't anticipate anybody else will be obsessed with the stupidity and patience to do what I did. But as long as I've gone this far, I might as well keep it up for as long as these industrial strength termites keep building more roads, and somebody's willing to haul my charred ass around.

* * *

The Frisco Highline Trail passes Wimpy's hamburger stand in Willard. The trail is an old railroad bed reincarnated into an exercise track for cyclists and joggers. It's a great trail, mostly, but it suffers from annoying intersections with country roads, where stop signs warn cyclists to yield or die.

Erifnus picked up the pace through Graydon Springs, birthplace of the late Wilford Crane. Willie is late only because he has a tombstone now. But in his heyday, he was rarely late, being the first race driver inducted into the Ozarks Area Racers Foundation Hall of Fame.

We raced north past Ash Grove, with a main street that looks like it's right out of a Jimmy Stewart movie. Just outside of town is Nathan Boone's house. He's a son of Dan'l and, like his dad, Nathan preferred to live in sparsely populated neighborhoods. His refined log structure still sits between two giant bookend fireplaces in the middle of nowhere.

During the age of rail, Ash Grove was a terminal for the Leaky Roof Railroad. Its real name was the Kansas City, Clinton and Springfield Railroad, but it was a haven for worn-out boxcars, welcomed there to serve their last days hauling mostly clay tiles. The tiles didn't care if they got wet. But other merchants along the route hated the railroad, including one flour miller who dubbed the railroad the Leaky Roof.

Ash Grove is the birthplace of Ma Barker, whose sons ran the Barker gang. They did their best to devalue banks in the 1930s. Despite J. Edgar Hoover's portrait of Ma's criminal activity, she was never arrested or even fingerprinted. According to gang members she couldn't plan supper, much less a bank heist. Her only crime was loving her sons and protecting them, when she could. The FBI gunned her down, supposedly putting a Tommy gun in her hands to justify killing an old lady.

But more important to civilization, Ash Grove is the home of Moses Berry, pastor of the Theotokis "Unexpected Joy" Orthodox Christian Church, an orthodox Catholic congregation that follows the old Julian calendar. Moses Berry's multiethnic parishioners include one Auschwitz survivor. Moses is also the founder and chief driving-force behind the Ozarks Afro-American Heritage Museum, dedicated to the history of slave families in the area. The museum's artifacts include quilts, tools, shackles and chains.

Nearby is a cemetery with the remains of "slaves, paupers and Indians,"—folks not allowed in the Ash Grove Cemetery. Buried there is Moses' great-great-grandmother Caroline, daughter of a slave owned by Nathan Boone.

Moses was right. It was unexpected.

The Road Less Traveled

It was an accident that I took the road less traveled, and went back in time.

Late one Friday afternoon, I pulled myself away from a lively festival in downtown Joplin. It was nearing the end of July 2006, and on this day Joplin was vibrant and alive. People seldom referred to the "Joplin Tornado" and when they did, they meant the tornado of May 1971.

I avoided I-44 since road construction had formed open wounds along its skin. With a zig and a zag, I rolled into one of the most pleasant experiences I've had in a car. At least by myself.

The courthouse in Carthage slapped my eyeballs with its white stone beauty. This might be the most beautiful courthouse in the world, its traditional stately lines contrasting with the modern architecture of the Powers Museum, which features famous Carthagenians including zookeeper Marlin Perkins and Harlow Shapley, the Organizer of Heaven.

The next 70 miles between Carthage and Springfield sent me back to the 1950's, as my wheels laid one more impression into the Mother

Road. Erifnus wore the road like a comfortable pair of slippers. For me, it was a mile-a-minute museum, as I entered the uncluttered simplicity of a road that hasn't changed one whit since the big interstate took the traffic away 50 years ago. Oh, some of the surviving roadside icons are suffering from weather and neglect, but they're still there.

Most Missourians—heck, most Americans—would pick Route 66 as the most legendary road this side of Burma. It unfolds over 300 Missouri miles and has received the highest tribute ever bestowed a route: Mother.

The surrounding pastoral beauty has a cleansing power. Few billboards, even fewer fast-stop conveniences. The Mother Road definitely has a slower pace than its hyperactive child, that sleek interstate on its southern flank, I-44.

Here is a historic highway, a narrow concrete time capsule, complete with ghosts of gas stations pumping out charm and skeletons of roadside diners serving up simpler times. For me, times were simpler back in the '50s because when adults asked my age, I used fewer than eight fingers to reply.

Just off the highway, whitewashed barns float on the rolling green hills. Soothing, nostalgic. And the tranquility hits home when you get an occasional glimpse of busy interstate traffic in the distance.

Route 66 is all attitude: Freedom. Adventure. Kicks. Its songs have become anthems. As the most famous road in America, the Mother Road is immortalized in chapter and verse—and movies. I stepped into the Route 66 Tavern while looking for movie stars in tiny Miller, Missouri, population 754. That's the town's population, not the tavern's, although the tavern's population gets close on Karaoke night. That's what I hear, anyway.

Miller is the unlikely set for a 1998 movie entitled "A Place to Grow," starring Wilford Brimley and Boxcar Willie. In the movie, a big recording star returns to his roots to sell the family farm after his brother dies. But he finds out the death might not have been an accident. The artist comes to the realization that many modern farming methods are in direct conflict with the survival of the American family farm.

While the family farm looks like it's dying, the Mother Road will live in eternity.

Old Route 66 is sacred indeed, dotted with a bevy of religious signs splayed along the road, Burma-Shave style. You can't go a mile without seeing at least one reminder that the end is near, like the warning in front of one hog farm: "Repent. Eternity is forever." Good thing hogs can't read, because they get only about 18 months before they're slaughtered.

Along the edges of old Route 66 I expected to see relics. I expected to see stubborn old roadhouses, stone structures that refuse to break down entirely, the wooden shells of taverns that fed the great auto migration west, and decaying tourist cabins that offered sleep to weary travelers. I expected to see those remnants that served the kinfolk of the Joads and the Clampetts and westward expansion.

Around this hallowed highway, I expected to see an old weed-framed concrete tarmac with nothing on it except a stubby concrete island with rusty bolts pointing up to where a Crown Gasoline pump once stood. I expected to see the wooden skeletons of old billboards and maybe a preserved succession of Burma-Shave signs.

I saw those things.

But I didn't expect to see this. Just off the Mother Road near Grays Point, an LP gas tank is painted like a calico cow, black and white with the bulbous tank-top cover painted pink. In effect, this calico cow has been tipped, its pink udder pointing up to the heavens. Just down the road, a big plastic life-size bull stands on the crown of a house, waiting for an opportunity, I suppose, to romance the calico gas tank.

Ah, the unexpected. It's what makes my car and its curious occupant go the next mile.

It was twilight as we passed the Friday night lights of Mickey Owen Baseball Camp. I couldn't see the ballfield, just the glow from the lights. Mickey Owen broke into baseball with the St. Louis Cardinals. He's a local hero—and not a goat, despite the latter label having been affixed to his name because of a dropped third strike in the 1941 World Series, back when he was a catcher for the Brooklyn Dodgers. Mickey's error gets the blame for letting the crosstown Yankees win the series. Leaving Bronx cheers behind, Mickey came home to Missouri and for four decades taught thousands of kids how to play baseball, including a young phenom named Michael Jordan, who went on to be a pretty good golfer.

Owen was so revered in these parts he was elected Greene County sheriff for 16 years. Mickey died a few years ago, but his legacy lives on in the hearts of his students.

I drove south and intersected I-44, where I stumbled onto one of the biggest auto junkyards I've ever seen. Acres of rusted automobiles can be accessed only through an entrance gate formed by two junked cars, their bumpers touching in a way they never expected. This field of broken dream cars, so close to the Mother Road, remains a reminder that nothing lasts forever. Punctuating that feeling, the car-gate was framed by trees still pointing to Hell after a thick ice storm a few years back bent the trees' trajectory.

First Families, Big Bangs and Whirlwinds

Route 66 delivered me to Marshfield, the nosebleed capital of Missouri. No, it's not because of past pugnacious newspaper editors or any current town bully. It's the nosebleed capital because the town describes itself as the "highest county seat in Missouri." I'm assuming they mean altitude. At a lofty 1,493 feet above sea level, Marshfield more than earns the nickname "Quarter Mile High City." Forget altitude, Marshfield should bottle and market its attitude.

Marshfield is the home of the oldest July 4th celebration west of the Mississippi. OK, every city west of the Mississippi has the oldest something-or-other. But get this: Marshfield is the home of the National First Families Library and Museum. Who knew?

A few years back, the town hosted the largest gathering of presidential relatives in the nation's history, including descendants of Presidents Washington, Adams and Adams, Monroe, Van Buren, Polk, Tyler, Buchanan, Jackson, Lincoln, Cleveland, Coolidge, Harding, both Roosevelts, Truman, Nixon, Ford, Clinton, and even a descendant of the union between Thomas Jefferson and Sallie Hemmings. Oh, and also one Kennedy half-in-law (Jackie's half-brother). They assembled to inaugurate the museum, located on the town square, which is within a horse shoe pitch of the Missouri Walk of Fame, a knockoff of the Hollywood Walk of Fame. Townsfolk undertook these projects all by themselves, mostly. Impressive for a town of 6,000 people.

Folks around here are proud of their history, even though some residents seem oblivious to it. I stopped in the courthouse to get directions to the Missouri Walk of Fame and asked several courthouse employees, even one county elected official, but nobody seemed to know much about the walk of fame. Somebody in the county assessor's office told me to consult Nicholas Inman, a writer for the local newspaper. Indeed, Nicholas knew all about the walk of fame. Nicholas knew about pretty much everything else in Marshfield, too.

There's a Nicholas Inman in every town. Usually a town's knowledge is kept by someone long in the tooth. Nicholas looked like he was 30. That's a sign of hope, at least for Marshfield. He directed me to some sweet spots, like Hidden Waters Nature Park, the headwaters of the Niangua River. Headwaters are sacred, and townspeople have preserved this spot where the Niangua breaks into daylight. The water rushes from its spring and splits the park in half, cascading downhill at the beginning of its marathon search for the sacred Osage.

But the spring only scratches the surface. Like the tornadic tragedy that scoured Joplin, legendary winds have blown across this spot, too, and they're recorded in vivid detail... not in video, but in verse. A local story adopted America's most-repeated lullaby. The song tells about a wind that blew a baby into the treetops during the Marshfield tornado back in 1880. Never mind that "Rock-a-Bye Baby," the most repeated lullaby in America, was first published in 1765. It has real significance to the mothers of Marshfield. It's a sad song, really, not something you'd expect a mother to sing to her child to make it sleep. The wind blows, and a cradle with a baby falls out of a tree. Yikes! But in a way, the song has prepared generations of children to accept other disturbing stories like "Jack and Jill," "Little Red Riding Hood," "The Three Little Pigs," "Ode to Billie Joe," "The Ballad of Billie Jack" and "My Girl Bill."

Marshfield has been a cradle to new ideas. Nine years after the tornado, a Marshfield mother sang "Rock a Bye Baby" to her child, and he grew up to formulate Hubble's Law, which posits that the universe was set in motion at a particular point, and continues in motion today. You know Hubble's Law as the Big Bang Theory. The Hubble telescope bears the name of Edwin Hubble, Marshfield's prodigy. The telescope dedicated to him enables us to look back into time and see the creation of the universe 14 billion years ago.

But the Hubble telescope is a lightning rod for the world's most uncomfortable conflict between religion and science. Many of Marshfield's good souls adhere strictly to the Book of Genesis. As such, believers accept on faith that God created the world in a succession of seven 24-hour periods about 5,000 years ago. The only Big Bang they acknowledge comes from the giant 40,000-square-foot fireworks wholesaler on Route 44.

Still, plenty of local citizens are proud of the replica of the Hubble telescope on the courthouse grounds. So once again, religion clashes with science, and this time Marshfield is its epicenter.

There's no scientific debate about the epicenter of the Marshfield tornado, though. That catastrophic tornado roared through thousands of lives and affected musician Blind Boone so deeply he recounted the event in nearly every concert until he died.

Blind Boone was an accomplished composer. Born John William Boone, he was another probable descendant of a Nathan Boone slave. He wasn't from Marshfield. He was from Columbia. But upon hearing about the Marshfield tornado, he wrote a gnashing piano piece so violent that simply playing the music caused destruction.

The tornado had struck with a vengeance. Around suppertime on Sunday April 18, 1880, a twister with winds topping 200 mph leveled much of Marshfield, leaving nearly 100 people dead. Folks still talk about it. Boone was 16 at the time, on his way to becoming the Stevie Wonder of his generation. According to historians, as his manager read a newspaper account of the tornado to Boone, the young composer hammered out what would become his signature piece.

Writer William Parrish described Boone's cyclonic masterpiece as beginning "with chime-like sounds, as if calling the people to church; then followed a soft strain of sacred music, imitating the congregation singing an opening hymn. Then came a loud imitation of thunder, and fire bells giving the danger signal as lightning flashed across the imaginary sky. Finally the storm died away, and Boone played softly, imitating water dripping from the eaves of the houses."

Boone visited Marshfield shortly after the tragedy to perform his masterpiece. Eyewitnesses report that when he played "The Marshfield Tornado," terror tore through the fresh wounds of the survivors who attended the concert. They believed that Boone's all-too-real rendition was bringing the twister back.

Why do such awe-inspiring performances get buried in obscurity?

Well, for one, among all the existing recordings and piano rolls by Boone, "The Marshfield Tornado" is absent. It seems his performance was so powerful, attempts to record it on piano rolls would destroy the piano roll machine.

"Rock-a-Bye Baby" survives. "The Marshfield Tornado" does not. Meanwhile, the forces of creation and destruction square off in Marshfield, a battle between blind insight and blind faith, in Edwin Hubble's home town.

Just in case, I kept an eye out for Hittites and Luddites and meteorites as I moved deeper into God's Country. It didn't take long to discover an odd sight. On the edge of town, in an empty parking lot next to a park, a lone van sat facing the swing sets and teeter totters in the playground. It was a prison van and the occupants, trusties and a driver—the lone guard—had stopped for a smoke break. They all stood outside around the van, looking relaxed, smoking. Some passersby undoubtedly shook their heads in disgust. Why are these prisoners outside in the fresh air, allowed to smoke?

Well, the answer is simple. They had just completed picking up after litterbugs who steal beauty by dumping their trash out the window and endanger the environment with burning-cigarette refuse. The inmates were still at least one cigarette away from their home, the rustic cabins of the Ozark Correctional Facility, built during the Great Depression by the Civilian Conservation Corps as a scout camp and later converted to a rehab center for low-risk offenders. Most of the prisoners standing outside the paddy wagon got busted for smoking pot or other petty crimes... not for attempting to set fire to the woods.

Regardless of the nature of their crimes, the inmates appreciated their driver, who was simply practicing the time-tested method of inmate control: keep them content. At Alcatraz, inmates were kept content with good food. In this parking lot, the driver kept them content with nicotine.

Across the road another parking lot looked packed. Marshfield's newest restaurant, the Southtowne Grill, had just opened. Even at 1:30 p.m., the restaurant was doing a land-office business. So I stopped. The maître'd, an elegantly seasoned citizen, told me that the restaurant has been open five days. "Sheila had a couple of restaurants in the past," the lady told me, "then she went away. Now she's back with this brand new restaurant, and word got around pretty fast."

The place has a bright future. It's a comfort zone, with plenty of TVs and a soda fountain-type lunch counter. More important, Sheila makes great pan-fried chicken, and everybody in town knows it. I broke a personal rule that says, "Don't eat at a new restaurant in its first 30 days. Allow enough time for the staff to work out the kinks and get into a restaurant rhythm." But Sheila had done this gig before, and her fried chicken is famous. Now I know why.

I drove out of town and into the forest.

Along Route BB, I approached a roadside park where an old man sat alone at a picnic table. Beside the man was a sign that said, "The Story Book Hour." As I passed him and waved, I glanced at my watch. Ten till 7 p.m. I hoped the story book hour began at 7 o'clock, and maybe the old man was a bit early. Old men are punctual, especially for dinner and story book hours.

He looked forlorn as he waited for listeners. Maybe they would come. Most folks enjoy listening to a story book. Especially children. But way out here, in the middle of the deep woods, mom and dad would have to make a special effort to bring the children, and stay with them.

Maybe the old man's marketing plan is flawed, and he should set up story book hour near a more populated area. But maybe the old guy sees himself as a story book pioneer on the edge of the deep woods, a one-man bookmobile, bringing "Three Little Pigs" to the outback. Or "Noah and the Great Flood." It wouldn't matter. A good story is a good story. Old men can tell good stories, most of 'em.

I should have stopped and listened. He might have found that odd, that a middle-aged stranger would stop. Or he might've used the opportunity to save my soul, if that was his mission. Maybe he would have been grateful for the attention. But his sign warned that the story book would last for an hour. I drove on, not sure if I should feel sad or guilty.

I circled north around the towns of Beach and St. Luke, which was also called St. Paul and might've been known as St. Mark at one point but now is known as Forkners Hill. I couldn't find evidence of a Saint Forkner. East of there, Dudley Town is named because "nearly all of the inhabitants were Dudleys," according to Vera Walton. Erifnus found a comfortable cadence as we crossed across Conklin and Crossway and Caddo.

Even further into the woods, Route DD unravels like every other road I've traveled: a crapshoot that might deliver something notable. Or I might see trailer trash.

My Missouri neighbors may resent my references to trailer trash. But I saw the trailers and the trash with my own eyes. Often times together. In fairness, most trailers are storage-challenged, since they can't stow stuff in the basement. So their yards become appliance orchards. It would take a million words to describe the images I saw. Lucky for me, there's visual proof on an independent website called missouritrailertrash.com, a site which is at once entertaining and humorous, sad and scary.

Anyway, Route DD uncovered a link to my past. I'd forgotten the path, but not the memory. It led to Camp Arrowhead, the first Boy Scout camp of my youth, where one weekend nearly 50 years ago, my scout troop planted several thousand pine trees along steep hills that had been ravaged by a forest fire.

Erifnus and I rolled into the unoccupied camp, which was awaiting the next scout troop. The log buildings looked much like I remember: a cluster of cabins in the woods, surrounding a big screened-in mess hall. After a look around, brief and unobtrusive to avoid the wrath of the caretaker, I turned Erifnus around and retraced our path, surveying the acres of pine trees I'd helped plant long ago, now a mature pine forest. It smelled green and I felt green, even as Erifnus converted fossils into forward motion.

We traveled around Niangua, down through High Point and High Prairie and Mountain Dale, also known as Love Ridge, home of an old seminary. I caromed south through Panther Valley and Panther Creek and along here somewhere to Panther Cave, but I couldn't find it, and didn't look too hard, either, because of its reputation. Decades ago a guy named Blunt Martin reported that it got its name because somebody killed a panther in the cave. Later, folks walled up the cave opening because "so many fine hunting dogs have disappeared in the cave," according to Martin. I guess the hunter who killed the panther didn't kill the panther's spouse. A bit unnerved by the specter of panthers, I drove west through the tiny town of All. Though small, All seems well. But just around a tight turn on Route PP, hidden atop a hill amid the trees, I might have found the riddle to Panther Cave.

Geologist Tom Beveridge says the place is called Devil's Den, one of eight such dens in Missouri that namers think must be occupied by Satan. This one is a narrow, deep sinkhole with steep walls that plunge straight down to dark water of unknown depth, thus gaining a reputation for being bottomless. There's something about bottomlessness that attracts beer and music, and this place is no different.

Beveridge repeats a story from Joe Clayton in the *Springfield News Leader* that a century ago a brass band from nearby Fordland used to perch on the ledge halfway into the hole and pump concerts out of the ground to picnickers. A railing around the hole's rim kept listeners from "toppling into a tuba." But the railings didn't stop the litterbugs, and Beveridge says that "Artifacts indicate that many modern picnickers respect the Devil and are amply supplied with liquid courage-builders." They offered their empty cans as alms.

* * *

Reaching Seymour, I ducked into Baldy's Café. It's home of the Big Baldy, two half-pound patties covered with melted cheddar cheese and grilled onions with four strips of bacon on a grilled wheat bun with fries or tots. Even though the wheat bun almost won me over, I opted for something more healthy, the chicken-fried steak with mashed potatoes and gravy and corn, and a sprig of parsley.

Parsley is the secret to life. Despite anything else you believe, know this: Parsley is the most valuable substance in the universe, besides oxygen and the TV remote. Yet it's the Rodney Dangerfield of leafy food. Contrary to the role it plays in the hands of chefs who use it to decorate a plate, parsley is not just another pretty face. Much more than a mere garnish, parsley is the pathway to preserving health. Pound for pound, it's the most powerful stuff on the planet. It's loaded with vitamins A, C and D, iron and antioxidants. And it's a breath mint.

Still, most people leave parsley on the plate. That leads me to believe that if people think the end is near, it's probably their own damn fault for leaving the parsley untouched.

Among the dozens of Amish homesteads along the road, it was wash day. Clotheslines became horizontal halyards with fluttering flags, an Amish rainbow of garments ranging from blue to brown to black and white and gray, all billowing brilliantly in the overcast breeze.

I stopped at Pam's General Store, a low-slung series of creosote log structures strung together into a narrow row just wide enough inside for a one-lane bowling alley, if Pam ever wanted to install one. Erifnus rolled into the empty parking lot, and I hopped onto the low veranda spattered with plastic lawn chairs. I opened the door and as I entered, a bird chirped. I looked around for it. Pam appeared from the back room. "May I help you?"

"Where's the bird?" I asked.

"No bird," she said. That's my signal that you came through the door." Pam told me she'd been in business at this outpost for 12 years. She sells supplies, including beer, to the neighbors, mostly Amish. I bought some supplies and thanked Pam and the phantom bird and headed back into Amish country.

Clown Country

Next day Erifnus took me along the back roads of Dent and Shannon counties. While bobbing and weaving between billowing thunderstorms, we crossed a series of routes beginning and ending with K. I consulted my map and realized that it's possible to drive a distance across parts of three counties touching only routes K to KK to K to KK. I'm just saying.

Route JJ is one of three sister roads that splay off Highway 17 like Lisa Simpson's fingers. It zigzags between two counties so many times that almost every view of the thick pine forest includes multiple highway signs announcing you've crossed another county line, and back again, like a slalom course. It's an unfortunate thing for taxpayers that the county road and county line intertwine like braids. Surveyors and lawmakers who keep track of this shit feel compelled to tell you every time you tip into the edge of the other county, with road signs from each direction. Obviously cops need the signs so they know where they're issuing tickets or finding dead bodies. I think they should move the county line so only one sheriff has to patrol the road.

Apart from its annoying signs, the road itself courses through beautiful wilderness. I saw a red fox crossing the highway, and down the road I found out why. Little month-old calves were jumping and playing, agitated after a scary hailstorm that had just passed over them. One calf had jumped the fence and was trying to figure out how to get back into the pasture to find mom. When I was a kid, all of southern Missouri was free range country. No fences. Although none of the Simpson fingers touch national forest land, the heavy woods offered a feel for the open range of a generation ago. But not for the calf that jumped the fence.

Turning up Highway 17, the road rolled through Eunice, where a lone house had folding tables in the front yard, set with what looked like 400 spray cans. Paint sale? Nearby, B&K Auto Repair listed its hours of operation: "Open by chance or appointment." By the looks of it, the Chit & Chat Grocery Store has been silent for many years, the chat having turned to chit.

This county has a proud name: Texas. And yes, it's the biggest county in Missouri, in terms of area, so Texas County fits the Texas profile. Its towns evoke vivid images with names like Huggins and Licking, Evening Shade and Windy Curve, Success and Solo and Slabtown, Cabool and Plato, Hattie and Oscar. There's a book inside each of those city limits.

A ton of talent touched this county, but its enduring legacy is clowning around.

Up past Yukon we headed for the stomping grounds of the world's most famous clown. Along the way we passed Raymondville, where years ago I attended an old-fashioned tent revival led by the one and only Freddy Gage, who calls himself the Underworld Preacher. He says he saved more men's souls for Christ than anybody but Billy Graham. No word about saving women. He's a self-described reformed drug addict from Texas, and star of an album called *All My Friends Are Dead*, which rose to #10 on Guardian Unlimited's "10 Worst Album Covers in the World." He's in marvelous company: Some of the other worst album covers include *Music to Drill Oil Wells By* and *Back to the Shit* with singer Millie Jackson sitting on a porcelain throne.

Anyway, Freddy authored a book called *Marijuana, the Weed of Death*, among other anti-drug messages. Still in college and off duty from our summer job of interviewing drivers on remote blacktop roads, my buddies and I had stopped to peek under the tent and listen to the cadence of old-time religion. Freddy was preaching up hellfire and damnation, and he worked his audience into a frenzy, and they truly feared that the Devil was among them. They all looked at us like we had pitchforks. We suppressed our collective coulrophobia—the fear of clowns—and visited with Freddy after his act. Freddy found out one of my buddies was Jewish and immediately condemned the Hebrew to Hell unless he gave his soul to Jesus. Golly.

From Raymondville it's not far to Houston—Texas County—hometown of the most famous clown in the world, if you exclude Ronald McDonald.

The clown's name was Weary Willie, but folks around Houston, Missouri, know him as Emmett Kelly. Emmett moved to Houston as a boy and spent his formative years here. He always considered Houston his hometown. When he grew up, he left for Kansas City and found work as a commercial artist and sign painter. In his spare time he developed his Weary Willie character and tried it out in local vaudeville theaters. That bit of clowning around marked a fork in the road for clowndom.

Before Kelly, clowns were slapstick. Weary Willie never smiled. He relied on sympathy and spawned a whole army of jesters who adopted the same sad shtick, including Emmett's good friend Red Skelton. Emmett joined the John Robinson Circus as a trapeze artist along with his circus acrobat wife, Eva. But the marriage—and the trapeze act—fizzled. That's when Emmett emerged as Weary Willie. He later remarried. His second wife was also a circus acrobat, named Evi. This guy knew what he wanted.

Every spring, Houston sets up clown college during Emmett Kelly Days, and for $25 you can learn to juggle and cry.

Hill Folk and Chickens, Rocks and Rabbit Heads

A few miles north, a little stream called Corn Creek runs between Highway 63 and Route T. During the Civil War, a man named Bill Wilson farmed beside Corn Creek. He kept to himself, but like most Missourians during that time, he was drawn into the conflict, victim of roving bands from one side, then the other. Wilson was attacked by Kansas Jayhawkers, his farm burned. Angry and looking for revenge, he joined the notorious Bushwhackers, led by Bloody Bill Anderson, and later fled to Texas. At least, that's the story people tell about him. The story has grown to legend over the years, becoming the basis for one of the greatest western movies of all time, "The Outlaw Josey Wales."

We moved up the back roads to rejoin the Mother Road, and headed east past towns with great Ozark names like Jerome and Sugar Tree and Doolittle.

Ah, Doolittle, a word that affects everybody. Some people fear it, others embrace it as a lifestyle.

The little town of Doolittle straddles Route 66. With barely more than a hundred residents, its homes blend into the roadsides, its existence barely noticeable to interstate travelers except for the big green signs pointing to the exit ramp for Doolittle. Cruising on I-44 at 70 mph, it takes only seconds to traverse the town's city limit signs.

For miles in both directions, drivers see hillbillies. Plastic hillbillies and wood hillbillies. Real hillbillies when you stop for gas. It's an
icon of Ozark culture, the hillbilly. And a money maker. Along an
archipelago of roadside novelty shops, folks can buy plywood cutouts
of pipe-smoking hillbillies or a deluxe model with moving parts. The
cutout's arms revolve backwards, making a silly hillbilly windmill.

With such suggestive cues and a city limit sign that says, well, Doolittle, travelers might be prompted to make fun of the town and its culture. But the town is a monument to bravery and heroism. It's named for
the famous Jimmy Doolittle, who dropped bombs over Tokyo. Jimmy's
squadrons flew so far that he knew his bombers didn't have enough
fuel to get back to their landing strips. That's the definition of heroism:
Knowing you're in big trouble before you start the journey.

By all indications, Jimmy Doolittle appreciated the little town's
tribute to him. General Doolittle even flew his B-25 Mitchell into
nearby Vichy Airport to dedicate Doolittle back in 1946. Today, like
most small towns that get bypassed by the superhighways, Doolittle
sees less of travelers.

But atop the hill at the end of the exit ramp, even a highway-
hypnotized driver will see the Cookin' From Scratch diner. The restaurant's delivery vehicle is called the Chicken Car, a red El Camino
with a giant rooster the size of a T-Rex towering in its cargo bed.
How can you pass a place like that? The chicken's chauffeur delivers
hot lunch to patrons in larger towns nearby. The cooks fry chicken the
old-fashioned way, in iron skillets.

Like any self-respecting restaurant that's also a gas station and
convenience store, they sell beer and wine and the stuff you forgot
when you left home. And hillbilly memorabilia: Outhouse salt shak-
ers. Droopy felt hats. Postcard pictures of fat hillbillies.

In the past, "fat hillbilly" was an oxymoron. When I was a kid
growing up in the Ozarks, I never saw a fat hillbilly. These remote
mountain folk worked hard to scratch life from the land and the water. They used all their corn for pone or moonshine, not for chips or
soft drink sweetener. They were strict conservationists, saving every
washing machine and motorized vehicle they ever owned, proudly
displaying these rusting hulks as yard art. But those are stereotypes, I
reminded myself, as I picked up a pack of GPC smokes and a Mountain Dew and some beef jerky, and headed off the beaten path.

The food at Cookin' From Scratch is tasty, but the greatest fried chicken ever in the history of civilization came from down the road. Route T descends out of Doolittle and winds down a steep Ozark mountainside for five miles to Newburg, home of the legendary Houston House.

Newburg blossomed during the Civil War, with a roundhouse that was the western terminus of the Frisco railroad until the war ended. The town hit its peak during the Great Depression, when thousands of hobos would congregate around the tracks in the shadow of the Houston House, awaiting the next ride on the Frisco to somewhere else.

As a bunkhouse, the Houston House cast a big shadow, but it used to cast an even bigger smell. The Houston sisters made the best fried chicken in the known universe, and fed a lot of paying customers, and some who could only pay by washing dishes. The old building still survives, but it's no longer a boarding house for railroad workers and passengers, since the passenger trains have long since forfeited the rails to freight. Hopefully, the Houston sisters left their fried chicken recipe in a cupboard somewhere.

A group of Newburg citizens recently pulled the old boarding house out of the frying pan. They have big plans. And another group is resurrecting the old hotel nearby. Townsfolk know their biggest strength. Hidden among the hills and streams, Newburg is too little, too isolated to take advantage of the highway-based economy. So it might just survive intact, without a McDonald's or a Walmart. That's just fine with most residents, as they turn to save the old relics.

Back on old Route 66, curtains of kudzu, a climbing vine, have begun to drape over trees and fences and power poles. While many rural landowners kept a sharp eye peeled for communist invaders, the creeping crud called kudzu gained a foothold in the south, and it's bent on taking Missouri before the armadillos do. The vine is not communist, but it is totalitarian, strangling everything in its path. Americans brought the plant from Japan to control erosion. But now it's out of control, and the "Little Shop of Horrors" comes alive.

Driving west on I-44, I overtook a convoy, but it wasn't the customary military convoy so common around Ft. Leonard Wood. This convoy was a tandem, two old pickup trucks loaded with a mountain of household belongings. At 42 mph, the old trucks labored down the highway under the weight of their junk piled high, looking like two rolling yard sales with the air squeezed out of them. The second pickup pulled a trailer with no tail lights, no license plate, and the most ingenious sign in the history of moving violations: "Headed for repairs." The leader of the pack was an old U-Haul truck, repainted a drab brown, pulling a Pinto with oxidized blue skin. The driver looked exactly like the guy who runs the Rock-O-Plane at the carnival. But I had the uneasy feeling that this convoy left despair in its wake. Bad roof repairs. Driveways sealed with waste oil.

They'll stay away from Rock Town, a name you won't find on the map because it's a nickname. The town doesn't need a nickname, since it's the sole Iberia in America. The only other Iberia is New Iberia, Louisiana, home of hot sauce. But this Iberia is salted with hot rocks, leftovers from a Civil War battle where the combatants ran out of ammo and fought the old-fashioned way, like David in the Bible, slinging stones at the enemy.

Breaking rocks and busting heads is a recurrent theme around Iberia. It's the old stomping grounds of one of the state's most legendary prison wardens. And the warden apparently was a good recruiter. Today they'd call him a job provider. At one time Iberia may have supplied the most prison guards per capita of any U.S. town that doesn't have a prison. I sense a pride around here that "It's the family business," handed down from generation to generation.

I crossed the Lenox Branch, although some folks still call it Rabbit Head Creek. Local lore says that back in the 1800s a hunter shot a rabbit and brought it home for supper. His wife cooked every part of the animal but the head. Instead, she threw the head in the creek. So he beat her. The abusive hunter is long gone, and so is his poor wife, and nobody remembers their names. But the name Rabbit Head Creek survives. It empties into Tavern Creek, so named by hunters because the game was so plentiful that it was like walking through a tavern.

A Different Kind of Hunter

Voltaire said that those who can make you believe absurdities can make you commit atrocities. Voltaire lived in volatile times. So do I. And it's not just the welling thunderstorm to the west.

On the fringes of this storm, on the fringes of civilization, along the deep isolation of back roads, there's a bizarre ritual that leaves signs....

Missouri's rural outback is infested with a destructive cult of sheet metal hunters. These hunters are skillful, able to shoot a highway sign multiple times before it can duck for cover. It's disturbing that these hunters don't eat the sheet metal they shoot. They should. By my count, Missouri road signs are air-cooled by 23 trillion bullet holes. Count 'em yourself if you think I'm kidding. It makes no sense. Some of these sheet metal hunters are anti-authority, anti-tax, anti-government. Their hate is in their handiwork. Yet their dead aim raises the taxpayer cost of maintaining the one service that guarantees they receive their food stamps in the mail box: roads.

The situation seems terminal, but I have an idea. As the highway department collects all those bullet-riddled signs, they can weld them together into a giant geodesic dome. The canopy will form a hillbilly planetarium, a tribute to the stars, where daylight shining through the bullet holes will offer viewers a panorama of the Milky Way. Never mind that the presentation will be woefully inaccurate.

Much of this neighborly gunfire is aimed at signs that show a horse and buggy, urging motorists to "Share the road." The signs are a simple warning that over the next hill, be careful, lest you smash into a buggy and its horse and its passengers, and create instant carnage. Yet the sheet metal hunters are not so tolerant. I really don't understand why. The Amish are among the hardest-working, friendliest, most unassuming folks I've ever met. True, they march to the beat of a different drum. So do most people in one way or another, including the sheet metal hunters. Why do these women use guns to shoot signs? Maybe it's some kind of penis envy. Same for the male shooters, I reckon.

I tried to rationalize that those bullet-riddled signs are a Show-Me State welcome to travelers, a gentle reminder that we're the daring descendants of Bushwhackers like Bloody Bill Anderson and Jesse James. That's bullshit. These sheet metal hunters are idiots at best, bordering on terrorism.

And their mangled handiwork is worse than the rattle of a snake's tail. So as I embroider Missouri with tire tracks and water the cracks where asphalt meets gravel, I'm cognizant of Missouri's beastly potential. No matter where I am.

The Ghost of Dance Hall Cave

During the clear-cutting of Missouri forests, men risked their lives to pluck pasture-sized log rafts from the Gasconade River. The logs were sent downstream by the toughest bunch of people since the Huns and the Hordes—the tie hackers, who cut down forests to make railroad ties.

But this same stretch of river has a softer side. High on the face of a bluff, the capital of culinary caverns offers one of the world's most unique adventures in dining.

A few miles outside of Richland, I traded the paved assurance of Highway 7 for a gravel road, a well-worn path that has delivered dancers and diners and witnessed at least one human tragedy over the past hundred years. The beaten path grows narrow as it winds down to the Gasconade River. Today, a strong concrete bridge anchors securely to both banks. But it wasn't always that way. ...

Back in 1918, Ed Steckle built a low-water bridge to entice travelers to his new resort, a series of log cabins beneath a towering rock bluff along the Gasconade. The resort was a hit, thanks to Ed's Dance Hall Cave, a cavern three stories up the face of the riverbluff. Every Saturday night, musicians would use ropes to haul their instruments up to the cave and lure hundreds of revelers up a makeshift ladder to dance the night away.

But the dance hall fell silent one day. Ed Steckel waded out into a swift current onto the concrete of his low-water bridge to dislodge snags that were collecting flotsam in the high water. From the downstream side, Ed loosed the giant pile of debris, and the rushing water moved the brush across the bridge, snagging him and trapping him underwater until he drowned. The dancing stopped, and nobody came to the resort for years. Ed's ghost roamed the area undisturbed while a succession of owners tried to run the resort. But it wasn't until 1984 that Dave and Connie Hughes struck on success. They opened Cave Man BBQ—a restaurant in old Dance Hall Cave—after blasting out 2,200 tons of rock and building an elevator to the cave entrance. Billboards enticed travelers to drive five miles off the interstate to try the experience. Dave and Connie eventually sold the business, now called The Cave Restaurant. Ed Steckle's ghost tolerates dinner guests, as long as they don't complain.

Erifnus didn't like it. I ditched her to take a shuttle to the restaurant. The shuttle's path along the river to the elevator is a billy goat's dream, with sheer cliffs above and below the narrow road to the cave. Patrons need the shuttle van not because of any danger from the towering cliffs, but because there's no place to park at the cave entrance, only a few paces from the river's edge.

Along the narrow pathway, I noticed the aging cabins still standing along the trail, propped against the steep hillside. Their old log walls are getting a loving rehab after years of neglect. The ghost of Ed Steckle approves, best I can tell. At least he hasn't put a spell on the three-story elevator, which raised me to the cave entrance where the restaurant's new owner, Gary Dyer, holds court. Gary looks like a restauranteur, a rotund host who knows good food and good fun, and treats guests royally.

The restaurant is intimate. It's a cave, for God sakes. So some folks avoid this experience if they fear heights or elevators or suffer from claustrophobia or speluncaphobia. Still, there's ample lighting, comfortable seating in booths if you want, and plenty of room to move around on carpeting while you look at trophy fish and trophy deer mounted on finished walls. And with a constant temperature just under 70 degrees and a dehumidifier, the place makes a dandy dining room, with a bar next to the wood stove. There are windows, and a door leads to the balcony with a railing made of wagon wheels, and a view through the treetops to the river below.

Gary knows how to put on a show. The piano player injects just the right amount of cheese. The menu fare ranges from fried walleye to a two-pound ribeye, and you can get fried dill pickles, fried okra and green tomato relish. There's even an emergency exit. The fire escape leads through the dining room to another hole in the cliff where an iron spiral staircase is attached. And yes, the restaurant has a bathroom.

Gary has big plans for the place. "A real fixer-upper," my buddy Vance would say. Maybe stay open year-round. Gary can do it, with the right mixture of savvy and showbiz marketing. But damn, this place is the poster child for "off-the-beaten-path." And in the restaurant business, that can be the kiss of death.

Still, Gary seems to churn out success. He has another restaurant in nearby Lebanon, with the unimaginative name of Gary's Place. But imagination runs rampant in other aspects of the business. They serve Italian food with a heaping side of murder mystery theater. The brochure claims that Gary's Great Grandma Bellini invented lasagna and fettuccine Alfredo and cheese ravioli and Sangria. Well, he's in show business. I happen to know that lasagna is an acronym for "let's all strip and get naked and..."

My story is as believable as his.

I took the back roads through the beautiful Coffin State Forest. It was near there that a sign pointed to HoHumm Canoe Rental & Campgrounds and its "Ole'-Time Country Store (stocked with what you need, or forgot)." I saw a sign recently that the place is for sale. In a world where sizzle sells, how do you sell HoHumm? I tried to access Coffin Cave, but it's fenced off and padlocked to protect native bats. So we turned away from the bats and coffins. Driving through this postcard dairy farmland, it reminded me of little Switzerland. We headed west through Plad and down to Long Lane, through Charity, across to March, through Tunas, and traversed the decidedly rural Urbana.

Those are six of the nine towns in Dallas County. Obviously, the residents didn't waste the opportunity to give each town a unique name. Along Highway 65, we came upon the seventh town, the tiny hamlet of Foose, which is so private it has an unlisted population number. The namers of this town must've had balls.

A neon buffalo greeted us as we drove past the Buffalo Motel in Buffalo, Missouri. It's the only surviving buffalo within miles, I suspect. Route YY drops down the side of an Ozark mountain. Before the drop, on the bald knob of the mountain I passed a stark image: an old house made of rock, a rugged ruin, a dwelling that harkens back to ancient Scotland. Dilapidated as it was, it had the character of a stone relic, and unlike its mobile home cousins, this ruin will stand against the elements to exhibit hillbilly ingenuity for generations to come. I remember riding the Flying Scotsman, a train from London to Edinburgh that zips past dozens of stone cottages on the bluffs overlooking the North Sea, with wind-swept seaside golf courses, and an occasional trailer court by-the-sea. Conversely, a drive through the hills along Route YY took me past trailers, and this stone ruin.

At the bottom of this steep hill where the highway turns to gravel, an old man sitting on his front porch stared at my car as if I was an intruder. Well, down here at the end of civilization, I am an intruder. I waved, then retreated. Erifnus made it up the long winding road to the top of the hill, then suddenly lost all power, as if a giant invisible wand had shut down her electrical system. No instrument lights, no radio, no juice at all. The car rolled silently to a stop next to the hillbilly ruin. I glanced at my cell phone. Blank. It's an eerie feeling to sit alone at the top of a deserted, treeless knob and be able to look in every direction but see nothing, no civilization, save one old stone ruin beside me. I turned the ignition key, and Erifnus fired up immediately. Her tires bit into the road, and we quickly reached cruising speed. Maybe the loss of power was caused by a solar storm. Maybe the Earth's magnetic poles reversed. Maybe it was the ghost of Coffin Forest. I don't know. I never looked back.

Throughout this area is a large population of Amish families, so many that the black asphalt is stenciled with dozens of white buggy wheel tracks and thousands of horseshoe marks. Along the road, back in among the trees, dozens of simple, clean, hand-painted wooden signs point to Amish shops: bakeries, furniture makers, general stores.

I passed a trio of peafowl, clucking and jabbering at each other—and at me—and drove through Windyville, which isn't even listed on the highway map. On cue, an intense thunderstorm struck Windyville. Wind whipped sideways and through the blinding rain, a faded mural on one Windyville wall struggled to get my attention. The scene depicts Noah and the Ark. I turned my wipers on high.

For the rest of the afternoon, we crisscrossed rain-swept blacktop, and the thought of losing power was never far from my mind. At the end of the last blacktop of the day, a gravel road took over the duties from the state road and immediately approached the bridge over Turnback Creek. High water crashed over the bridge, which was closed. I turned back.

America's Mathematical Middle

I felt a comfortable sense of balance as we approached Edgar Springs, Missouri. The exact middle of our American population is just 2.8 miles east of this little town along the edge of the Mark Twain Forest. Or it was after the 2000 Census. The town's reign as the U.S. population center is over now, and the 2010 Census moved America's mathematical middle 22 miles southwest.

On the roadside in Edgar Springs, there's a bait shop with a giant wooden ice cream cone in the parking lot to catch the eyes of kids. I stopped. The bait shop proprietor was frustrated that nobody had done much to promote America's mathematical middle.

Another Edgar Springs resident downplayed the importance of being the exact middle: "I don't see too much to get excited about. There's not much to play up because there's not much here."

He's right in terms of population and motels and shopping centers. There are no man-made tourist hooks, no giant ball of string, no world's largest pencil. But within a short radius of downtown Edgar, the anatomy of the earth takes some interesting shapes. The Devil's in the details. Down the road from Edgar, not far from Devil's Elbow, is a spot called Devil's Tongue. It's also called Lizard Rock in polite company, but some folks think it looks like another part of the Devil's anatomy. I'm not sure how they know. Anyway, nearby there's a Devil's Tea Table and a Devil's Punch Bowl and a Devil's Sugar Bowl, and not one but two spots called Devil's Backbone. All that Deviltry was unsettling enough, but just north of Edgar, I stepped in quicksand.

The quicksand sits along the Little Piney River as it courses past a spacious U.S. Forest Service campground called Lane Spring. This stuff is genuine quicksand, not the fake Hollywood stuff. Locals assure visitors that it's difficult to drown in real quicksand. I tested it with a toe, then a step into its sandy suction. But I ventured no further, being by myself, without a lasso, remembering all those tragic quicksand scenes in countless cowboy movies.

The real danger came later that night as I sat around the campfire with friends who had come here to camp. A storm approached. Thunder got louder and lightning got closer, eventually unleashing torrents of rain that pelted us for hours. We took shelter in a pair of trailers, high enough on the riverbank to avoid the flash flood that tore through the area. North of us that night, campers weren't so lucky. Along Saline Creek, the same storms dumped several inches of rain, and the flood flashed through suddenly, sweeping two little girls downriver, still inside their tent. It took almost a week for searchers to find one body. They never found the other.

Nature's fury can strike with devastating consequences. It's the same force that forged all these Devilish formations that surround

Edgar Springs. And while the little town has yet to find its tourism mojo, that's okay. The Devil is patient. Lizard Rock isn't going anywhere.

Meanwhile, the clock kept ticking toward a new census that determined a new population center. This time it's another tiny town, with a big name: Plato, Missouri.

Plato, of course, is the world's greatest philosopher, whose Republic suggests that the best ruler of all is a wise and gracious philosopher-king. Folks who founded Plato, Missouri, envisioned a utopian town, ruled by thinking leaders.

The first car I saw in Plato was plastered with bumper stickers saying, "Don't Tread On Me" and "Our Ancestors Left Europe to Get Away from This Crap" and "I'll keep my guns and money... you can keep the change" and "Even God only asks for 10%" and "Don't touch my junk" and "Somewhere in Kenya, a village is missing an idiot" and "Hey President, looks like you could use a good cup of shut the hell up."

Bumper slogans don't solve problems. But they do identify the driver. I was more than happy to heed the bumper car's warning: "Shut up and leave me alone." Personally, I'll vigorously defend the First Amendment rights of any bumper-sticker brain: red, blue, left, right or stupid.

The dumb luck that Plato is the population center of America offers an opportunity for America to focus on something more than slogans, and perhaps to read Plato's Republic again, or maybe for the first time. But I'm not holding my breath for that bumper-sticker driver to discover the real Plato.

Knowing she was tipping the balance of America's population, Erifnus rolled me up the road through the old Rock Island Railroad town of Crocker. I remember a scary incident from my childhood, back when this territory was free range. It was late night, and I was asleep in the back seat of our car when I awoke on the floorboard after a crash. A horse had darted onto the highway, and our old '58 Biscayne hit her, broadside. The horse fell to the ground, stunned, and then got to her feet and fled into the woods.

As we sat in the darkness with a busted radiator, the beam from a farmer's flashlight bobbed and waved in the woods, searching for the wounded mare. By the time a wrecker reached our remote location, the farmer hadn't found her yet. The wrecker towed us to town, me in the backseat looking out the back window for a horse that never appeared again.

Free range ended in the '60s, as the middle of America realized that it had to organize its shrinking wilderness. Today, good fences make good neighbors. Except that a fence can't stop smells or hold back pollution.

Or frogs. The back entrance to Waynesville is guarded by an Army fort. But the sentry along the east approach is the world's greatest frog, if size means anything. Sure, to most folks it looked like a giant rock outcropping, but to the tattoo artist who painted the rock green and yellow, it's a frog. The highway department—or somebody—erected a sign that warns "Frog Crossing." It's hard to miss, this 20-ton hopper, poised to jump across the highway from its perch four stories above the road, or perhaps flick what might be a 90-foot igneous tongue to zap passing traffic.

Liquor, Ghosts and Ammo

A half-day's drive northwest of America's mathematical middle, between neatly organized orchards that drape the hills overlooking the Missouri River, I could smell the apples. Along the river, two towns combine to form the Wellington Napoleon School District. It must be fun to be a history teacher there.

The historic Santa Fe Trail follows the river, and crosses Terre Beau Creek. The phrase "Terre Beau" is a lovely attempt to say, "beautiful land" in French, although the French would shudder at mixing two words with mismatched genders. No matter. In a short time, locals shortened the words to Tabo Creek. But entering the edge of Dover, Terre Beau surfaced again in a most delightful form.

An old pre-Civil War Presbyterian church now houses the Terre Beau Winery. Inside, this church-turned-winery is beautifully restored. Tables draped in linen stand on wood floors, and a tile floor supports the old altar site. It's an inspirational spot to relax and soak in some wine and history. During a Civil War skirmish, a riverboat fired a cannon ball into the church's steeple. Union forces turned the building into a makeshift jail for Southern sympathizers.

The Tulipana family makes this winery a labor of love, so I didn't ask if they advertise on the radio, where "terre beau" sounds, well, terrible.

But what do I know? At the easternmost end of this same road, on the banks of the Mississippi, a casino called Terribles seems to be raking in the chips.

We drove the 16 streets of Dover, most of them only a block or two long. When early Doverites laid out the town, there must've been a reason they named one street Mulberry and another Mulbury. The two street sit side by side, offering a challenge for the mail carrier. But with only 48 households in the whole town, the carrier probably can figure it out.

Down the road, between Dover and Waverly, many ghost hunters want to believe there's a haunted house. The Dover Mansion probably gets its haunted reputation because of its outward appearance and not so much because of any paranormal apparitions inside. The mansion is gargantuan, an odd sight along this rural stretch of highway. The house is crowned by a Monticello dome, and its huge columns show their age. Some folks said it was a cult house, which probably helped fuel the ghost stories. But I was skeptical about all this chatter as we drove toward this mansion.

I pulled over to the narrow shoulder, rolled down my window and took a photo of the haunted house. The photo didn't turn out. Of course, that's because when I loaded my camera, the film did not advance properly, and I lost the whole roll. The mansion looked spooky from the outside. I didn't go to the door. That's not because I'm afraid of ghosts; I just had a sixth-sense warning that if I sneaked up to this house and peeked in the windows, apparitions would appear from behind me with guns and handcuffs, and they'd whisk me away to some dungeon where I'd be booked and fingerprinted. Besides, Erifnus has no use for such folly and wouldn't appreciate being abandoned on the roadside while I negotiated bail.

Ghost hunters persist with up-close eyewitness reports, most stories revealing more about the spookee than the spook. Online, one lady said she approached the mansion, and lights went on inside the house. She said she peeked in the windows and saw a newspaper with that day's date. Just then, a big spotlight shone down on her from near the peak of the house. Well, duh. I wouldn't want a peeper around my windows either while I got up from reading the paper and went upstairs to take a dump. Another online confession read, "Me and my friends was at a party and about 1:30 am we decided to go to the Dover Mansion 'cause we heard it was haunted. When we got there, no lights were on, but as we peeked in the windows, all the lights went on, and we ran because it was spooky." I wonder if those kids are registered to vote....

Too bad John Newman Edwards can't get to the bottom of all this ghost stuff. John's long dead, buried in Dover cemetery. When he was alive, he was one of the best storytellers in America. A staunch Confederate, Edwards wrote running eyewitness accounts of the Civil War as he rode with General Shelby against the Union. After the war, he helped found the *Kansas City Times* and as its editor, used barrels of ink to glorify the Bushwhackers and instill pride in a defeated South.

His most lasting legacy was exalting Jesse James to the status of Robin Hood. Newman reached out to the James Gang, and Jesse wrote letters to Newman explaining why he still fought to right the wrongs against his family and against Southern sympathizers. Edwards published the letters and—as much as any other single individual—built up the legend of Jesse James. After Jesse was murdered, Edwards worked to help negotiate Frank James' surrender to the governor of Missouri.

Nowadays, while rural areas throughout Missouri still tell tales about the James Gang, there's a good chance that any rural crime can be traced to a meth lab.

But the Dover Mansion suffers another insidious infestation. From stories I heard, ghost hunters would get their courage up in the wee hours to trespass on the grounds of this home. They'd get spooked by the oddity of incandescence, and text all their friends that they peed their pants. It's a self-fulfilling prophecy, fueled by an OMG to BFF, and pretty soon ghost stories persisted all along the river and the Santa Fe Trail. Sensing an epidemic, ghost hunters list other suspected haunted towns within the immediate area, including Alma, Concordia, Corder, Hardin, Henrietta, Higginsville, Lexington, Mayview, Odessa, Richmond, Waverly and Wellington. In other words, the whole freakin' area is haunted. The end is near. But it ain't because of no ghosts.

Leaving the ghost busters, we weaved through back roads to a spot that goes beyond haunted. Where I-70 crosses Route 65, the area is known as Marshall Junction. Unlike many major highway intersections, this crossroads is desolate. The only gas station sits a quarter-mile south, across from the ghostly shell of a shuttered dance hall.

Country Palace, they called it, and when they built it back in the '70s, it was a beautiful, spacious brick-and-concrete monument to folly and dally. But the nearest big town is 16 miles away, too far to sustain such a business built on the profits from booze. So the dance hall went silent, long ago abandoned, standing vacant and spooky. Its blank marquee presides over prairie weeds growing up through the cracks in its ample parking lot. But the dance hall is not the haunted spot.

Minutes from there, hidden from sight by layers of thick woods, the Marshall Junction Conservation Area's remote location makes it a great place to practice target shooting with firearms. The Missouri Conservation Department set up a shooting range for just that purpose.

On September 9, 1986, the shooting turned deadly. Donald Reese was in the parking lot minding his own damn business—preparing to dispose of two dead bodies from his trunk—when Conservation Agent James Watson and Chris Griffith drove into the lot and got out to go to the target range. Acting quickly, Reese pointed his rifle at Watson and buried two bullets in his chest. Griffith turned to run, but made it only a few yards when the weight of five bullets in his back finally felled him. Less than a week later, the trail of evidence led authorities to Reese, who was arrested, tried and convicted. He was executed 11 years later.

Reese's death-row mugshot reveals vacant black eyes over a Mona Lisa smile, a visage of satisfaction about his deeds.

Agent Watson's son, tormented by the events, later took his own life. The six ghosts mingle at this spot, and in between the sharp crackle of practice gunfire, I could hear their silence.

I shivered, saluted, and turned away, back toward life.

A Star and a Steak, Four Daughters and a Card Game

Arrow Rock sits on the bluffs above the Missouri River. Or it used to. About a century ago, the river meandered a mile away from the town. But the bluffs of Arrow Rock are still there and from their shoulders, in the distance I could see the Boone's Lick, the salt lick where Daniel Boone's sons operated their successful salt business.

Arrow Rock used to be bigger than its population of 79. Back before the Missouri River meandered away, it was a bustling river port, luring an enterprising bunch of settlers including the guy who discovered that quinine would quell malaria.

It's also the home of George Caleb Bingham, a Renaissance Man, and one of America's foremost portrait artists, whose paintings of frontier stump speeches and jolly flatboatmen feature characters that seem to exhibit the dangers of taking botox injections while smiling. During the Civil War his painting of *Order #11*—a gut-wrenching depiction of the tragedy brought on by the systematic burning of four entire counties—stirred strong emotions at the time. Bingham also is connected to another Civil War tragedy. He owned a house in Kansas City, which, unknown to him, would turn this ugly war even uglier in Missouri. The house caved in, killing and maiming a group of Bushwhackers' girlfriends who were held captive there. The acts of revenge for that cave-in rained Hell on Missouri for decades.

Bingham seemed a proper gentleman. But don't get the idea that he was artsy-fartsy. He'd kick your ass, figuratively, in a disagreement. In fact, he routed out the Ku Klux Klan in southern Missouri—and the Baldknobbers too. And he had very public feuds with a bunch of colorful characters, including the man who coined the term "Man's Best Friend." Bingham loved the dog in the case; he just didn't like the dog's attorney.

Arrow Rock descendants point out that Bingham was such a dog lover that he put a dog in every genre painting but one. Asked why there's no dog in "The Jolly Flatboatmen," Bingham replied, "He's in the hold."

Also on hold, down the road from Arrow Rock, the remains of a whole family of Bingham haters await the Rapture. Sappington Cemetery is the eternal resting ground for physician John Sappington. Ol' Doc Sappington is known for two things, primarily. He discovered quinine as a treatment for malaria. And he had four daughters who each married a Missouri governor. One married the rotund Meredith Miles Marmaduke. The other three married wily Claiborne Fox Jackson. After Jackson outlived the first two and married the third, Sappington advised Jackson, "I'm all out of daughters." Anyway, they're all dead happily ever after in the same cozy cemetery. Bingham didn't care much for those damn governors. Their faces show up ugly, shiny and goofy in his political paintings.

There's another reason Bingham hated Jackson, I suspect. Jackson was governor at the beginning of the Civil War, but he refused President Lincoln's request to raise an army in defense of the Union.

When Jackson fled the state capitol building, he took the contents of the state treasury with him. Some time after a new slate of pro-Union leaders took office, the steadfastly pro-Union Bingham became state treasurer. He was painfully aware of the depleted treasury. Among all the reasons the vast majority of his neighbors were pro-Confederacy, one of the biggest was money. If they were going to get any of their tax dollars and investments back from Claiborne Jackson's government-in-exile, the South had to win the war.

On this trip I bypassed Marshall, but my CD player begged for me to play "Touchdown," the seminal CD of Marshall's favorite musical son, Bob James. You know the music, if you've ever hummed along to the theme from the television show "Taxi." I drove north to Slater, the tiny town which everybody knows is the boyhood home of Steve McQueen. Well, you know it now. I preempted my Bob James music and plugged in a CD ballad about Steve McQueen, performed by another worldly Missourian, Sheryl Crow.

These back roads make a perfect drive for Steve McQueen's motorcycle. Their swerves and knolls led me to Salisbury, a town I'd been told was the home of the Salisbury steak. Well, not exactly. Salisbury is a delightful little town that oozes pride. New sidewalks and street lamps frame the downtown, where McTag's Bar rocks on weekends. That's when the Pizza Hut wagon rolls into town to do a brisk business. Talk about delivery. And to deliver the soul, the religious bookstore known as Mary's Call gets you pointed in the right direction, offering a 15-decade rosary tape with meditations. Because the end is near, I didn't purchase the tape, figuring I won't have time to absorb 15 decades of the joyful, sorrowful meditations on the glorious mysteries.

But one mystery is solved. The story that Salisbury is the home of the Salisbury steak is slightly wrong... by one generation. The town was named for the steak's creator, a Civil War doctor with an idea for a special diet. An easterner, Dr. James Henry Salisbury worked with Union troops during the war and found himself treating battle wounds in tiny Constantinople, Missouri.

The folks in Constantinople had another problem: Diarrhea had reached epidemic levels, and townspeople turned to the doctor for help. Doc Salisbury had long promoted the idea that food should be ground up to help with digestion, and prescribed ground beef as one of the prime staples of a healthy diet. He convinced townspeople to try a diet of ground beef and hot water. There's no proof that the diet worked, but the diarrhea stopped, and Dr. Salisbury must've got the credit, because years later the townsfolk renamed the town after him.

Thanks to Dr. Salisbury and a bit of luck, the town narrowly avoided the alternative name: Hersheysquirtsville. Good thing. That word is too long for a highway sign and would cause car wrecks when drivers tried to text their location.

I drove to Macon, home of lions and tigers and bears, stuffed and on display. Sometimes in the past, you'd see a live one. But Macon doesn't see the big cats in the auction barn like they used to. Still, Lolli Brothers Auction is known far and wide as the spot to buy a camel or a llama—or something more exotic, maybe a giraffe. It's reassuring here in the middle of America that if the Great Flood II washes over the world, locals can get most of the passengers for their Ark right here, along with pretty much all the critter chow they'll need, too, from the Checkerboard Farms down the road. I didn't have room in my trunk for a zebra, so I left without any exotic passengers and headed east to Ten Mile.

Hay's Ten Mile Store is only eight miles from Anabel, six miles from Economy. Fact is, it's not 10 miles from any town. The largest town in the area is Macon, and it's a lonely six mile drive from Macon to the Ten Mile Store, but enough folks find it to keep the doors open. It was shuttered for a decade, not long ago. But now it has a fresh coat of paint on the tall wooden facade. A King Feed sign sits next to the spokes of an old iron wagon wheel that borders a 100-year-old awning beneath the Coca Cola sign that announces, "Hay's Ten Mile Store." The awning shelters the old screen door, and a walk through that door takes your eyes back more than a century.

The store's role may have changed over its 11 decades, but the turn-of-the-century décor is preserved. It used to provide life's necessities for folks who arrived by wagon. Nowadays, Wade and Megan King sell antiques on weekends, and a few dry goods here and there. Four old unmatched chairs team together around an ancient wooden table that supports a game of cutthroat pitch that's been going since some time back in 1902. The game appears to include some of the original players: old men who, with decades of practice, have settled comfortably into a seamless rhythm of pitch and bullshit. On the wall, a mule deer watches from under its orange hunter's hat, keeping the card players honest. The deer no longer seems to mind the hat, since the animal has lasted longer than any of his brothers and sisters.

Sub Warfare, Racism, Marxism and Oysters

Primo's reminded me that on the road there are two ways to eat: federal or local. Some restaurants are instantly identifiable because they proudly display their corporate brand. Food corporations are federations with the same colors, the same drive-thrus, same uniforms, same menus.

On the other hand, Primo's shows its local flavor.

Occupying a main street building in Canton that's probably witnessed a dozen Mississippi River floods, Primo's offered me a menu with great pizza and soups and subs. But it also whet my eyeballs' appetite. Primo's might be a chain. I don't know. But it doesn't look like a chain. Its biggest competition, at least in sub warfare, is the Subway perched at the interstate exit atop Canton's formidable Mississippi River bluffs. Hey, Subway serves a good sandwich. But its major selling point is consistency. You know what you're going to get, right down to the décor.

When I walked into Primo's, I entered an art studio. Brenna Phillips seated me at a table standing on a floor with those tiny white tiles you find in old hotel bathrooms. We began a conversation that ranged far from the menu. The walls are adorned with several paintings by a local artist, and the paintings are provocative, not in a lewd way, but disturbing in their subject matter. One painting features the unexpressive faces of a dozen people, their blank stares curious because all of them are clinging to a bare tree, its limbs fleeced by a tornado, twisting off in the distance.

"Yeah, those paintings are by Richard Baily," Brenna said. "I'm surprised he's not here right now. Comes in all the time."

"Art professor?"

"Nah, but he knows a lot of stuff."

She told me the story of the paintings. Apparently, somebody burned down Richard's garage a few years ago. He found out who did it, which is usually fairly easy in a small town. But proving your case is another matter. Nothing was done about the vandalism, at least to the artist's idea of justice. He received no restitution. So he painted a canvas drama entitled "Justice," an angry scene showing the sacred goddess named Blind Justice getting mugged in a surreal Salvador Dali-style scene. The people in the treetops of the adjacent painting are the folks who know about the garage fire but did nothing.

It's not something you'd see on the walls of a Subway. I ordered a tenderloin sandwich and ate among the tornadoes and tree huggers and Blind Justice, who couldn't see me, but probably could smell my french fries.

I thanked Brenna and walked onto the street, around a corner where a lady was painting a mural on a blank wall next to a vacant lot. I sidled up behind her left shoulder, keeping a respectful distance, admiring her art. I was about to speak when I realized that she was talking, even as she brushed white highlights onto her river scene filled with birds cavorting in lush wetland vegetation. Nobody else was around. She was talking on a hands-free cell phone. I started walking again, and that's when she noticed me. I nodded, gave her a thumbs up, and kept going.

Around the corner, parked along a curbless streetside was a black buggy, signaling an Amish dwelling. Behind the house, a horse munched hay in the corral next to a well-tended garden. I circled the block, dodging horse droppings, admiring the stately old homes mixed among modest dwellings and the occasional house with a chronic condition of yard sale.

Back on Main Street, I sneaked up on Erifnus. She didn't startle. She never startles. At the city park we passed an old red brick building that sits alone in its own rich and troubling history. Some day the old Lincoln Colored School will become a Civil Rights museum with help from some of the town's Culver-Stockton College professors. That's the plan. But for now the building sits empty, its paneless windows covered with tin.

The old school was built in 1880 in response to "a petition from the colored citizens of Canton asking and praying for a better school building for the accommodation of the colored children of Canton School District." The school board responded by building the structure for $800. Still, when children graduated from the school, Canton had no high school for blacks, so students commuted 40 miles to a high school downriver in Hannibal. To get a high school diploma, those children had to exchange a significant amount of play time for travel time.

Chances are those kids probably didn't have the luxury of playing with any of the 10,000 toys that ended up at the Remember When Toy Museum, a roadside lot where things just seem to collect inside and outside an aging one-story building painted a can't-miss canary yellow. Five bucks buys a glimpse of what the museum calls the world's largest collection of Marx toys, 60 years' worth. But best I could tell, the museum is not the Official Marx Toy Museum. Among toy collectors, apparently there are Marxist cells everywhere, which should give some satisfaction to conspiracy theorists. Anyway, Canton's version, the Remember When Toy Museum, was closed when I drove into the parking lot, which is a museum itself, packed with Edsels parked in parquet rows facing a fleet of old Cadillacs. It was car lot chic, against that bright yellow stucco backdrop.

Pointed south on old 61, we paralleled the Avenue of the Saints. To our left we could nearly touch the ancient Snicarty Slough, the long river pool that used to be the main channel of the Mississippi. Ahead: La Grange. Not the La Grange in the song, which is about the best little whorehouse in Texas. This LaGrange doesn't have a world-famous whorehouse that I know of, although it was the first place I ever saw a rubber machine, in an oily old gas station bathroom. I was nine at the time, and we were taking my sister to college up the road at Culver-Stockton, and I went to the bathroom and there it was. I didn't have a quarter, or I'd still probably be carrying a rubber from that machine in my wallet.

No, the chicken ranches around La Grange have nothing to do with prophylactics, and the only vice in town sits down on the river at Terribles Casino. Like all casinos in Missouri, Terribles is called a riverboat, but it never sails, permanently attached to terra firma. When Missouri reintroduced gambling back a generation ago, voters limited the purpose (school funding) and the location (rivers): According to law casinos had to be functional riverboats, and the gambling tables could be open only when the boats were traveling on the river. The rules relaxed when Missourians realized that riverboats could sink, and therefore the casinos' insurance policies had shot through the roof. Nowadays, the riverboats are as stationary as riverfront hotels. But they still must touch the river, or at least sit next to one. I'm not sure what Mark Twain would have thought. Oh, he wouldn't mind river-boat gambling. He was used to that. But gambling on a riverboat that can't sail? That's a terrible idea.

La Grange used to have four button factories. Sitting beside the Mississippi River, the button makers could dredge a billion mussels and make buttons from their shells. But now the shell buttons have been replaced by plastic buttons. And the old button machines have been replaced by the one-armed bandits at Terribles Mark Twain Casino. So the mussels filter sighs of relief that few gamblers display mussel shells on their shirts.

Just south along the old Oyster Prairie, Oyster Branch Creek flows into Oyster Pond, and nearby the old town of Oyster once thrived. On a clear day you could almost see Oyster Island, where migrating waterfowl stop to rest and feed, though probably not on oysters, since there aren't any oysters in this river. These landmarks were named for a guy named Oyster. For some reason, the state park, a haven for the waterfowl, isn't called Oyster Park or Mussel Park. It's called Wakonda State Park. Wakonda comes from the Sioux word for "home of the Great Spirit."

Surveying the park, I was disappointed to learn that Lone Tree is gone. It was a landmark in Mark Twain's day and as the name implies, it was a solitary tree on the west bank of the Mississippi, used by riverboat pilots to tie their boats. The tree was ripped out of the ground by a boat in 1874, so I couldn't be upset that I had just missed seeing it.

Neither did I see the ghosts along Sunflower Road just north of LaGrange, but I assume they saw me. Some of the ghosts come from the old Wayside Inn, an ancient traveler's oasis that's been gone for decades. In its heyday it was a well-known stop along the old Memphis-LaGrange Road. Culver-Stockton College students who party along the nearby creek know the ghost stories, passed down for generations. One story tells of the innkeeper's daughter who fell in love with a traveling salesman staying at the inn. The salesman disappeared, never to be seen again. Soon after the salesman vanished, the innkeeper filled and sealed the inn's well. For months, locals say, the water tasted like chicken.

* * *

I was damn near the Iowa border when I came to a dying breed: a two-newspaper town. There aren't many American towns left with two newspapers, especially towns with fewer than 2,500 people. In

Kahoka, business tilts toward seeds and fertilizers and farm implements. And two weekly newspapers battle head-to-head. The *Kahoka Media* tilts Republican, the *Kahoka Hometown Journal* leans Democrat. Obviously, some people are getting both papers, broadening their views. It's refreshing to see some local media competition, although to be honest, the battles to cover the police blotter and the city hall beat might take a back seat to the bigger fight for advertising dollars.

Kahoka is named for the Cahokia tribe. With this unique spelling of a tribal name, it's the only Kahoka in the known universe.

Passing the stately old courthouse, I shook my head, lamenting its perch atop a preservationist group's top ten most endangered places. Built in 1870 for less than $19,000, the courthouse remains one of the few examples of Missouri courthouses built in the immediate aftermath of the Civil War.

The courthouse needs a benefactor, a sugar daddy, to save the building from the ravages of time. But Clark County, like most of its neighbors, has no extra funds. With a population of only 7,400, it's a challenge to raise money. A mere dozen Missouri counties have smaller populations. Nine of those are proximate to Clark, in a region where hogs outnumber people.

Some locals held hope that big hog operations in the county would donate money to save the courthouse. Others just wished the hog operations would go away. It was a battle brewing, and the stench of battle wafted over the Battle of Athens State Historic Site similar to the way it did on August 5, 1861, when Union Colonel David Moore and fewer than 500 troops held their ground against an invasion by 2,000 soldiers of the pro-Confederate Missouri State Guard, led by Colonel Martin Green.

When Confederate spies reported that a shipment of Union supplies had just arrived in Athens, Green made plans to invade the town, capture the supplies and liberate the Southern sympathizers, called Sesesh, a contraction of "secessionist."

The townspeople knew the invasion was coming. Many of the Sesesh women in the town baked chickens and pies, to celebrate their impending liberation. On the morning of the battle, civilians gathered across the Des Moines River on a slope that formed a perfect amphitheater to watch the fight. They assumed they would be safe....

The battle commenced at daybreak. Green's Confederates surrounded the town on three sides, leaving the river as the only option for a Union retreat. Two Confederate cannons fired on the town but overshot their marks, their shells landing on the opposite river bank, scattering startled onlookers. Less than two hours later, when the battle smoke cleared, Green's troops had failed to rescue the town, an outcome foreshadowed by Confederate Captain Moore, son of the opposing colonel: "I know dad, and he'll give you all the fighting you want."

True to young Confederate Moore's premonition, his father's Union soldiers repelled the invaders. That night, the Union troops enjoyed southern fried chicken and southern baked pies, but probably didn't feel much southern hospitality.

And the Sesesh? Well, Athens (pronounced, wouldn't you know, with a hard a) never recovered. A thriving river town in 1861, with 500 residents and 50 businesses, the town has dwindled to a handful of people and even fewer buildings.

Erifnus rolled across Sweet Home Township and through Revere and delivered me to the Battle of Athens State Historic Site. In this northeasternmost part of Missouri, we're closer to the state capitals of Iowa and Illinois than to Missouri's capital. But descending into the park, a beautiful setting along the Des Moines River, I knew why we came.

I saw the Cannonball House, so called because at least one Confederate cannon ball found its mark, crashing through two kitchen walls. A few other buildings survive, standing like cuspids in a mouth of missing teeth. The park superintendent was only too eager to show me around and explain the battle.

I can understand why people would want to settle here, and I promptly nestled into a secluded campsite myself, and explored the Des Moines River Ravines Natural Area. The park enjoys a 1.5-mile river front and enough hills and woods to get lost in. The rolling hills and beautiful scenery stand as irrefutable proof that north Missouri is much more than flat farmland.

Geese flew over my head in expansive V's, drawn across the sky as if they came from the hand of a five-year-old. The geese are attracted to the wetland estuaries of the Great River National Wildlife Refuge, seen better from aloft, along their Mississippi River flyway.

I could only see it from my two-dimensional view along Highway 61 between Alexandria and Gregory Landing. Still, I knew the value of these wetlands, and the fights these lands have sparked between developers and preservationists, who both sense that the end is near. Developers want to make a killing before Armageddon. Preservationists want to avoid killing until Armageddon.

The Civil War is long gone, but battle lines persist.

Driving south from Athens along the Des Moines River, I came upon a preservationist victory. It's a historic site that once was a summer village inhabited by the Indians of the Illiniwek Confederacy. The Illiniwek, or Illinois Indians, were prevalent when Europeans first came to Missouri. The village looks different today than it looked back in 1673, when Marquette and Joliet first introduced Europeans—and disease—to the 8,000 villagers. Today the 300 lodges along a network of streets are reduced to an archaeological dig. Still, this village is the biggest and best-preserved museum of the Illiniwek culture.

Erifnus is a Pontiac, named for the most famous Native American nobody knows. Oh, they know the name. But few can recount the history of Pontiac, the legendary leader of the Three Fires Confederacy who led the siege of Fort Detroit back before there were cars or provinces or states united. Chief Pontiac was assassinated by a member of the Peoria tribe, and his remains lie beneath the streets of St. Louis. His name lives on as a hood ornament. Alas, even that hood armament will disappear beneath the streets, relegated to museumhood. It's a troubling reminder to Erifnus Caitnop that the end is near. I assured Erifnus that when her time comes, she'll be buried beneath the streets of St. Louis with Chief Pontiac.

My car doesn't care that I'm the great-grandson of an Irish Catholic priest. Still, she obliged as I took a circuitous route from Illiniwek along the Dempsey Highway to the village of St. Patrick, not far from the Wyaconda River. St. Patrick is the only place in the world where you can send a letter postmarked with the name of this legendary evangelist. As I sealed a dozen letters, I wondered how many people don't know about St. Patrick, or about Illiniwek and Joliet, or about the Battle of Athens. Erifnus, the Pontiac, knows.

But she will never see the old courthouse again. They tore it down.

Killers and Carnies

I drove into Memphis. No, not that Memphis, with its barbeque and Beale appeal. This Memphis was wide open, wild and woolly. At least it was when it produced the most prolific killer in the entire saga of the Wild West. Tom Horn was born and raised around Memphis, Missouri. Destined to ride tall in the saddle, Horn grew to nearly seven feet. But oddly, he was more than a foot shorter than the tallest woman in the county.

As a child Tom grew up in the family's rural home between Granger and Etna, just outside Memphis. Their family was churchgoing, God-fearing, but Tom looked to escape a strict father who beat him, and his yearning for adventure lured him to the Southwest. He left Memphis in his teens and headed for New Mexico, where he became Leonard Wood's chief scout during the Apache wars. His gang tracked down Geronimo, who finally surrendered because the chief tired of the chase. Tom later served as a deputy marshal, and an agent for Pinkertons, where he's credited with killing 17 souls.

"Killing men is my specialty," Tom bragged. And he was just getting started. Some wealthy cattle barons in Wyoming wanted to eradicate neighboring homesteaders, whom they regarded as cattle rustlers, and Tom was the cattle barons' most trusted exterminator.

He later rejoined Leonard Wood, and was set to ride with Teddy Roosevelt's Rough Riders during the war in Cuba. But Tom contracted malaria before he made it to Cuba, and returned to Wyoming to resume killing homesteaders.

He was smitten by another Missourian, barely half his height. Glendolene Myrtle Kimmell came to Wyoming from Hannibal to teach school and chase cowboys. They fell in love and would have lived happily ever after. But Tom, in his quest on behalf of cattle barons to terrorize settlers, killed the young son of a homesteader. Glendolene warned Tom to flee, but authorities tracked him down and brought him to trial.

He was represented by the best lawyer available to the wealthy cattle barons: the chief counsel to Union Pacific Railroad. But the jury found Tom guilty, and despite attempts to get him to roll over on the cattle barons who'd hired him to kill homesteaders, Tom went to the gallows. Steve McQueen played the lead role in the 1980 movie "Tom Horn."

All this talk of death and doom made me hungry.

Keith's Café has a lock on the most strategic location in town, where two highways intersect, and Keith doesn't squander the opportunity. The fresh ground steak burger and homemade fries live up to their best-in-galaxy status. And judging from the memorabilia on the walls, every famous Democrat in the world has stopped in for a meal.

On this visit, the presidential debate was on TV and everybody, including Keith's mom, the cook, was watching with intense interest. I watched and ate and laughed and cheered along with the other patrons, paid my bill and my respects to the cook, and strolled back out into a rainy night, hopeful that the only horn I'd come in contact with was the one in the middle of my steering wheel.

As tall in the saddle as Tom Horn rode, he wasn't the tallest in the county. One person looked down on him: the world's tallest woman.

Not far from the warmth of Keith's Café, Ella Ewing is secure in her final resting place. Ella was born near Gorin, and spent her childhood in the same stomping grounds as Tom Horn, though she was a dozen years younger than Tom. So she was still little when he left. But when she grew up, she really grew up, so much that she traveled with Buffalo Bill and Barnum & Bailey as the tallest woman in the world. Best I can tell, Ella still holds the record, at 8 feet 4 inches tall, though her name rarely shows up on anybody's official list.

It wasn't her choice to be that tall, but it made her famous. Reluctantly, she finally realized that she could capitalize on her height, so she joined the circus to make a living. She knew the wages of fame, so when her 10 pallbearers lowered her extended cab casket into the ground, her father told grave diggers to pour extra concrete over the vault to keep body snatchers from extracting her. She was afraid entrepreneurs would reintroduce her skeleton to the carnival sideshows. For 95 years, Ella has rested peacefully in a cemetery next to Harmony Grove Baptist Church, in a remote spot in remote Scotland County. So far Missourians have protected Ella's heritage from carnies.

Another carny regular was born down the road near Ravanna, an unincorporated area within spittin' distance of the Vandyke Conservation Area. It boasts 248 residents, but its most famous product is Martha Jane Cannary.

When she was 13, Martha's family moved to Montana. Maybe it was the Big Sky or hormones or fate or some damn calamity. Whatever it was, Martha morphed into Calamity Jane and made a living on the Wild West show circuit as a storyteller.

Erifnus and I passed the Calamity Jane Roadside Park. Soon we found the parking lot at the Crossroads Bar & Grill in Princeton. Crossroads gets good marks from folks for miles around. It's a neighborhood bar with a great selection of beers and a better selection of characters who call you by name and make you feel at home. Home is the way the food is cooked. I ate a steak and a fist-sized loaf of bread, but try as I might, couldn't stir up any further Calamity.

* * *

To get to the tallest deer stand in North America, we had to cross Pole Cat Creek. We passed up the Toot-Toot Family Restaurant & Lounge in Bethany, a good bet to be a railroad museum. We passed a boat, a runabout stuck stern-first in the ground, buried up to its steering wheel. The rest of the boat stuck out of the ground at the angle of a ski ramp, and the boat's gunwales formed a perfect fiberglass flower pot. We drove through Blythedale, where the population beneath headstones easily doubles the number of breathers. And then I saw it....

Up near the Iowa border, where the prairie affords long views, the deer have a clear view for a long way. They just naturally seem to avoid buckshot, and multiply like crazy ("concupiscent as rabbits," Steinbeck would say). From a mile away, I spied a wooden structure that was taller than a fire tower. A ladder propped against the top of the deer stand like a hook-and-ladder truck, forming an isosceles triangle with the ground, a good 40 feet per side.

For anything else, you probably wouldn't need a hook and ladder in Harrison County. Nothing's that tall, save that deer stand and one grain elevator. As I drove through this vast farm country, I could see for miles. In the distance, the grain elevator stood tall on this prairie landscape, maybe 20 stories tall. I circled it, on four different highways, and I could see it from every vantage point, even half a dozen miles away.

I shook my head in sadness as I passed more abandoned farm houses. Then I came upon the biggest black field I'd ever seen. Must've been 1,000 acres. I drove through miles and miles of the blackened fields of Harrison County, burned off after the harvest to reinvigorate the soil. It's a rite of renewal, a fiery, smoky episode in the cycle of life that sets the stage for rebirth in the spring. But it makes the landscape look like the Book of Revelations' front yard.

After miles of blackened cornstalks, we came to a front yard with a particularly unique carcass, saved from the scythe of the Grim Scrap Heaper....

For old highway bridges looking for purpose and meaning in their sunset years, Harrison County is a retirement villa. On Route B sits a house with its own steel bridge, a giant in the genre of personal private front yard bridges. The span must be a salvaged highway bridge, spending its golden years crossing over a small creek, its overhead superstructure nearly as tall as the dwelling to which it leads. Not far from there, on Route D is another steel bridge sitting in a ditch alongside the road, spanning nothing, leading nowhere, waiting to be useful again. I turned down Route UU and passed Mt. Pleasant #2 Baptist Church. A sign near there was damaged by a shotgun. Hopefully it wasn't the result of any unpleasantness with Mt. Pleasant #3.

There's a sad phenomenon in so many of these precious old towns. Generally, more people lie under the ground than walk on top of it. It's a natural progression, I guess, as Earth's population pushes toward eight billion, that we must find more space for our dearly departed loved ones—and more granite to mark their resting spots.

I thought back to an experience I had in London a few years ago. The date was November 11, and a crowd had gathered at the entrance to Westminster Abbey. I walked to the gate, where a guard turned me away.

"Special Armistice Day ceremony," he said.

I told him, "I'm an American, and I came to pay my respects."

He graciously let me in, even though I was dressed in shorts and a T-shirt. Once inside, I took a seat in the corner of a nave, in an empty row of folding chairs. As the mayor of London spoke from a lectern all the way across the abbey, I looked around at the Britons nearest me. I couldn't see them, because they were buried in the floor and the walls. But I saw their names: Charles Dickens. Alfred Lord Tennyson. Isaac Newton. From Edward the Confessor in 1163 to Sir Laurence Olivier in 1991, the walls of this abbey hold the bones of Britain's brightest.

But there's little more room. Even the abbey's current owner, Queen Elizabeth II, will likely be buried somewhere else. At least out here along the American back roads, there's still plenty of space to bury dead people.

Outside Ridgeway I happened upon what I thought was a really crowded cemetery, with anonymous headstones all crowded together. Turned out to be a monument sales company. Business must be booming. And the marble orchards are spreading like kudzu vine. The end is near.

And then I came upon Fillmore, a town that wears its sense of humor. Fillmore sits far off the interstate, hiding where the signs for routes H and A come together to share a post and a laugh. Grandpa's Bar is across the street from Floyd's Antiques, which is next to the Fillmore Opry, which advertises that it's "next to the pop machine" in beautiful Fillmore, Missouri.

Well, sure enough, there is a pop machine on the half-block-long main drag, with an opry next to it. And on the other side, the highway signs spell, "HA" and point to the opry. Must be a fun time. But I couldn't wait for the curtain to rise for the next performance. That would be Sunday, and this was smack-dab in the middle of the week. There just isn't half a week's worth of stuff for me to do in Fillmore, besides hang out at Grandpa's Bar or Floyd's Antiques. Too bad. I later saw a picture of the opry orchestra on a marquee, and I'll just bet my pop bottle that the orchestra hoots and howls in this wide spot in the road.

Heading straight north on the back roads, I happened upon a town where citizens have a reputation for shooting at problems.

Skidmore is tattooed with a legend. Most people don't talk about it. Matter of fact, they never talked about it, even when quizzed by prosecutors and CSI and FBI agents. Books and movies tell the story of their tight-lippedness. They killed the town bully, shot him full of different caliber bullets from different angles. In broad daylight. Downtown. Nobody knows who did it. Nobody's talking. The town is nothing like the movie "In Broad Daylight," except that it's small, and has a half-block main street with a general store. Back then the town was what it's always been: a place for country folk to get their groceries and mail and chat with neighbors.

During a dispute, the bully had shot and wounded the town grocer right in the store. Ken Rex McElroy was arrested and convicted of the crime. But the judge let him out on bond. He quickly violated the terms of his release by terrorizing townsfolk with a shotgun. A judge set a date for his bond revocation hearing. The townsfolk were content to end the bully's terror by legal means.

But news accounts say the bully's lawyer employed an obscure rule: If your attorney is in the legislature, you can postpone a trial until after the legislative session. So the defense hired a state senator. The hearing was delayed while the legislature met. And the bully stayed out of jail. He continued to threaten folks. The townspeople couldn't wait for justice.

Hey, the defense team was just using the rules. But being outsiders, the defenders misread the mood of the locals. Yep, the defense knew how to buy time. They just forgot Missouri's bloodthirsty history and penchant for mob justice. In one sense, though, the defense was successful: They assured that Ken Rex McElroy never served a day in prison.

Skidmore is quiet again, not much going on, except the occasional murder. The last victim, just a few years ago, was a pregnant woman whose fetus was lifted from her dying womb, kidnapped by a Kansas woman who wanted a baby all her own. The killer got the death penalty. The end is near.

It's a perversion that, given enough time, folks grow fond of legendary killers, or at least the legends. Jesse James. Tom Horn. Bonnie and Clyde. People can make money on those legends. So far, from the looks of the tiny town, Skidmore hasn't capitalized. As we left town, I saw the sign saying that trash on this section of highway is cleaned up by Skidmore Community Betterment. Community betterment, indeed. Sometimes Skidmore's community betterment packs a wallop.

Worth the Trip

It's an irony, for sure, that Worth County has the lowest per capita income in the whole state. The lack of economic development assures miles of green rolling farmland, and not much congestion. Where I found them, the people were friendly, and it's obvious that people in this area like to have fun.

In this out-of-the-way world a million miles from interstates and fast food joints, I found the world's greatest small town. It's not a tourist spot. There's nothing that immediately grabs you by the eyeballs. Yet Allendale may be the cleanest, neatest, most functional little town I've seen.

In the quiet downtown, only a block long just off Highway 46, a curious sign hangs on one building front: B&W Widget Industries. Nobody answered the door, so I peeked into the windows to see tidy tables, ready for people to assemble widgets or eat dinner. The proprietor of the restaurant next door, the Oldtowne Café, said she'd been doing business next door to the widget company for six years and knows the owner but still isn't sure what the company does. It's refreshing, albeit a bit mysterious, that in a town of 54 people the neighbors don't know everything about each other.

The town might be tiny, but it has a website, promoting the Allendale Community Betterment Club, which has "one mission in mind, making Allendale a better place to live, work, play, and visit." It's working. Across the street from the widget-maker, I heard the crack of a cueball busting the billiards at Allendale Pool Hall.

The town surrounds a nice city park, with a big red corkscrew slide in the middle, and fronted by a monument commemorating Allendale's centennial, 1955. There's a tire store and a volunteer fire house and some other tidy buildings. And excitement? Every year, 2,500 rodeo fans pack the town for the Allendale Rodeo. There are dozens of rodeos in Missouri every year, even in towns with fewer than 400 people, like Hume and Downing, Green Castle and Bible Grove, even tiny Barnard. But this double-digit town is the smallest venue.

Not far from there, I found one source of nocturnal entertainment. Just off Highway 169 a low-slung sprawling white frame building dominates the roadside. Paint peels from its windowless walls, but the sign on its side reveals the secret to life: "The 169 Club. Beer. Food. Dancing." The place looks abandoned, but resurrectable when the mood hits. I'll bet that when the time is right and the moon is full, and the broncos have been busted, this place howls. Down the road toward Siloam Springs is a big hand-painted Obama logo across an entire side of a shed. It always surprises me when I travel through what seem to be bright red patches of a red state, and there are glimpses of blue out there.

Siloam Springs is barely a wide spot in the road, on the dead-end of a black top. At least its name is popular, being one of two settlements in Missouri with the same name. Like so many towns, both Siloams spring from a Biblical name. The two are 300 miles apart, as the crow flies, so there's little worry that if you find yourself in Siloam Springs and your spouse sends you out for a quart of milk, you'll return to the wrong town.

We sliced down through Albany. Near the beautiful red brick court house, the Rigney Theater sits on a corner just down from the Carnegie Public Library. Both are notable. The Carnegie Library is not named for Dale, even though he was born down the road in Maryville. It was named for Andrew Carnegie, who donated the money. Thus I was reminded of the most influential tool in the effort to win friends and influence people.

The Rigney Theater is a gem. Its Moorish style and warm salmon color promise great entertainment for locals who nowadays come on weekends to see movies. But this old opera house felt vaudeville on its boards, if you go back to its birth in 1914.

Erifnus found out she could get anywhere fast in Albany; It takes only two minutes to travel from 18th Street to 336th Street, which has to do more with skipping numbers than speed. Don't tell Erifnus.

* * *

Savannah's town square is picturesque, what you'd expect from a town named Savannah. Old, well-preserved buildings surround a courthouse that can be described as stunning. If I were found guilty of loving one courthouse over the others, the verdict would be delivered under the roof of this red brick wonder. Of course I felt that way about Albany's courthouse, and Carthage's too, and a half dozen others, and I'll favor Savannah's until I see the next stunning courthouse. There are plenty, except for the cold concrete boxes built in the 1930s by the WPA.

This one is a beaut, with its cupola dressed in white sandstone and a clock tower adorned with wrought-iron lamps that illuminate the clock faces. Atop the building stands a statue of a woman who looks a lot like Eleanor Roosevelt, though I could not verify her identity with any of the half-dozen folks I asked on the street.

I drove past the tiny one-room waiting station for the old St. Joseph and Savannah Interurban Railway. The tracks are either long gone or sealed beneath pavement, but this brick-and-stone sweetheart with the tile trim roof will last another hundred years. It's an outpost now, isolated in time and space, sitting quietly in a mostly residential neighborhood, waiting for passengers to make the 11-mile rail trek to St. Jo. Not any more, old friend.

Near the bend in Highway 71, the Andrew County Museum opened my eyes. Oh, I'd seen dozens of county history museums before. This one is better than most. Its "Rural Way of Life" exhibit uncovers a lifestyle that's long gone: Fireplace cooking. Steel-wheeled Farmall tractors. Old hotels before the interstate era. But it was the tribute to home funerals that dropped me in my tracks.

In my driving, I've tasted home cooking and helped with home canning and visited the homes of hundreds of folks, living and dead. I've learned the histories of tragic deaths and murders and suicides, and I've stood over countless graves, but I never really thought much about how the dead were prepared for burial. Isn't that what funeral homes are for? This museum made me think, with its frank presentation of death in the 1800s. Back then it was common to die in the home, not in a hospital. And families played a much bigger role in performing burial preparation in the home, before they started paying thousands of dollars for somebody else to do it.

We reentered the land of the living, and passed Avenue City Elementary School in Cosby, with more students and teachers than the town has people. The Avenue City Aces represent what's good about our youth. Sure, this bunch is smart: They've read more than 10 million words so far this school year. But when they heard the news that neighboring Amazonia School had burned down, the Aces jumped into action. They donated supplies for the Amazonia teachers and students, who were meeting temporarily in a Savannah church. The Aces are always doing something to help: a food drive for the homeless; the Pennies for Patients campaign with the slogan "Kids Making Change."

Outside of Avenue City, I followed Route W past a string of nice old farm houses. One in particular caught my eye: a white-frame beauty with a unique dairy barn that had giant picture windows facing the highway, for people to see in—or for cows to see out. Contented cows give better milk, and surely they're content to stand as God intended, in a brick building with hoses attached to their teats, watching traffic pass by.

Highway 59 approaches St. Joseph from the north, where I entered a needier side of St. Jo: proud old buildings, run down. Each building is a clue to the rise and fall of an empire on the western edge of American civilization. St. Jo grew so fast in the early days and so much money flowed through town that artistic innovation and opulence crystallized in the form of elaborate buildings. Almost as fast, the boom ended, and over the years through recessions and depressions, few folks had the money to maintain their architectural heritage. The troubling truth comes to mind: "Once those proud old buildings are gone, they're gone for good."

I got out of town and doubled back north.

The new Highway 71 took a long time to put in place. And it wasn't without gnashing teeth. From earlier travels, I remember a nice little mom 'n' pop motel in Maryville. Stayed there once. On the south edge of town, the owner owned a billboard for years that promoted the motel, straight ahead. Because of the billboard's age and location, the owner didn't pay a dime for anything besides a coat of paint now and then. That all changed with the new highway. Plans called for the highway to go right through the billboard. And federal and state billboard laws guaranteed that any replacement billboard would be costly, and in a less desirable spot. End of billboard. But it's a nice new highway.

Not far from there, a house outside of town is near a target shooting range. The target range is operated by the local department of public safety. The homeowner sued the city of Maryville, saying that city property, in the form of ricocheting bullets, trespasses on her property. So far, the courts haven't agreed with the complainant. I ducked as I drove the back roads around Maryville's purported flying bullets, fearing that the end might be near.

I sought a higher power—and was surprised what I found.

A Higher Power

I warmed my hands by the fire. The crisp fall day had ushered me through rolling loess hills, past newspaper offices whose names are as vibrant as their communities: *Stanberry Headlight. Fairfax Forum. Tarkio Avalanche.* I learned that Tarkio is a Native American word that means, "Wikipedia thinks Tarkio is the place where walnuts grow." Now, pausing briefly beside a roaring fire in an honest-to-God fireplace at the Missouri Welcome Center outside Rock Port, I reflected on my discoveries so far.

Even from a distance, Conception Abbey peeks above the horizon. The giant 120-year-old brick basilica rises from the pastoral landscape.

It's home to 65 Benedictine monks, who comprise nearly a third of the population of Conception, Missouri. Back in 1893, the building was only two years old when a tornado hit it. So the monks lovingly restored it, using what must be a billion bricks. Only a few blocks away, the Benedictine Sisters of Perpetual Adoration set up shop in Clyde, Missouri, proud that they possess more documented saintly artifacts than any other spot in the country.

The edifices that house the monks and sisters used to be the tallest elements on the skyline along this rolling prairie. No longer. Their newest neighbors tower above them, giant wind generators which have sprouted like dandelions on nearby farms. Still, there's absolutely no truth to the rumor that the Sisters of Perpetual Adoration will change their name to the Sisters of Propeller Adulation.

The windmills are worthy of awe. The towers rise 250 feet in the air, their three blades resembling 90-foot-long airplane propellers. I'd heard about 'em, but I'd never seen one. So when we drove into the countryside, I could see them in the distance. As we came closer, more and more appeared, each one sitting on a solitary stilt, planted on the landscape. These graceful creatures looked a bit like aliens from "War of the Worlds." The propellers are so big that each blade looks like it's moving in slow motion.

Some people don't like them, say they don't belong on the landscape. They're ugly, folks protest as they cling to their cell phones, which bounce their signals off of ugly cell phone towers. Granted, the wind turbines make more noise than cell phone towers, but less chatter.

We drove down the road, and I could see in the near distance a lady walking from her farm house to her mailbox. Behind the house, not a quarter-mile away, was a giant windmill, each of its three propeller blades slicing through the air with an audible whoosh, a low roar like wind forcing its way through a mountain pass. We approached her and rolled to a stop by the mailbox. She turned to face me, and I asked, "Does the noise bother you?"

"Oh, yes," she said. "I have trouble sleeping at night. Even in the spring and fall, when we would normally open our windows for some fresh air, we keep them closed to shut out the noise."

I'd heard her argument before. Some folks are incensed by the noise of a dozen generators; others are angered by the smell of 10,000 hogs. Each has a point: Good fences make good neighbors. But what happens when the wind farmer can't keep the noise inside her fence, and the hog farmer can't contain the smell? I wished the woman well and drove down the road past a half-dozen of these monstrous wind catchers, thinking about the price of progress.

From his tomb in Westminster Abbey, 4,000 miles away, Sir Isaac Newton whispered a reminder to me: "For every action, there's an equal and opposite reaction." The windmills generate electricity and a new profit for farmers. But their noise brings an equally noisy reaction from some neighbors and naysayers.

The windmills are working. As I drove through the countryside, the wind speed hit 13 mph, near peak efficiency for these giant generators. Nearby Rock Port made national headlines a couple of years ago as the first American town totally powered by wind. And after its 1,300 residents get all the electricity they need, they sell the excess power to other communities. A University of Missouri natural resource engineer says that Rock Port residents won't see an electric utility rate increase for a dozen years. Farmers love windmills because farming wind is a lot easier than raising cattle or corn. The windmill company sends a rent check every month.

I made a stop at the Opp Hotel, which isn't a hotel anymore but rather a part-time art gallery. When local entrepreneurs can keep the doors open, it's the Prairie Hills Museum. But even while the grand old building gets a facelift and a tuck, it remains host to an 80-proof history. When George Opp ran the place, folks called it "the best hotel between Kansas City and Omaha." It was best at something else, too, according to several locals: The hotel served as a major player in the underground distribution of illegal booze during Prohibition.

Clarence Schaffner is working to restore this proud structure with the Spanish facade. "We were having a problem with the wiring," Clarence told me. "While I was examining all the meters, I saw a desk blotter fastened to the ceiling. It was connected to a trap door, which opened into a small space. Inside that crawl space was a dinner plate with chicken bones on it and some empty whiskey bottles. Sometime in the past, somebody was living above the hole in that ceiling.

"The building had quite a few secret passageways," Clarence continued, "and a tunnel that ran underground all over town. There was a tunnel burrowed under the street, across to a car dealership. During Prohibition, people would go into the dealership as if they were car shopping and take the tunnel to the hotel. Nobody would suspect that folks were picking up their liquor that way."

Of course, few folks had the cash for a car during the depression. When they left the dealership, they weren't carrying auto parts in those brown paper bags. The system apparently worked well enough to avoid scrutiny from revenuers. The tunnels still exist, although Clarence warns, "You can go a little ways but not far. We're working on opening them up, as far as we can go."

And maybe they'll find more evidence of this underworld industry built on the shoulders of moral intolerance. But no need to call Geraldo Rivera; the loot is probably long gone.

From local lore, I learned that loot flowed like whiskey from George Opp's fingertips. Long after Prohibition ended, George continued his penchant for spreading joy. Back in 1961, George paid almost $20,000 in taxes... for the whole town. Opp is gone now, but his legend and legacy live, and his hotel avoids the wrecking ball, waiting for funding so loving hands can bring it back to 80-proof.

I suspect George Opp would be intrigued by the big corn liquor distillery south of Rock Port. The Craig distillery plant makes ethanol for your car. Newton's law applies here, too: Some folks point out that it takes major energy—and a lot of water—to make ethanol. What if we have a drought, and the corn crop fails? And why in the world with so many starving people are we using cropland for fuel?

But there certainly doesn't seem to be a lack of corn in our fast food and soft drinks. Regardless of your view, local farmers have demonstrated one thing: With cooperation and technology, America can find ways to achieve energy independence. Some ways are more efficient than others.

Northwest Missouri continues to be a leader in alternative energy. Ethanol and windmills tell only part of the story. For nearly three decades, Northwest Missouri State University has recycled wood chips, paper and animal wastes into pellets they burn to fire the school's boilers.

The school doesn't waste any energy inside or outside the classroom. Its Bearcats football team turns its fuel into a perennial powerhouse in the NCAA Division II. And it was Saturday afternoon, so I tuned to their game on the radio as I drove around northwest Missouri. The team was playing for the national championship, a tight game. The announcer relayed every strategic move by coach Mel

Churchman. At least that's what his name sounded like. What a great name for the team's leader: Churchman!

Turns out his name is spelled Tjeerdsma. It sounds like Churchman on a car radio. More importantly, he's their very successful spiritual leader, no matter what Tjeerds he attends. Anyway, Tjeerdsma recently retired. Within months, his successor suffered a heart attack and died. Considering all that has happened, the next coach might find it useful to be a churchman.

Even more important than all that oblong-ball stuff, the school became one of the first American institutions with a comprehensive electronic campus. Each dorm room has a computer workstation and dedicated TV channels. Each student living in a residence hall gets a laptop, access to high-speed Internet and access to instructional sites and hundreds of software programs, databases and electronic research tools. Not impressed? They've been doing this since 1987. Not bad for a university that a Missouri governor almost closed and consolidated into another school.

A few blocks from the university's power plant is the school president's residence, the 140-year old Gaunt House, a mansion built of bricks made of mud dredged from the 102 River. Having crossed the 102 River many times on my travels, I'm always intrigued by its name, incorporating the world's three most popular numbers, arranged in no apparent order. Some people think the river got its name because it's 102 miles from Iowa. Others say it's because the river is 102 miles from the entrance to Heaven, according to Mormon belief. One historian thinks 102 is simply an Anglo translation for an early French settlement on the river known as "Cent Deux". Fine, but "Cent Deux" means "102," so what did the French mean by it?

The 102 isn't the only riddle associated with the president's house. Around back, on the second story exterior wall, white bricks form the number 187. Many folks think its code, maybe even some sinister signal. The real answer is less creative. Major edifices often have cornerstones with chiseled dates. The old Gaunt House displayed its date in a more unique fashion, when bricklayers used white bricks to pattern the date into the wall. Today, only three quarters of the date remains. The number 187 used to be 1870, until a new window was added a few years after construction. Still, some folks hold fast to the conspiracy that the building was built by a Kenyan Muslim.

Some time ago I stayed overnight in that house as a guest of the university's first family. Dean and Aleta Hubbard are what you'd expect from a couple in that position, gracious and accommodating, insightful and reasoned. They gave me a close look at the recently refurbished old house. It's a treasure.

But another treasure just blocks away was hearing shouts for its demolition. The old Nodaway County Courthouse is two years younger than the Gaunt House and just as beautiful, dressed in red brick with white sandstone trim. The clock tower pierces the sky, with a clock that still keeps good time. The building looks like a prop in a Von Trapp musical.

But some folks wanted to tear the building down. The building costs too much to repair and keep, they said. Too expensive to save. But it's on the National Register of Historic Places, so the destroyers might have to jump through some hoops to raze the building.

Maybe they need to take a Dale Carnegie course and learn how to win friends, influence people and raise money. Poor Dale would be discouraged today by the number of disputes settled not by diplomacy, but by wrasslin'. Well, wrasslin' has a proud tradition around these parts. Pro wrestling legend Handsome Harley Race hails from Quitman, a town of 46 people just north of Highway 46. It's an oxymoron that Handsome Harley is from Quitman, since he rarely quit. I know, you probably think wrasslin' is fake. Don't tell that to the growing number of lawmakers and constituents who seriously consider using Handsome Harley's patented moves—the diving headbutt, the piledriver, the gutwrench suplex, the swinging neckbreaker—to impose their will on the people.

Wherever I drive, my radio gets there inches before I do. So I make it speak to me. As it scans the intolerant diatribes up and down the radio dial, it seems that the aggressive style of Handsome Harley Race has Dale Carnegie's charm in a headlock.

South by Southeast

It was one of those times where life imitates art.

The furious buzz startled me, as the intruder plunged toward me from the treetops. Before I could react, the bright yellow winged creature zipped over my head and landed in a flat field next to my car.

I should've anticipated such a surprise. Earlier in the day, this same crop duster zigged and dived like a nighthawk, tracking invisible roller coasters as it completed its rounds in the cotton fields south of Poplar Bluff.

Right out of a Hitchcock movie—sans the mistaken identity—the spectacle provides cheap entertainment, for sure. Every crop duster pilot is one part business, one part showman and eight parts guts. In my mental b-roll, this aerobatic demonstration shattered the thrill meters of scores of air shows I've seen over the years... good ones, too. Crop dusters win because of, well, guts. And reality. These guys do this stuff for real. It's business.

It's a precise business, dropping inches over power lines and tree limbs to spread critter-killing cocktails on cotton. And it's dangerous business, too. At the end of almost every season, the pilot roster gets shorter.

I'm not surprised crop dusting theatrics don't draw bigger crowds. They don't publicize the show times.

Down here, the Missouri map dangles a strange appendage that looks like a Bootheel, thanks to the "Czar of the Valley," a rancher named Walker, who wanted to be a part of the new state of Missouri, and not the Territory of Arkansas. So Congress carved out the Bootheel.

Truthfully, I wasn't expecting much as I drove south into the Bootheel, on terrain that varied little across miles of cotton framed by drainage canals and dotted with sleepy little farm towns. As far as I was concerned, the Czar of the Valley and his cronies in Congress just gave me an extra 88 roads to drive. The Bootheel is influenced more by Memphis than by St. Louis, and the area definitely is a member in good standing of the Old South. Stuck like a hatchet in the forehead of Arkansas, the Bootheel and its people, for the most part, feel alienated from the rest of Missouri.

I have no control over that, since the issue was settled generations ago by Walker, Bootheel Ranger. So I formed a plan to crisscross these 88 roads in the most efficient manner, and peel back the cotton curtain to reveal real life. I drove down to tag the very bottom of Missouri, paralleling the Pole Cat Slough past Senath, through Bucoda and Europa, a town built for the purpose of selling whiskey. I didn't stop to buy any.

The old cotton gin at Pascola looks abandoned, but a flatbed wagon in back betrays cotton balls stuck in its cage. The gin itself is a giant on the flat landscape, a sprawling rusted two story tin shed. But come cotton harvest, contraptions like this one will come alive, digesting enough cotton seeds to panel your basement.

I've heard stories about the rigors of picking cotton, but never in the excruciating detail described by a friend who offered a first-hand account.

"As a kid, it's one of the first things I remember," Bob said. Picking cotton is hard to forget. It's hot, backbreaking knuckle scraping work. Children have one advantage: They don't have to bend over as far to pull cotton off the scrubby plants. "We were dirt poor, and the cotton harvest was one of the biggest opportunities to make some money to buy food and shoes. Mom had us kids out in the fields at dawn, with our gunny sacks, ready to start pulling cotton bolls off the plants. Mom was smart. On the first day, she told us kids, 'I'll give you two cents a pound.' We picked like crazy, and she paid us at sundown. Next day we were up early again, ready to go, and she said, 'Now, you must pick as much as you did yesterday.' She didn't pay us for that." Life's lessons are hard.

* * *

Tucked in gentle rolling hills on the brink of the Bootheel, the Bloomfield Cemetery tells a story. The chapters unfold one-by-one on the white tombstones of Confederate soldiers from around Bloomfield who died during the Civil War. Many are now laid to rest on this beautiful spot atop Crowley's Ridge, a towering geologic oddity that slices across southeast Missouri, separating the hill people from the flatlanders.

Some of these headstones represent soldiers who were killed in action. Some never made it home to rest in the cemetery. Regardless, all have a story to tell, and the tombstones provide a glimpse. Some soldiers were "executed by parties unknown," or "murdered while en route home." But the vast majority died of illness. Alas, details on headstones can only scratch the surface of deep family tragedies. Private James Horton died of illness in the Union's Rock Island Prison. Private Johnathan Horton died of illness at Gratiot Prison in St. Louis. Private Jesse Horton died of illness as a POW in Alton, Illinois.

And a man old enough to be their father, John Horton, died in Gratiot Prison. All were cavalrymen in the same unit. Reading the inscriptions, I sensed that in the 14 months spanning the deaths of these POWs, there were four widows in the same family.

So far as I know, this is the only Civil War cemetery in the nation where the tombstones tell how each soldier died. "Noted guerrilla" John Fugate Bolin was captured, imprisoned in Cape Girardeau and hanged by an angry mob on February 5, 1864. Private George Baker "Deserted CSA, Joined USA, Captured by CSA, Hanged by CSA." Private Jacob Foster "died of wounds received at Christmas dinner, Doniphan, MO, Wilson's Massacre." One inscription reads, "Accidentally killed. Kicked in head by horse."

A long view of the rows of tidy white stones belies the chaos that reigned over this area during the Civil War. Up close, the stones tell personal stories. Aboard the ironclad C.S.S. *Arkansas*, Private Smith Minton saw a shipmate decapitated by an enemy shell. When the captain ordered him to "throw that body overboard," Smith Minton replied, "I can't sir, that's my brother."

It seems natural that Bloomfield would put extra information on tombstones. Long before there was an Armed Forces Radio, the town spread news to uniformed troops through the *Stars & Stripes* newspaper, first published here on November 9, 1861. That's when young Brigadier General Ulysses Grant was prosecuting the nearby Belmont campaign against the Confederates. Grant ordered 2,000 troops to eradicate the rebel forces in Stoddard County. Union invaders found the abandoned newspaper office of editor James Hull's *Bloomfield Herald*, where they cranked up the press to publish some camp news. Today, Bloomfield's Stars and Stripes Museum Library honors that event and nearly 150 years of subsequent issues of the newspaper, delivered into the hands of America's service men and women worldwide.

Editor Hull is buried here, too. An orderly sergeant in the Confederate 6th Missouri Infantry Regiment, he died in 1863. The headstone doesn't say how he died; it simply lists him as "editor, *Bloomfield Herald*, Birthplace of the *Stars and Stripes* newspaper."

I hadn't planned on staying so long in Bloomfield. But the exhibits in the Stars and Stripes Museum combined with the gravestone engravings had a strong gravitational pull on my curiosity. The sun was low in the sky when I finished reading the tombstone testaments. I headed a few blocks down the road to dine.

My approach up the gravel trail to the genuine rawhide ambiance of the Cowtown Café was a step into country living, complete with a barnyard greeting from goats and donkeys and such. On the inside, antiques dot the rough-hewn wood framing and giant fireplace. I had a delightful home-cooked meal, a rarity on the road. And I got a history lesson. The friendly folks in Bloomfield told me the history of Crowley's Ridge. Before engineers came along to drain the hundreds of square miles of swampland in the Bootheel, early pioneers followed the ridge along the narrow Chalk Bluff Trail, between the swamps, to reach Arkansas and Texas. They called this town Bloomfield because they found a big field of blooming wildflowers here.

I made a promise to return to the chuck wagon races. From where I sat, I could toss an egg and hit the race course, a field at Holly Ridge Ranch that would soon transform into a kind of backyard Roman Coliseum, with serious chariotry, though the chariots are small buckboards and Conestogas, and the steeds are smaller than Ben Hur's white horses. Hell, some of them are mules. But the races are serious nonetheless. A few years back, a rider was killed on this very spot. Don't know if they erected a tombstone in the Bloomfield Cemetery for his valor. Probably not.

Some folks believe the tall tale that chuck wagon racing began 90 years ago at the Calgary Stampede, when two drunken cooks got into a pissing match over who could cook faster, and serve faster and, finally, drive faster. In reality, chuck wagon races began much earlier, when westward wagon trains would divide up the cutlery and the cast-iron skillets and do their damnedest to outrun the Sioux. Lately, the races have been commandeered by a group representing Cowboys for Christ. It seems that chuck wagon races had become a bit rowdy and, well, not very gentlemanly. So to restore the good reputation of cowboys who, as we all know, never swore, stunk, puked, bought drinks for whores or shot each other, the chuck wagon races have been sanitized for the unknowing. If the end is near, these cowboys will be wearing white hats when the blinding light of Rapture serves them up in that big skillet in the sky.

The Pad of the Heel

Even with no swamp surrounding it, Crowley's Ridge cannot hide as it cuts across the Bootheel's instep. This unusual geologic phenomenon towers an average 200 feet above the surrounding flat farmland along 42 Missouri miles of designated National Scenic Byway. We could view the ridge from Mingo National Wildlife Refuge, and just about everywhere.

Mingo preserves a part of the old swamp, and features a surprisingly accessible glimpse into a vibrant ecosystem, with all of its critters. Migrating waterfowl appreciate the courtesy of this preserve, and they reward visitors with up-close views of their habits and habitat.

The visitor center presents the single most awesome display I've ever seen anywhere in my life. Walking through the front door, I saw two buck deer, giant antlers locked together so their snouts are inches from each other. Their ritual territorial fight had changed into a fight for survival when they realized they were hopelessly locked together. They were found in the swamp, where they drowned when they couldn't cooperate for a drink of water.

"We wish more people knew about this place," a ranger told me. I agreed. I had anticipated that the swamp would be inhospitable to humans, but it's a delightful opportunity to see wildlife. We drove past critters of all types along the 27 miles of roadways, and many more miles of foot paths. Just as important, this preserve shows what the land looked like before what may be the most dramatic transformation of swamp land to farm land in North America. The feat was performed by engineers including teams that had just dredged the Panama Canal.

We skittered along Highway 51, past Idlewild and a place called Bottomless Pond, which I couldn't find, much less fathom.

But I found Bullwinkle's, and discovered the secret of the airplane. "You can't miss it," the guy at the senior center had said. Sure enough, there it was, in the middle of nowhere. Bullwinkle's Bar, with an airplane crashed straight down into the top of the roof. It was rigged, of course, but an effective attention getter.

Airplane crashes, even fake ones, have an unnerving effect. So we drove as safe as we knew how, crossing the Castor River, crossing the Castor River again, crossing it again, and again and again. We crossed the Castor River so many times that I stopped to study my map. On the map there are two Castor Rivers, at one point flowing within five miles of each other. Apparently, when they drained all this swampland, one Castor River became two.

Castor is French for beaver, and the beavers built dams all through this swampy region. Despite being the hardest working hydraulic engineers on the planet, beavers don't get a paycheck, so they have a right to be the namesake of multiple waterways. It beats names like Crackskull. Anyway, the beavers must've been disappointed when engineers turned the lower Castor River into a drainage canal, sucking precious swamp water away.

Henry Schoolcraft, the first chronicler of the Ozarks, had another name for the Castor. He called it Crooked Creek. It's a simple name. One can understand why he preferred simple names. His wife's name was Obabaamwewegiizhigokwe, which in her native Ojibwe language means "the sound that the stars make as they rush across the sky." Henry called her Jane, which means "Jane." I think I know why. Her mother, Ozhaguscodaywayquay, probably didn't object, since she herself adopted the Anglo name Susan Johnson.

Despite his prominence in exploring Missouri's Ozarks, I have yet to drive past a sign or a town or any place named Schoolcraft. He's in good company, though, since there isn't a Moses, Missouri, or an Austin either. There's no town named Yogi in Missouri, although there is a Jellystone Park. There's no Shapley, no Blow, no Dice, no Wilder, no Sacagawea or Calamity. Ah, but there's a Jane.

Before it was drained, the area provided great cover for Confederate General M. Jeff Thompson, the "Swamp Fox" of the Civil War. As a result of clear-cutting and a complex network of drainage canals, the Swamp Fox would have precious little cover today among the cotton fields and rice paddies and the occasional shrimp farm. Yet there's still one more place to hide in the Bootheel.

To get there, I drove from Mingo across the crown of the Bootheel, headed southeast through Cobb and Ives, over open flatland from Penermon to Frisco, past Canalou and Noxall. Most of the time you can see the next town before you leave the last one. I passed through Kewanee and Tallapoosa, through Buckeye and Dogwood, Anniston and Airline Acres, through the cotton fields from East Prairie past Pulltite and Pinhook to the hiding place: Big Oak Tree State Park.

This thousand acre forest is mother nature's secret recipe for greatness, blending swamp and soil so fertile that a remarkable variety of trees grow to steroidal proportions.

I assumed the centerpiece of Big Oak Tree State Park was a big oak tree. Well, it used to be. Back in 1937, when the state acquired the land, the big oak tree was the alpha tree among the other giants. Even then, it was 481 rings old, having germinated in 1456.

When residents around Mississippi County began the effort to save this bottomland virgin hardwood forest, they faced a dilemma. What would they name the park? It could easily be Big Oak, Hickory, Swamp Cottonwood, Green Ash, American Elm, Black Willow, Silver Maple, Giant Cane, Persimmon and Bald Cypress State Park. Fact is, six state champion trees have towered over the park's visitors, including two national champs. Now, sadly, that roster doesn't include the big oak tree. A few years back, it bit the dust. But I found a cross section of the mighty oak at the visitor center.

By far the most common visitors to Big Oak Tree are birds. More than 150 different species, some rare, have clutched a branch in the rarified air, dropping an occasional present onto what might be Missouri's longest boardwalk. The park makes a great rest area along the Mississippi flyway. With a treetop canopy reaching 140 feet, there's plenty of room in the high-rise and an unobstructed view for miles and miles.

The sun was setting, and Erifnus and I were still more than an hour away from our campsite. Darkness fell as we drove through the flat farm fields of Mississippi county, where even at night, you can see for a dozen miles in any direction. In the distance, I saw strange lights. They looked like low-slung ball field lights, five of them spaced equally apart. But they were moving. Around them the dust rose like an eerie fog. They were harvesting cotton. Up close, the harvesters look like mechanical crabs, with a row of close-set beady eyes and fearsome pincers. Or maybe they look more like the betentacled Davy Jones in one of those ghastly "Pirates of the Caribbean" movies. Regardless, they're fearsome monsters, able to chew up just about anything in their paths.

We stopped at a roadside convenience store to get a 12-pack for my campfire vigil. The beer cooler was at the back of the convenience store, a position as strategic as a baptismal font. I stood before the cooler searching for my brand, Busch Beer. I scanned the cooler over and over again, shelf by shelf. Busch Light. Busch NA. I could find no regular Busch. I grabbed a 12-pack of Stag, the godfather of Busch, and took it to the counter. "I can't find regular Busch Beer," I whined. The clerk left his register and walked back to the cooler. It would've been the perfect time for a thief to dash in and pilfer the cash register.

"There." He pointed to the Busch 12-packs. The packages were dressed in camouflage. So were the cans. I honestly didn't see them. This camo shit works.

* * *

If you wanted to hide from hit men or creditors, Lake Wappapello would do nicely. Isolated in rugged hills, wholly surrounded by the thick woods of Mark Twain National Forest, the lake stands apart from the crowd. Literally. The nearest three towns—Williamsville, Wappapello and the county seat of Greenville—combine to fall short of a population of 900, and falling. Local fishermen hope it stays that way. Less competition for fish.

Driving to the campsite, I knew I was in for a lonely night. Winter was nigh, and Erifnus and I had Wappapello State Park to ourselves. The park already had cut their seasonal employees, and only a caretaker couple and I shared opposite ends of the 1,800 acres of land surrounded on three sides by water. Here I was, on a peninsula overlooking a beautiful lake, all by myself. It was dark, of course, and I'd built a good fire. I drank a beer and tended the fire. But I was tired from driving 600 miles of crisscross through the flat terrain of a drained swamp.

Late autumn chill was creeping through the layers of clothing. I crawled inside my tent and zipped the flap shut, slipped inside my sleeping bag, and drifted off to... wait a minute. What was that?

Footsteps in the leaves. It was unmistakable. Something was walking toward my tent. I knew it probably wasn't human. Maybe it was a deer. Or a bear. Mountain lion? I hear they're making a comeback in these hills.

My curiosity grew with each approaching footstep. The intruder passed between my campfire and me, casting a huge shadow on the wall of my tent. The monster ambled off down the narrow peninsula. I knew it would have to come back, since there was only one way out. In the meantime, I jumped out of my sleeping bag and threw every stick of wood within reach onto the fire.

Sure enough, after a few minutes I heard the rustle of leaves, getting louder as the animal approached my tent. I shone my flashlight, and saw the reflection in its eyes. It was low slung, with two white stripes down its furry black back. A skunk.

"You little shit," I scolded her, not too dramatically. She was unfazed, and kept doing what she was conditioned to do around the discarded trash from hundreds of careless campers... look for food scraps. I had none, and told her so. She didn't take my word for it, but once she was satisfied that I was telling the truth, she ambled off up the hill. I went back to my sleeping bag and slept like a baby, snoring sweet fresh air.

A Whuppin', A Gypsy and the Wonder of Lard

I'd had a bad day. After my 5th-grade teacher paddled me for the second time in four hours, I knew I'd face the music again at home. My teacher would tell the principal, who would tell the superintendent, and that's where my troubles would multiply.

The superintendent was my Dad.

My transgressions were not capital crimes. I don't even remember what they were. Talking. Chewing gum. It didn't matter. In the halls of honor, I was a goner.

So I postponed the inevitable for as long as I could. I rode my bike around town, past the fresh-ink smell of the newspaper office, where I imagined tomorrow's headline rolling off the presses: "Truant Burned at Stake." I whistled through the Rolla Cemetery, past a grave covered in flowers. That grave is always covered in flowers. Not likely for me... I rolled past the ball field where I got my first base hit, and past the old Frisco steam locomotive I always wanted to ride. And I wondered why I hadn't just let those boxcar wheels cut me in half when I'd crawled under that moving train. That would've spared the misery I felt now. I said goodbye to the icons of my childhood and went home to plea for mercy.

The events of that day led to a teachable moment. My parents, as teachers, branded the lesson into my memory: Respect teachers.

Branded just as deep from my Rolla childhood are the three elements that led to this book: trips with my mother to the library; my deep genetic attraction to lard, and the spirit of a wandering Gypsy. The Gypsy was a real person. He died on the road, not far from my house. And he's buried in that grave that's always covered with flowers.

* * *

Rolla was an idyllic place to grow up. A college town in the woods, it sits on the nation's most storied road. Steady streams of knowledge and wisdom spill on and off Route 66. In pleasant weather, shoppers and diners browse the bookshelves that line the sidewalk along Pine Street, the town's main drag. Pine Street turns green every St. Patrick's Day, when the college students celebrate their patron saint of engineering and do a lot of vomiting.

The rest of the year, the town is quiet, for the most part. But it has always served up good food. From my early days in Rolla, my favorite café is gone. The legendary monument to lard, Chub And Jo's, ascended to that blue-plate diner in the sky.

Chub And Jo's was the kind of place you don't really miss until it's gone. Then you really miss it. They made the usual stuff: roast beef, meatloaf, fried chicken. But they made the meals with unprocessed ingredients, and lard. Buckets of lard. The rolls came out hot and fresh, and it didn't occur to anybody to throw them. If either Chub or Jo were ever hauled into court for the charge of assault with lard, and I was on the jury, I'd vote for acquittal. Truth is, I would never be able to pick Chub or Jo out of a lineup. But I miss them all the same.

In the same shotgun store, another restaurant has holed up. Leonna's Kitchen serves home-style cooking. And in the great tradition of Chub And Jo's, I don't think they've changed the walls, or the floors or the ceilings. It's one of those places where the smoking section is the main floor, and non-smoking is relegated to a couple of tables by the window at one side of the entrance. Pretty much everybody was smoking but me, but I sat at a booth away from the non-smoking section, to lower suspicion that I was a goody, and thus become a pariah.

The waitress called me "Hon," a clue that she was a hail fellow well met. I ordered the catfish special with hush puppies and fries. It was good, but it wasn't made with lard.

Eateries come and go. Some stay. On the edge of town where Route 66 travelers can see it, Zeno's is an institution. Since 1959, Zeno's Motel and Steak House has launched a billion prom dates, for better or for worse. Some prom dates even ended there, in the motel that connects to the restaurant, although realistically most high school students didn't have the money or the nerve to rent a motel room to test their abstinence.

At Zeno's, travelers along the Mother Road still can order a great steak from a menu cut in the shape of an Angus steer. And although the restaurant shows its age, there's comfort in its well-worn surroundings, like the feel of old Route 66 under Erifnus Caitnop's tires. Unlike the plastic chain restaurants, Zeno's offers real comfort, the kind of comfort only attainable by eating aged beef in an aging dining room beside an aging Mother Road. And the age-seasoned motel room still gave my aging frame a good night's sleep.

Almost next door, one of Rolla's brightly painted bookends stands as a sentinel on the sunset side of Route 66. It's a big tall billboard version of a totem pole, and the corresponding entrance to the other side of town is guarded by a towering mule with an accompanying hillbilly: two local trading posts take visitors back to a world that predates the sameness of pit stops. It was a time when Route 66 travelers could buy gas and groceries and immerse in the local hill culture. They still can.

It doesn't take much to encourage Scott Jones to talk about the Totem Pole Trading Post. The trading post has been in his family for three generations now, and he's just taken the reins to the business. We stood in the organized clutter that surrounds the counter: horse saddles and white-oak baskets, Minnetonka Moccasins and old relic postcards and hillbilly trinkets. Looking down on us were eight giant photos of old Route 66 and 11 hornets nests and, yes, a giant totem pole with a painted pelican on top of a stack of painted bird beaks and god faces.

Scott told about the past. "We were a convenience store back before there were convenience stores." Sixty years ago his grandfather left the comfort of his Chesterfield home, where he sold coal by the bushel from his front yard, to take over this business on the edge of civilization, where the terrain was so rugged that Route 66 slimmed from four lanes to two.

When Route 66 turned its traffic over to I-44, Grandpa eventually moved the trading post closer to town, but he kept the kitsch. For decades, he and his son sold Standard Oil gasoline without a lease, until Standard wanted them to conform to standard. When Grandpa refused to adapt to the form-fit, brand-driven plastic world of the modern interstate, Standard cut Grandpa loose.

No problem. Grandpa switched to Shell Oil—the last Shell station between Rolla and Oklahoma. Alas, eventually Shell demanded Grandpa's business look like a company store, too. So they parted ways. Now Scott has inherited the trading post, ready to make a go of it. He sells a local brand of gasoline. And his walls are still adorned with trinkets and saddles and baskets and Minnetonka Moccasins, all for sale.

Scott has added a body shop to restore classic old cars that still cruise along old Route 66. It's refreshing to see somebody resist conformity, and stay true to the history of this legendary highway. It's especially refreshing to see a young person resist. Scott Jones knows the road ahead will be rough, with no support from a major corporate brand and no skyscraping sign luring travelers to the feeling of comfort that comes from a billion dollars of advertising. But thousands of vacationers who scour old Route 66 for the remnants of the real thing will see his billboards and find him and trade at the trading post and thank him for preserving this outpost of nostalgia.

* * *

Before there was a Totem Pole, or even a Route 66, Benton Elementary School started cranking out knowledgeable products. Alas, the old school shut down, victim of the progress that comes from successful school bond issues. The big brick structure stood mostly dormant for decades, an occasional tenant here and there. But mostly its deep red skin awaited the fate of the wrecking ball.

But on its 100th birthday, the building morphed into Benton Square, the postmodern world's most elegant amalgam of shops, spas and dining. It's the centerpiece to Rolla's burgeoning arts and entertainment district. Seriously, artists have always flocked to this part of the Ozarks. They included the likes of world-class sculptor Louis Smart, painter Ellen Pearce, songbird Luce Myers and even a pair of Ozark Mountain Daredevils.

The Benton Square developers are daredevils, too, rescuing the old building, combining their own artful vision of classic design with classy services and betting on the draw. They drew from their obvious business sense—and deep pockets—to dress up the old school like Auntie Mame, and treat Rolla like royalty. For my taste, the makeover is a bit gaudy. But I'm grateful that somebody saved this building, because it's where my life turned around.

Yes, this is the same building where my 5th-grade hide got blistered twice in one day. So in a semi-triumphal return, I walked in a side entrance. From nearly five decades ago, I still remember the hiding places: The basement furnace room has become a spa. The old cloakroom—where I used to share a coat hook with a kid whose fingers had been blown off by blasting caps—opens into a dining room. The well-worn wooden stairs I trudged as a youth still fit my feet, although they've been shellacked to a blinding shine. I climbed to the rooftop… legally, this time around.

From the rooftop, I could almost see the Gypsy king's flower-bedecked grave. As long as I can remember, I've heard legends about its origin. Everybody around town knows the legend, but nobody can tell the story with any certainty. Local reporters and historians have tried to dig into the facts, with little success.

Still the legend persists: Decades ago, the King of the Gypsies died along Route 66, folks say, and they buried him here. I'm not sure what a Gypsy king might be, though likely he was a king of the road. Even among locals, the term Gypsy inspires a multitude of reactions. One thing is certain: Around Memorial Day each year since the passing of this mortal, somebody shows up to decorate the plot, and the companion graves that have surrounded it over time.

Like all legends, the mystery may eclipse the true story.

I walked back down the old Benton School stairs. Even though the building has a new name and a new purpose, among the diners and revelers are folks who remember their own stories about time served in that building. Some stories are good, some painful.

I left the building again—nearly 50 years after my servitude there—with much the same attitude: Don't know if I'll ever return. The end is near, you know, lubricated by gravy. And my soul follows the path of the Gypsy.

Erifnus is fine with that. She's in the parking lot, ready to roll.

CPSIA information can be obtained at www.ICGtesting.com
Printed in the USA
LVOW131415221212

312906LV00003B/5/P